Differentiation
for the
Adolescent Learner

Accommodating Brain Development, Language, Literacy, and Special Needs

Glenda Beamon
CRAWFORD

CORWIN PRESS
A SAGE Company
Thousand Oaks, CA 91320

For information:

Corwin Press
A SAGE Company
2455 Teller Road
Thousand Oaks, California 91320
www.corwinpress.com

SAGE Ltd.
1 Oliver's Yard
55 City Road
London EC1Y 1SP
United Kingdom

SAGE Pvt. Ltd.
B 1/I 1 Mohan Cooperative Industrial Area
Mathura Road, New Delhi 110 044
India

SAGE Asia-Pacific Pte. Ltd.
33 Pekin Street #02-01
Far East Square
Singapore 048763

Printed in the United States of America

Library of Congress Cataloging-in-Publication Data

Crawford, Glenda Beamon.
Differentiation for the adolescent learner: accommodating brain development, language, literacy, and special needs/Glenda Beamon Crawford.
    p. cm.
Includes bibliographical references and index.
ISBN 978-1-4129-4053-5 (cloth: acid-free paper)
ISBN 978-1-4129-4054-2 (pbk.: acid-free paper)
  1. Individualized instruction. 2. Cognitive styles in children. 3. Mixed ability grouping in education. 4. Learning, Psychology of. 5. Adolescent psychology. I. Title.

LB1031.C73 2008
371.39′4—dc22   2008008421

This book is printed on acid-free paper.

08   09   10   11   12   10 9 8 7 6 5 4 3 2 1

Acquisitions Editor:	Hudson Perigo
Editorial Assistant:	Lesley Blake
Production Editor:	Veronica Stapleton
Copy Editor:	Gretchen A. Treadwell
Typesetter:	C&M Digitals (P) Ltd.
Proofreader:	Dennis W. Webb
Indexer:	Molly Hall
Cover Designer:	Rose Storey
Graphic Designer:	Karine Hovsepian

Table of Contents

Foreword

Education is a vast and complex set of interactive processes for teachers and students alike. Teachers have the daily challenge of educating and preparing students' minds and talents for what lies ahead. Teachers must also remain current with new discoveries in how different age levels learn and understand how to translate these findings into viable classroom procedures. Students must learn to understand each new level of the curriculum and how to use these new understandings to progress to the next level.

These challenges and classroom procedures are perhaps most difficult with adolescents. Many parents fear the onslaught of adolescence in their children. Many teachers believe they should receive hazardous duty pay for teaching adolescents. Adolescence is for many—adolescents, parents, and teachers alike—a time of turmoil, rapid growth and learning, as well as shifting emotions and searching for personal and social identities. But, at the same time, adolescence is a time when new capabilities open new vistas and learning opportunities. It is a time when learning levels increase in dramatic fashion. It is a time when intellectual, social, emotional, and academic development is ripe for blossoming. During these often tumultuous years, adolescents need a trusted guide and a haven for exploring new learning, as they begin to understand their needs, interests, and changing emotions and come to grips with their personal identities.

Glenda Crawford addresses these issues in an integrated and interactive manner in this book. The primary focus of the book is how to improve learning in adolescents. This is, obviously, a complex task that demands learning and understandings from a variety of areas. She treats these issues in a concise and understandable manner. She integrates those important factors that impact adolescent learning and development that mutually interact with teachers of adolescents in their efforts to assist their students' continuing development.

Dr. Crawford also identifies and addresses critical new findings. These include recent brain research centered on changes occurring in adolescent brain structure that allow more reasoned emotional judgments and social controls in adolescents. She also discusses how brain operations affect learning in adolescents. She describes the importance and need for having a safe and secure classroom for learning where each individual student is respected by the teacher and peers alike. The importance of a classroom climate that encourages and supports learning and emotional/social development is strongly related to an adolescent's need for academic understanding and personal meaning.

Dr. Crawford goes beyond just describing these critical issues and discussing how they are interrelated. Using Universal Design for Learning (UDL) as a model, she describes how differentiated instructional approaches can capitalize on student variability to maximize learning in all students. She provides excellent instructional techniques that are consistent with brain function, effective learning, the UDL principles of differentiated instruction, and the developmental needs and interests of adolescents.

Two other elements of this book need to be noted. First, Dr. Crawford discusses how the principles of UDL can be used effectively with three types of student groups: fast learners, English language learners, and those that may have learning challenges. She assumes that most classrooms will have students from each of these groups in them. The suggestions for curriculum and instructional approaches are practical and possible for all teachers and, in fact, can be used in any classroom.

Second, Dr. Crawford utilizes technology extensively in her suggestions for implementing UDL in classroom instructional practices. Her suggestions and the many technological references she provides offer a teacher of adolescents a rich and varied set of excellent resources.

This is a must read book for teachers of adolescents. It would also be an excellent guide for parents and parents-to-be of adolescents.

David H. Reilly
Professor and Dean (Ret.)
School of Education
University of North Carolina @ Greensboro

ACKNOWLEDGMENTS

I owe deep appreciation to several individuals for supporting me in this publication . . .

To my students and educators who contributed outstanding adolescent-centered learning ideas. We share the belief that all adolescents should have the opportunity to learn at the highest potential.

To Judith, my valued colleague, for so graciously sharing the fine work of the Project T2 Team at Elon University in North Carolina.

To my sons, Michael and Brent, "daughter" Dodi, and new granddaughter Piper. They are my most spirited and faithful supporters.

To my mother, Polly, and in memory of my father, Claude. Their love has sustained me.

To Dave, my mentor for twenty years. His insightful ideas and consistent feedback continue to shape my written words.

To Larry, my husband. His patience and support through the months of writing were constant.

Corwin Press would like to thank the following individuals for their contributions to the work:

Maria Timmons Flores
Assistant Professor
Lewis & Clark Graduate School of
    Education and Counseling
Portland, OR

Cynthia Grindy
Chemistry Teacher
Duluth East High School
Duluth, MN

Hope J. Hartman, PhD
Director
Center for Excellence in Teaching
    and Learning at City College of
    New York and Professor of
    Educational Psychology at City
    University of New York Graduate
    School and University Center
New York, NY

Carol Kirkwood
French Teacher
Albany County School District #1
Laramie, WY

Mark A. Springer
Teacher
Radnor Middle School
Wayne, PA

Patricia Long Tucker
Regional Superintendent
District of Columbia Public Schools
Washington, DC

About the Author

Glenda Beamon Crawford's experiences with young adolescent learners span nearly thirty years. She has taught Grades 4 through 12 and currently coordinates the Middle Grades Education Program at Elon University where she is a professor. She has written three books, one in its second edition, and published several articles on structuring classrooms for adolescent thinking and learning. Dr. Crawford consults and presents regularly at state, national, and international conferences. She has conducted professional development in Tajikistan and has taught in London and at Southeast University in the Peoples Republic of China. Her research and teaching honors include the 2002 North Carolina Award for Outstanding Contribution to Gifted Education and the 2004 Award for Outstanding Scholarship in the School of Education at Elon University.

*To my friends Sylvia and Hank, Dave, Craig
and Jennifer, Tony and Helen, and Han*

Introduction
and Overview

Differentiation for adolescent learning is grounded in the premise that all students have the capacity to learn and achieve *if* they have the opportunity to access, process, and demonstrate knowledge of content and skills in ways that are personally meaningful. Whereas teachers have little control over the wide range of diversity in contemporary middle and high school classrooms, they can seek to know their students developmentally as learners with similar and differing strengths, preferences, and interests and design a context for learning that is responsive and supportive for their academic success. This context is shaped by the dynamic interaction of strategic instruction and learner engagement. The ultimate goal of differentiation in the adolescent classroom is to empower students with the cognitive strategies and personal efficacy to manage their own learning.

This book introduces a differentiation framework for adolescent-centered learning that incorporates research from the field of neuroscience on the developing and learning adolescent brain. This framework is sustained by adolescents' developmental needs for personal connection, appropriate intellectual challenge, emotional engagement, guided social interaction, metacognitive development, and a supportive learning environment. The six components of the adolescent-centered differentiation model are these:

Evaluation: Diagnostic, ongoing formative, and culminating assessment of students' knowledge, skills, interests, preferences, and progress that informs curriculum design and instruction and promotes student learning management.

Expectation: Curriculum designed around age-relevant themes, essential content understandings, key concepts, and cognitively compelling learning experiences.

Engagement: Authentic and relevant learning experiences that intrigue and motivate by building on students' knowledge, experiences, interests, strengths, and preferences.

Exploration: Structured and flexible social interaction that promotes collaborative inquiry and individual academic and behavioral accountability.

Extension: Explicit instruction to promote students' metacognitive development, self-regulation, and learning transfer.

Environment: A classroom learning community responsive to adolescents' physical, social, intellectual, and emotional development.

Differentiation for adolescent-centered learning is a proactive, developmentally appropriate, and student-centered approach to assessment, curriculum design, and instruction. It is based on current pivotal research on how adolescents' brains learn developmentally and individually. It provides a commonsense guide for teachers to determine adolescents' differing learning strengths and needs and to respond strategically through varied, multiple, and flexible strategies for engagement, involvement, and evaluation. It constitutes teaching so that all adolescents in mixed-ability classrooms have cognitive access, opportunity, and support for academic competence. Differentiation for adolescents further involves metacognitive coaching so that students attain and know how and when to use pertinent cognitive strategies for self-regulated and independent learning. Ultimately, adolescent-centered differentiation is about good teaching practice.

CHAPTER 1: DIFFERENTIATION AND THE LEARNING BRAIN

Chapter 1 addresses the many and varied differences among adolescents that impact learning strengths and needs. It includes a discussion of new research on differences in the way the learning brain receives, processes, and emotionally relates to content, materials, and instructional experiences. The chapter defines differentiation as curriculum and instruction design that builds strategically and meaningfully on adolescents' learning strengths, interests, and preferences. The chapter gives an overview of the differentiation model, Universal Design for Learning (UDL), and introduces the concepts of technology-enhanced cognitive tools, or digital accommodations, which provide flexible scaffolding to enable more equitable access to learning by the range of adolescents in mixed-ability classrooms. Chapter 1 identifies six differentiation design principles for adolescent-centered learning. These are the "Six Es" of Evaluation, Expectation, Engagement, Exploration, Extension, and Environment.

CHAPTER 2: DIFFERENTIATION AND ADOLESCENT DEVELOPMENT

Chapter 2 identifies six developmentally-responsive, brain-based elements that support adolescent learning and align with the components of the adolescent-centered differentiation framework introduced in Chapter 1. These developmentally appropriate elements are personal connection, appropriate intellectual challenge, emotional engagement, purposeful social interaction, metacognitive development, and supportive learning environment. Chapter 2 also examines pivotal findings from the field of neuroscience that shed light on the developing adolescent brain and related cognitive and emotional development. It explores the interrelationship among adolescents' developmental tendencies, brain functioning during the learning process, and compatible classroom practices.

CHAPTER 3: ADOLESCENT-CENTERED DIFFERENTIATION: EVALUATION, EXPECTATION, ENGAGEMENT, AND EXPLORATION

Chapter 3 broadens the discussion of adolescent-centered differentiation with focus on four of the design principles: Evaluation, Expectation, Engagement, and Exploration. These principles present a differentiation framework for adolescent-centered teaching that is based on six research-based elements. It suggests ideas for evaluating adolescents' interests, abilities, and learning preferences and in setting high curricular expectations accompanied by pertinent support. It also describes instructional approaches that motivate and engage adolescent learners and enable them to interact collaboratively. Chapter 3 provides differentiation classroom examples in the disciplines of science, social studies, English/language arts, and mathematics, builds on the differentiation examples introduced in Chapter 1, and adds others appropriate for contemporary heterogeneous secondary classrooms.

CHAPTER 4: METACOGNITIVE EXTENSION IN ADOLESCENT-CENTERED DIFFERENTIATION

Chapter 4 elaborates on the fifth "E" of the adolescent-centered differentiation framework, Extension. It explores ways in which teachers instruct so that adolescents attain important cognitive strategies that enable them to take ownership and management of their own learning. The chapter showcases two integrated, technology-enhanced problem-based learning (PBL) units that incorporate the principles of UDL, cognitive strategy development, guided reflection, and metacognitive extension.

CHAPTER 5: A DIFFERENTIATED LEARNING ENVIRONMENT: THE AFFECTIVE, SOCIAL-EMOTIONAL, AND PHYSICAL DIMENSIONS

Chapter 5 describes the interrelated affective, social-emotional, and physical dimensions of the adolescent-centered learning environment. Adolescents learn and think better in a flexible, yet structured, community-oriented environment where they move, talk, act, and interact. They thrive in a learning environment where they are motivated personally, guided socially, challenged intellectually, and supported intentionally as they engage in relevant and meaningful learning experiences. Adolescents also need a *safe* learning environment defined by respect for and acceptance of students as individuals, however diverse. Essential to the social dimension is instructional use of flexible grouping that enables adolescents to interact with peers on a variety of engaging, appropriately complex tasks. Adolescents also learn better in a physical setting characterized by order, cleanliness, movement, and structure. Chapter 5 further offers research-based strategies for managing the differentiated adolescent classroom.

CHAPTER 6: THE INTELLECTUAL DIMENSION IN THE DIFFERENTIATED LEARNING ENVIRONMENT

Chapter 6 continues the conversation of the adolescent-centered learning environment with a focus on the intellectual dimension. Adolescents thrive in an intellectually charged environment where they are appropriately challenged and intentionally supported. The chapter illustrates key instructional strategies that differentiate for student readiness and stresses the critical connection between affective and cognitive competence. Chapter 6 also emphasizes the important interplay of knowledge acquisition, understanding, and meaningful assessment in shaping the intellectual dimension. It suggests grading principles that support adolescent-centered differentiation and intellectual growth and mastery. Chapter 6 further features instructional technology as a cognitive scaffolding tool for adolescent learning and intellectual development.

CHAPTER 7: LEARNING PATTERNS AND PROFILES

The underlying message of Chapter 7 is that teachers view all adolescents as contributing members in the learning environment. Rather than thinking in terms of labels and students "at-risk," teachers in differentiated classrooms regard students' learning strengths as starting points for instructional design. At the secondary level, where adolescents are expected to read more complex content, many students need explicit instruction to attain the skills for critical literacy. This chapter focuses on instructional differentiation for three clusters of adolescent populations prevalent in contemporary mixed-ability classrooms. These are gifted, or advanced learners, English language learners, and adolescents with learning challenges that affect reading comprehension and literacy development. The chapter reiterates the goal of adolescent learning that they become metacognitive managers of their own thinking and learning. It describes many differentiation approaches, including explicit cognitive strategy instruction, to help students activate prior knowledge, build connections, construct meaning, and attain pertinent cognitive strategies.

EPILOGUE: A SHARED COMMITMENT TO EQUITY

The Epilogue brings closure to the discussion of adolescent-centered differentiation with a focus on collaboration. Through collaboration, teachers in heterogeneous classrooms encourage high levels of respect and concern among students in high levels that transcend intellectual, cultural, and economic differences. The section showcases project-based learning as a collaboration strategy that works well with all adolescent learners.

GLOSSARY OF DIFFERENTIATION TERMINOLOGY

The final section of the book is an annotated Appendix of relevant differentiation terminology. Throughout the book these terms are boxed and highlighted to denote their importance in adolescent-centered differentiation.

Differentiation and the Learning Brain

Welcome to Ms. Rickard's eighth-grade classroom. The thirty students range from accelerated gifted, to those on grade level, to those with special learning needs, and to those who are English language learners. She has the choice: teach to the middle and hope not to bore the advanced learner or frustrate those struggling with information processing or attention, or vary instruction in ways to meet the range of adolescent learners. She chooses the latter. Not wanting to compromise essential content for anyone, she works with the media specialist to find materials with varied reading levels. Knowing her students differ in how they receive and process information, she uses varied and multiple ways to present subject matter, including auditory, visual, and kinesthetic. Not wanting to make any of her students feel categorized as "slow" or "disabled," she designs tasks that vary in complexity but not in challenge, meaningfulness, or relevance. Wanting to create and maintain sense of community, she groups the adolescents in multiple ways, depending on abilities and personal preferences. Wanting to tap into her students' talents and interests, she gives them choices in how to show their learning. Wanting to motivate, she takes time to assess each student's learning style and preferences, interests, and readiness levels. In Ms. Rickard's classroom, one size does not fit all. Differentiation is apparent.

Differentiation in the adolescent classroom is a commonsense approach that takes into account the learning and development needs inherent in a range of academically diverse students. Adolescent learners differ in cognitive ability, social and economic status, literacy and language proficiency, race, ethnicity and culture, background, prior knowledge, quality of family support and degree of opportunity, motivation, learning preferences, and interests. Who adolescents are, the complex composite of biology and experience, determines the learning strengths and academic challenges they bring to the classroom. Neuroscience further reveals distinct variations in the way adolescents' brains receive, strategically process, and emotionally relate to content, instructional delivery, and assessment (Rose & Meyer, 2002).

IT'S ALL ABOUT GOOD TEACHING PRACTICE

Many of the instructional practices suggested for differentiation are familiar ones. Best-practice teaching (Brandt, 1998) has shown that students learn best when what they learn is personally meaningful, challenging, and appropriate to their developmental level. They learn best when they have choices and learn in their preferred way, when they have opportunities to interact socially, use what they know to construct new knowledge, acquire strategies for learning, and receive helpful feedback. They also learn best in an emotionally positive and supportive environment where they are valued and respected as worthy individuals.

As a matter of necessity, the majority of teachers already make adjustments in curriculum and instruction to allow for student differences in the classroom. They may give students choices of books to read, vary journal prompts, incorporate discussion groups based on interest or ability, ask multiple levels of questions, or arrange for reading buddies. These are examples of good teaching practices that value student choice, student talk, and student differences. Other practices that take more preparation time include tiered activities and products, literature circles, interest centers, learning contracts, compacting, simulations, group investigation, and problem-based learning, to name a few (Tomlinson, 2001).

Tomlinson suggests that teachers begin to differentiate with the more time-consuming strategies at a comfortable pace. She encourages teachers to start small and build on what is familiar. A teacher might collaborate with the media specialist to find varied reading sources or multilevel supplementary materials for a social studies unit already developed or previously taught. Another might incorporate small literature circles based on interest or ability. A math teacher might tier a word problem based on complexity; a science teacher might tier a task. Still another might give students choice on the format for culminating products. Teachers who teach multiple subjects are advised to begin with the one they enjoy the most. By working in a cumulative manner from semester to semester and year to year, differentiation is more manageable.

Adolescent-Centered Differentiation

A strategic approach to curriculum design and instruction that builds meaningfully and responsively on adolescents' unique developmental needs and learning strengths.

Chapter 1 explores innovative research associated with the adolescent learning brain, describes the differentiation philosophy of UDL, and introduces key terminology related to classroom differentiation. It defines differentiation as a strategic approach to curriculum design and instruction that builds meaningfully and responsively on adolescents' unique developmental needs and learning strengths. The chapter identifies and illustrates six key design principles that characterize adolescent-centered differentiation.

THE LEARNING BRAIN

Although human brains share the general characteristics of intake and sense making, individual brains "differ substantially" in the way they recognize, internally process, and assign emotional significance to new information, teaching strategies, and materials within the learning environment (Rose & Meyer 2002, p. 13). Brain imaging of neural activity during learning discloses an astonishing multifaceted communication network that is comprised of three smaller networks, each functioning distinctively and collectively as students learn. These smaller brain systems are (1) the recognition network, which enables students to identify clues and patterns and to associate meaning with information, ideas, and concepts as they attempt to understand (the "what" of learning); (2) the strategic network, which specializes in executive functioning and allows students to plan, carry out, and monitor actions and movement (the "how" of learning); and (3) the affective network, which evaluates and assigns emotional value to incoming information and impacts students' level of engagement (the "why" of learning). These networks parallel Vygotsky's (1962) three prerequisites for learning: information recognition, strategic processing, and learning engagement.

> ### The Learning Brain
>
> The multifaceted communication network comprised of the smaller networks—recognition, strategic, and affective—which function distinctively and collectively as adolescents learn.

Specialized tissues within each of the three neural networks perform certain tasks (Rose & Meyer, 2002). Different tissues in the recognition network, for example, respond to visual stimuli, and other tissues recognize auditory patterns. Different parts of the strategic network control goal setting, and other parts direct people to execute these. Similarly, specialized areas in the affective network may associate positive or negative emotions with subject matter, instructional strategy, teacher style and presentation, learning conditions, and assessment method. During the learning process, students' brains make rapid and simultaneous associations as incoming information is distributed and processed. The recognition network takes in information through multiple sensory avenues (visual, auditory, olfactory, tactile). The strategic network identifies a learning goal, selects and executes a strategy, and evaluates the outcome. Negative or positive emotional responses in the affective network influence students' motivation and ability to engage and progress.

These pertinent findings in neuroscience reveal that adolescents' learning brains specialize in complex and varied ways. "Learners cannot be reduced to simple categories such as 'disabled' or 'bright.' They differ within and across all three brain networks, showing shades of strength and weakness that make each of them unique" (Rose & Meyer, 2002, p. 11). To maximize the chance for more students to succeed academically, teachers are challenged to rethink how they present new information, the opportunities they give students to process and express learning, and the ways they engage and motivate. They need to have multiple and varied methods of presentation, offer more flexible ways for students to make sense of and represent learning, and seek to accommodate their varying interests and learning preferences. Building on individual learning strengths through multiple means of representation, expression, and engagement is the underlying premise of UDL.

UNIVERSAL DESIGN FOR LEARNING (UDL)

UDL is a differentiation approach to curriculum design and instruction that responds to the learning brain (Rose & Meyer, 2002). UDL interjects variety and flexibility into the way information is represented (in support of the recognition network); the skills and strategies students employ to learn and demonstrate competence (in support of the strategic network); and the emotional engagement and enjoyment in the process (in support of the affective network). When teachers provide multiple and flexible representations of a concept and multiple ways for students to participate and engage, they accommodate students with learning challenges *and* create a more flexible and cognitively stimulating learning context for other students in the class.

> **Universal Design for Learning (UDL)**
>
> A differentiation approach to curriculum design and instruction that responds to the learning brain. It encompasses flexibility in information representation, strategic learning and demonstration of competence, and emotional engagement.

[handwritten margin note: Stems from Architecture]

UDL in Practice

Ms. Dixon, an eighth-grade math teacher, plans to teach students the numerical phenomenon of the Fibonacci number. Some of the students will process the concept readily if she shows pictures of nautilus sea shells or arrangements of seeds on flowering plants. For a student who is visually impaired or has difficulty discerning spatial relationships, however, the use of visuals as a representation strategy would be limiting. Acknowledging the ranges of learning strengths and challenges among students in the class, Ms. Dixon offers multiple and flexible ways for them to learn the concept. She accompanies visuals with verbal descriptions; brings in example specimens from nature for students to touch and examine; has students work in pairs to construct the Fibonacci sequence tactilely with simple manipulatives, such as dominos; instructs them how to plot the ratio points on a graph to determine the golden number; and allows them to explore the concept interactively through Web games. She also activates an e-text reader for students who need assistance in reading and processing information.

By offering flexible and varying opportunities that accommodate differing patterns of learning strengths, Ms. Dixon additionally provides a more stimulating environment for all students in the class. She more cohesively activates the recognition network, for example, through multisensory stimulation. She prompts associations across the strategic network by stating learning goals and directions clearly and by giving students instructive feedback. She presents and allows students to process information through varied and multiple learning tools: examples, illustrations, models, and games. She motivates the affective network offering by accommodating student's interests and learning preferences and by allowing them choices in how they process the new content and how they express what they have learned.

COGNITIVE ACCESS FOR LEARNING

[handwritten: COGNITIVE ACCESS]

Universal Design for Learning has its origins in an architectural movement called universal design (UD). Rather than "adding on" unattractive ramps to buildings for handicapped users, architects anticipate the needs of special populations and "build in" accommodations in the design stage (Curry 2003; Rose & Meyer, 2002). Universally-designed architecture and commercial products, critical for persons with disabilities, provide better access for all. Decoder chips in television design, for example, benefit people with hearing impairments *and* any viewer in a noisy restaurant, airport, or health facility. The curb cut in airport parking lots makes navigation possible for those in wheelchairs, mothers with strollers, people on crutches, and travelers pulling wheeled luggage.

[handwritten: better access for all]

Applied in the mainstreamed, regular classroom, universal design provides critical *cognitive access* to curriculum, materials, and instruction for students with learning challenges and enhances access to learning for all students (Howard, 2003; Kame'enui & Simmons, 1999). Central to this differentiation approach is the use of digital technology as a powerful and flexible scaffolding tool (Curry, 2003; Rose & Meyer, 2002). Digitized books and readings, portable word processors, electronic whiteboards, handwriting recognition tools, touch keys on computers, text enlargement, highlighters, translators, read-aloud features on computers, and other multimedia curricular materials and assistive technologies provide learning access for students who struggle with the traditional print versions of content. Numerous software programs and other resources are available for use as "cognitive tools" for screen reading, concept mapping, graphing, model construction, mathematical exploration, content organization, and other learning visualization opportunities (Rose & Meyer, 2002).

> **Digital Technology**
>
> The host of digital media tools that provide flexible scaffolding for cognitive access to learning. These include digitized books, computer-enhanced features for translation, highlighting, and text manipulation, as well as numerous software resources for screen reading, content organization, and visualization, to name a few.

EVOLVING CONVERSATIONS ABOUT DIFFERENTIATION

The UDL premise that all students can learn if given appropriate cognitive access and opportunity based on learning strengths is characteristic of fresh conversations about differentiation in contemporary classrooms (Rose & Meyer, 2002; Scherer, 2006; Tomlinson & Jarvis, 2006; Tomlinson & McTighe, 2006; Weiner, 2006). Deficit terminology such as "category," "label," "dysfunction," and "disability" is evolving into the more positive and action-oriented language of *inquire, discover, reframe, celebrate, build, nurture,* and *encourage.* As Scherer (2006) writes:

> The assumption that students' misbehavior and poor achievement are caused by learning disabilities or are the effects of growing up in poverty or of having dysfunctional families often precludes teachers

from recognizing their students' strengths and appreciating their own power to change the classroom dynamic. (p. 7)

Rather than measuring students' capabilities against a so-called "construct of normalcy," educators are focusing on the strengths each brings as learners.

Tomlinson and Eidson (2003) define differentiation as "a way of thinking about the classroom with the dual goals of honoring each student's learning needs and maximizing each student's learning capacity" (p. 3). It is an inclusive approach to curriculum design, instruction, and classroom management that anticipates and builds on students' learning strengths and supports learning needs. It is ongoing, formative, and assessment-driven as teachers monitor, match, and make learner-responsive instructional decisions and adjustments. It offers varied, multiple, and flexible options for students to learn, work together, and succeed academically.

Tomlinson (2001) describes the teacher's role in differentiated classrooms as one who "proactively plans and carries out varied approaches to content, process, and product in anticipation and in response to student differences in readiness, interests, and learning needs" (p. 7). She identifies several distinguishing elements of differentiated teaching:

1. Qualitative. Differentiated teaching is qualitative rather than quantitative. Students who have demonstrated mastery of a math skill, for example, do not need more practice but rather need to move to a subsequent skill. Conversely, a student who struggles with reading comprehension does not need fewer pages to read but needs support in organizing and making meaning of the content or reading material on a more appropriate level. The teacher's role is to adjust the nature of the task to match students' learning needs so that tasks are:

2. Grounded in Assessment. Differentiation is an ongoing effort to design instruction that opens the learning pathways of readiness, interest, and learning preference. Assessment in differentiated classrooms assumes multiple forms: diagnostic and pretests; informal measures, such as observation, journal entries, discussion, and group reporting; more formal formats, such as quizzes, tests, and papers; and more authentic products, such as mock trials, debates, and multimedia presentations. The teacher's role is to use assessment routinely to learn about students and to monitor their learning progress so that tasks are:

3. Student-Centered. In differentiated classrooms, learning experiences are relevant, engaging, interesting, and appropriately challenging. Students are encouraged to take responsibility for their learning and to make evaluative decisions about it. The teacher's role is to guide and provide direction, support, and feedback, as needed, to help students stretch, grow, and achieve success and competence, academically and socially, with tasks that are:

4. Approached in Multiple Curriculums. In any classroom, teachers have the "power" to make decisions about these curricular elements: (1) content, or

what students learn; (2) process, or how students make meaning of concepts and ideas; (3) product, or the way students demonstrate learning and understanding; (4) learning environment, or the use of physical space, time, and resources. In differentiated classrooms, the teacher's role is to vary these elements in ways that maximize student learning with tasks that are:

5. Flexible. Differentiation is an appropriate and flexible blend of whole-class, small group, and independent learning experiences. Students work in both heterogeneous and homogenous groups based on learning needs and interests. The teacher's role is to provide multiple and varying grouping options with tasks that are:

6. Dynamic. Differentiation is an ongoing inquiry into how students learn best in order to maximize learning and academic success. The teacher's role is to plan proactively to meet students' needs and to adjust and refine learning opportunities continually in response to students' readiness, interests, and learning needs.

Benjamin (2005) delineates several features of differentiation. These include pacing, the degree of structure provided by the teacher, the degree of independence given to the learner, the number of facets in a learning task, the level of concreteness or abstractness, and the level of complexity and depth. Depending on the needs of the learner, teachers can adjust each of these areas.

DEVELOPMENTALLY RESPONSIVE DIFFERENTIATION

Differentiation for adolescents considers students' developmental and individual learning needs. Developmentally, it is important to remember that adolescents are transitioning between concrete and abstract thinking. Younger adolescents are beginning to think logically and to see varying perspectives, yet they are still developing the metacognitive skills more characteristic of older adolescents and adults (Piaget, 1928). Psychologically, adolescents are in the process of defining who they are sexually, religiously, and politically (Erikson, 1968).

A unique goal of adolescent-centered differentiation is that they attain the cognitive strategies and the personal efficacy that enable them to manage their own learning. Adolescents are cognitively "ready" to think strategically and reflectively, the metacognitive capacities that are associated with the brain's developing prefrontal cortex. Learning efficacy evolves as adolescents recognize their personal learning strengths and acquire the cognitive strategies that further their learning goals. For adults, learning strategies are more practiced and automatic; however, for adolescents, these skills are in an experimental, formative state, often below their level of recognition. It behooves a teacher to provide multiple strategies for intellectual interaction and to schedule time for processing and reflection. In response, adolescents recognize and learn in a manner that leads to success and personal competence (Crawford, 2007). This cognitive apprenticeship relationship among adolescents and teacher, described in Chapter 2, is an important element in differentiated classrooms.

THE LANGUAGE OF DIFFERENTIATION

Differentiation is shaped by the dynamic interaction of strategic instruction and learner engagement. It suggests that teachers concentrate on understanding the nature of the student in the design of curriculum, instruction, and assessment. Adolescents' individual learning differences are influenced by biology (gender, brain development, personal proclivities, and cognitive ability) and the environment (family, culture, opportunity, support structures, previous experiences, and prior knowledge). The teacher's goal is to design instructional experiences that build on and meaningfully challenge adolescents' knowledge, skills, and experiences, as well as to provide the necessary supports to help them succeed academically.

Differentiation involves understanding adolescents' varying learning needs as determined by their interests, readiness, and learning profiles (Tomlinson, 2001; Tomlinson & Eidson, 2003). These student characteristics are briefly described below.

- **Personal interests**, or what students enjoy learning, thinking about, and doing. The teacher's goal is to motivate by tapping into adolescents' interests and helping them connect with content that is relevant, intriguing, meaningful, and personally appealing. The teacher's goal is also to try and generate new interests in students.
- **Learning readiness**, or students' current knowledge, understanding, and skill set with regard to the content or skills a teacher is teaching on any given day. The teacher's goal is to make the learning task difficult enough to challenge at a given point according to students' readiness level and to provide the necessary supports that enable that student to succeed.
- **Learning profiles**, or students' preferred learning mode and intelligence strength. Factors that impact learning profile are learning style, such as audio, visual, tactile, kinesthetic preferences, and intelligence strengths (Gardner 1993, 1999, 2006) (see Box 1.1, "Intelligence Strengths"). Learning profile also includes differences in gender proclivities (see Box 1.2, "Gender Profiles"). The teacher's goal is to enable adolescents to learn in a natural and efficient manner, to recognize personal learning preferences, and to develop new avenues of learning.

Tomlinson and McTighe (2005) note that "[r]esponsive teaching necessitates that a teacher work continuously to establish positive relationships with

---

❖ BOX 1.1 Intelligence Strengths

Multiple Intelligences Theory

Linguistic. Understanding and use of written and spoken communication.

Logical/Mathematical. Understanding and use of logic and numerical symbols and operations.

Musical. Understanding and use of concepts of rhythm, pitch, harmony, and melody.

Spatial. Orientation and ability to manipulate three-dimensional space.

Bodily/Kinesthetic. Coordination of physical movement.

Naturalistic. Ability to distinguish and categorize natural objects and phenomena.

Interpersonal. Understanding and effectual interaction with people.

Intrapersonal. Understanding and use of personal thoughts, feelings, preferences, and interests.

Existential. Contemplation of phenomena or questions beyond sensory or empirical experience.

Source: Gardner, (1993, 1999, 2006). *Multiple Intelligences Theory*. New York: Basic Books

Triarchic Intelligence Theory

Analytical. Preference for linear learning based on memory ("schoolhouse intelligence").

Practical. Preference for learning within an authentic and relevant context ("contextual intelligence").

Creative. Preference for solving problems and creating innovations ("problem-solving intelligence").

Source: Sternberg, R. (1988). *Beyond IQ: A triarchic theory of human intelligence*. Cambridge, MA: Cambridge University Press.

❖ BOX 1.2 Gender Profiles

Gender and the Brain

Verbal/Spatial. Boys' brains are more spatial-mechanical and girls' brains are more verbal-emotive.

Optical/Neural. Boys' brains are more responsive to movement and girls' brains are more sensitive to color variety and fine sensory activity.

Frontal Lobe Development. Girls' prefrontal cortices (the part of the brain responsible for decision-making, literacy, and writing skills) are more active than boys', which tend to be more impulsive.

Neural Rest States. Boys' brains go into neural rest states that create a lower tolerance for boredom.

Cross Talk Between Hemispheres. Girls' brains structurally generate more communication between hemispheres enabling better multitasking abilities.

Natural Aggression. Chemical and neural differences associate boys with more competitive, aggressive, and less nurturing tendencies.

(based on findings from Blum, 1997; Gurian, 1996; Gurian & Stevens, 2005; Havers, 1995; King & Gurian, 2006; Rich, 2000; Sax, 2005; Taylor, 2002)

individual learners and come to understand which approaches to learning are most effective for various learners" (p. 18). Critical to the differentiation process is initial and ongoing assessment (Tomlinson, 2005). Teacher-designed inventories and surveys yield valuable early information about adolescents' interests, learning preferences, and attitudes toward subject areas. Quick-checks gauge reading comprehension, writing, and vocabulary levels, for example, while pre-unit assessments inform teachers of students' content-related knowledge and skills. Students demonstrate learning and understanding through varied and multiple opportunities for expression, including projects, authentic products, and performance-based debates or presentations.

The key to effective differentiation is to adjust the curricular components of content, instructional strategy (process), and assessment (product) continuously in response to adolescents' interests, readiness levels, and learning profiles. A discussion of these curriculum differentiation components with supporting examples in instructional practice follows.

CONTENT DIFFERENTIATION

Content, or the "what" of teaching, stems from several sources that include state and local standards, recommendations of professional organizations, curriculum guides, textbooks, and other curriculum materials in the learning environment. The teacher's challenge is to discern from these sources the essential knowledge, skills, and understandings that are *enduring* in the discipline, *relevant* to adolescents' lives, and *pertinent* to the unit or lesson under construction (Crawford, 2007). Wiggins and McTighe (2005) suggest that teachers choose concepts, "big ideas," and core processes that (1) have lasting value beyond the classroom, (2) are central to an understanding of the discipline, (3) have basis in students' misconceptions, and (4) potentially engage students' interests.

According to Maker (1982), the role of content differentiation, or modification, raises the expectation for students to learn and mentally organize knowledge in a more sophisticated manner. The focus is not on discrete facts, dates, rules, names, formulas, and words but on powerful organizations of content that are more abstract and complex and that are meaningful and transferable to students' lives and other learning contexts (Tomlinson, 2001).

Classroom Application

In planning a high school social studies unit, Mr. Wirt considers curriculum standards related to an understanding of the impact of social, cultural, and political context on human perspective. Adolescents may realize that historical accounts are based on personal interpretation; however, they may lack the ability to discern the validity of varying perspectives or the contextual factors that influence them. He formulates the following essential understanding that becomes the entire class's learning goal:

Human perspectives are shaped by complex historical, cultural, social, and political factors.

Mr. Wirt also determines that all students should develop the critical thinking skills to analyze and evaluate the credibility and authenticity of sources. He decides to use the Tiananmen Square incident of 1989 as the historical event to anchor the unit of study. He decides on the following learning goals for all students:

- Students will determine the validity and credibility of historical and cultural events by critically analyzing the varying accounts of the 1989 Tiananmen Square event.
- Students will think critically about the role of propaganda to distort the reporting of current events by examining news coverage in newspapers and on the Internet.

The next challenge for Mr. Wirt is to find ways that ensure student access to this essential understanding and skill set (Tomlinson & Eidson, 2003). Knowing the range of readiness, he selects texts and supplementary materials at varied reading levels. He considers the complexity, abstractness, depth, and breadth of resource materials and the academic needs of his students. He determines multiple ways for students to interact with and make meaning of, the content, including resources on the Internet. He builds in varying support or *scaffolding* strategies, such as highlighted text, videotapes and audiotapes, graphic organizers for note taking, and digests of spotlighted vocabulary and guiding questions. He realizes that translations of key concepts may assist students who are learning English. Box 1.3, "Example Strategies for Differentiation of Content," illustrates the content differentiation strategies Mr. Wirth uses to meets his students' varying readiness, interests, and learning profiles.

❖ BOX 1.3 Example Strategies for Differentiation of Content: Readiness

- Has students read from sources at **varied reading levels** about historical events (the Cultural Revolution, Mao's reign, the pro-democracy movement) that set the context for the Tiananmen Square incident
- Has students read conflicting accounts and excerpts in **different formats of varying complexity** of the 1989 Tiananmen Square incident in Beijing, China
- Builds in supports such as **highlighted text** and **translation**
- Supplements presentations/lecture with online **visuals** from the Encarta Learning Zone (photographs of Tiananmen Square, the protest, and a Beijing map) and **audiotapes**
- Allows students to work together as **reading buddies/partners**
- Provides students with **digests of key concepts** (for example, cultural and political context, propaganda, cultural stereotyping, cultural and historical perspective)
- Asks **task-specific questions**
  o Is there an account that seems closer to the truth?
  o Are there similarities in any other accounts?
  o How can any account be justified?
  o Why would Chinese officials be surprised at the protests?

(Continued)

(Continued)

- o How might the people's roles or ages influence the perspective?
- o Does the date of the reporting make any difference?
- Varies **levels of questions** during ensuing discussions
- Implements **reteaching methods** for students having difficulties

Interest

- Sets up an **interest center** with books, a computer, and list of pertinent sites for further exploration
- Uses **students' questions** to guide mini-lectures
- Uses **examples and illustrations** based on student interests and prior knowledge
- Develops a **learning profile**
- Shows a video of the news coverage of the 1989 Tiananmen Square incident for an **alternate presentation mode** (visual, auditory)
- Involves students in activities that involve choices related to **intelligence preferences**
- Has students research **other cultures** for instances of biased historical interpretations, such as Native Americans in U.S. history books or the debates over slavery between the North and South
- Provides **time** for students to think about and reflect on new content

Source: Adapted from instructional ideas in G. B. Crawford (2007). *Brain-Based Teaching With Adolescent Learning in Mind.* Thousand Oaks, CA: Corwin Press.

PROCESS DIFFERENTIATION

Just as students need multiple ways to take in new content, they need multiple and diverse opportunities to process, internalize, and consolidate new learning (Kaufeldt, 2005). Willis (2006) refers to the brain's need for periodic rests to process new material with the wordplay "*syn-naps,*" or "restorative breaks that are as important for successful memory retention as surprise, positive emotional state, sensory memories, and other relational memories" (p. 26). Furthermore, preteen adolescents can pay attention for approximately ten to fourteen minutes before they need time to actively process new ideas; secondary students, ages 13–18 can attend for approximately twelve to eighteen minutes (Kaufeldt, 2005). The stimulation, complexity, and frequency of processing opportunities improve the chance that new information will move from short- to long-term memory and be retained for future use.

Although the line between content and process is not a distinct one, it is useful to think about process as the time when students make meaning of content by applying it through a learning experience (Tomlinson & Eidson, 2003). When teachers differentiate for process, they find multiple and appropriately challenging ways for adolescents to think about, grapple with, and make sense of content related to important ideas and learning goals. A worthwhile learning experience is one that takes students beyond recitation of memorized information to "seeing how things work and why they work as they do" (p. 5).

Appropriate process experiences take adolescents to a more complex level of understanding, are designed with students' interests in mind, engage students' thinking at a higher level, and relate authentically to the real world

(Tomlinson, 2001). These learning tasks are further designed to align in complexity with students' readiness levels and to give students choices about where to put their learning energy. They additionally encourage students to use their preferred mode of learning, such as whether to work independently or collaboratively; whether to explore or express learning verbally, spatially, creatively, musically, or kinesthetically; or whether to work at a table, on the floor, at the computer, or at their desks.

Implications for Practice

Many adolescent-centered strategies support flexible and responsive processing (Benjamin, 2002, 2005; Crawford, 2007; Heacox, 2002; Kaufeldt, 2005; Tomlinson, 2001; Tomlinson & Eidson, 2003). A few are listed below:

- **Process partners,** when the teacher pauses and students discuss for a couple of minutes what they are learning with a preassigned partner. Prompts ask students to recall new ideas or concepts, orally summarize, or listen to the partner's interpretation.
- **Interactive response journals,** when the class is reading a common novel, for example, the teacher gives prompts varied according to students' interests or academic needs. For adolescents, free-response journals encourage more general or personal emotions to be expressed, issues related to health or relationships to be explored, or concerns about specific subject areas to be addressed. Math journals, for instance, enable students to reflect on how they approached and solved a problem, and associated questions.
- **Thinking maps or graphic organizers,** which give students a visual framework to display and organize ideas and information. According to Willis (2005), [g]raphic organizers coincide with the brain's style of patterning . . . to create meaningful and relevant connections to previously stored memories" (p. 16). These take the form of Venn diagrams; PMI (a graphic for listing the Positive aspects, the negative aspects or Minuses, and the Interesting aspects of an issue under discussion); decision matrices, flow charts, fishbone diagrams, T-charts, and multiple other organizing frames. Ed Ellis has published a wide repertoire of thinking maps ("think sheets") for content areas on his CD, *Makes Sense Strategies—The Works,* available at www.GraphicOrganizers.com.
- **Collaborative learning groups,** when small groups of students collaborate on a learning task. These include literature circles, when students read and discuss common readings; think-pair-share; Jigsaw, where students become experts on various aspects and "pool" their knowledge to construct a group understanding; and inquiry-based structures such as problem investigation, problem/project-based learning, and collaborative lab experiments.
- **Cooperative controversy,** in which students argue both sides of an issue. Adolescents could debate, for example, differing sides of relevant issues such as homeland security, immigration control, or deforestation.

- **Guided note taking,** when students are encouraged to take notes from an overhead or chart by adding their own visuals or personal touches.
- **Tiered assignments or parallel tasks,** in which students work at different levels of difficulty on the same key learning goals. *Tiered assignments* can be adjusted by challenge level, complexity, resources, outcomes, and products (Heacox, 2002). Students can be assigned to a tier or given a choice based on interests or learning preferences. Box 1.4, "Tiered Research Task for the Tiananmen Square Unit," provides an example of tiered research assignments.
- **Interactive technology,** including VCRs, DVD players, Internet, digital cameras, recorders, and presentation programs such as Hyperstudio, PowerPoint, and Inspiration.

Within each processing opportunity, teachers differentiate learning based on students' interests, readiness, and learning profile. In the Tiananmen Square unit, for example, Mr. Wirt differentiates for readiness in the following ways.

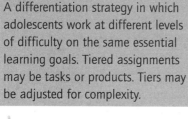

Tiered Assignments
A differentiation strategy in which adolescents work at different levels of difficulty on the same essential learning goals. Tiered assignments may be tasks or products. Tiers may be adjusted for complexity.

- The use of a **pro-con graphic organizer** helps students compare and contrast varying cultural and historical perspectives on the incident.
- The selection of URLs at **varying reading levels** facilitates student research.
- **Variation in the make-up** of cooperative learning groups, to include same and mixed ability levels, provides flexibility and support.
- A **tiered research assignment** provides differing levels of complexity.
- **Mini-workshops** offer students assistance on research skills, as needed.
- The use of **research partners** allows students to work together.

He differentiates by interest in these ways:

- Students take perspectives on varied issues related to **individual interests,** such as animal rights, mandated drug testing, the death penalty, stem cell research, bioengineering, censorship.
- Students conduct polls with peers on **selected, relevant issues.**
- Students write a persuasive letter or editorial to a pertinent source that reflects a **personal perspective** on a current issue.

He also differentiates by learning profile when he allows students to work together and independently and gives students choices in learning tasks and in the way they express their learning.

Processing for Transfer

Also important to adolescents' information processing and retention is their ability to connect new learning with events, phenomena, and circumstances

---

❖ BOX 1.4 Tiered Research Task for the Tiananmen Square Unit

With your research partner, follow at least three of the URLs below to read differing accounts of the Tiananmen Square incident. Prepare a one-page response based on the assigned task.

- Encarta Learning Zone, an interactive site that shows panoramic photos of Tiananmen Square: http://encarta.msn.com/media_701765791/Tiananmen_Square.html
- Tiananmen: The Gate of Heavenly Peace, contains several links to video and audio clips, articles, essays, and book excerpts on the incident: http://www.tsquare.tv/
- Berkeley University: News accounts from the US: http://globetrotter.berkeley.edu/clips/1989/XI1IIa.html
- Pekingduck Archives: A college student who participated in the event: http://www.pekingduck.org/archives/000063.php

Task One (for readiness level learners)

- Choose one of the accounts (Chinese, American reporter, student participant, others) and record the series of events about the incident on a flow chart diagram. Discuss why you think the account represents the person's point of view from a cultural or political perspective.
- Write this person a letter that contains at least three questions you'd like to ask related to this perspective.

Task Two (for advanced learners)

- Use a Venn Diagram to compare two differing accounts of the incident (Chinese, American reporter, student participant, other). Discuss why you think the account represents these persons' cultural or political perspective.
- Pretend you are a French reporter covering the event for your newspaper. Write your own account. Be prepared to justify your perspective.

Task Three (for grade-level learners)

- Use a Venn Diagram to compare two differing accounts of the incident (Chinese, American reporter, student participant, other). Discuss why you think the account represents these persons' cultural or political perspective.
- Pretend you are a reporter covering the event for your local newspaper. Write your own account. Be prepared to justify your perspective.

---

beyond the immediate learning context. Transfer of learning to new situations does not come naturally to adolescents. Their metacognitive skills for seeing the "big picture connections" are developing. Teachers thus are challenged to use explicit processing strategies to help them realize how the essential understandings that shaped a unit's design have lasting generalization in their own lives. Mr. Wirt, in the Tiananmen Square example, extends adolescent learning through reflective questioning and parallel activities. Examples of metacognitive questions that extend learning follow.

- Why do people see and interpret events differently?
- How do personal emotions affect one's perspective?
- Why is it important to consider historical and cultural context?

- What is important to consider in the critical analysis of sources?
- Do you think that what you read in the United States is always credible?

Mr. Wirt also heightens transfer by asking students to use critical analysis skills to contrast the coverage of current events in local, regional, and urban newspapers, or to compare editorials, articles, Web sites, or news coverage that give varying viewpoints on current issues such as the justification of the Iraq war, immigration control, or stem cell research.

PRODUCT DIFFERENTIATION

The term *product*, or learning evidence, generally refers to students' culminating demonstration of understanding the essential knowledge and skills of a unit or extended study. A product can be a unit test or a more authentic measure of learning, such as a presentation, a performance, a newscast, a newspaper, a museum exhibit, a musical interpretation, a multimedia presentation, a reenactment, a portfolio, a Web portal; a speech, a project or some other less traditional, alternative measure (Beamon, 1997, 2001; Crawford, 2007; Gardner, 2006; Tomlinson & McTighe, 2006; Wiggins & McTighe, 1998). Beamon (2001) offers several ideas suggested by teachers of adolescents. These include

- A travel brochure to show understanding of environmental concepts
- A trial simulation to show understanding of the judicial system
- Survival backpacks for a chosen biome to show understanding of the concept of survival
- A math bridge to show understanding of weight and equations
- A plan to attract businesses to a community to show understanding of economic principles
- A carnival game to show understanding of probability
- A children's book to show understanding of literary perspective and voice

Several elements are key to the design of assessment products for adolescents. First, the product is a meaningful, challenging, and a natural extension of the learning experience. Gardner (1993) proposes that a good assessment instrument be a learning experience in itself as students reshape and synthesize ideas within a real-world context. Second, the assessment conveys students' genuine understanding of or insight into important content knowledge. Third, guidelines and criteria for evaluation are clearly defined and understood, generally in the form of a rubric.

An additional critical element in product design is to allow adolescents to demonstrate learning in ways that reflect personal learning differences (Tomlinson & Eidson, 2003). Just as content and process are differentiated, products can be designed to vary or give students choices in response to readiness, interests, or learning profiles. Products can be tiered for depth or sophistication, as illustrated by Mr. Wirt's research task in the last section, or products can

Table 1.1 Differentiating Products for Multiple Intelligences

Linguistic	Logical/Mathematical	Musical	Spatial
Poem, Speech	Flow chart, Diagram	Song, Rap	Illustration
Letter, Essay	Strategy game	Musical score	Model, Diorama
Crossword puzzles	Graph, Checklist	Multimedia presentation	Comic book
Persuasive papers	Timeline, Sequence		Poster, Brochure
Intrapersonal	Bodily/Kinesthetic	Interpersonal	Naturalistic
Editorial, Opinion	Role play, Drama	Discussion, Debate	Travel brochure
Journal, Log	Interpretive dance	Opinion survey	Display, Collection
Reflective paper	Demonstration	Interview	Experiment

allow students to use a range of talents, interests, and preferences, including learning style and intelligence strength. Table 1.1, "Differentiating Products for Multiple Intelligences," provides ideas for products that differentiate for eight of the multiple intelligences.

POWERFUL LEARNING EXPERIENCES

Although the various elements of differentiation are discussed separately in this book, each constitutes an integral part of the learning cycle. Kaufeldt (2005) writes that "[t]his integrated approach to orchestrating content, grouping, environment, presentation, process, and products, when done well, should appear simply as a *powerful learning experience* to the students" (p. 116). Teachers who differentiate for adolescent learning structure meaningful, relevant, and appropriately challenging learning experiences that provide multiple pathways for students to acquire knowledge, demonstrate understanding, and be successful academically. Teachers who teach responsively understand the way in which student differences influence the way they learn. They develop curriculum, plan instruction, and structure the learning environment so that all students have access to, relate to, and make sense of essential ideas and skills and demonstrate understanding in personally meaningful ways. Accordingly, they support and maximize the success of all learners. If teachers hope to meet adolescents' changing and disparate developmental needs, they have no option but to create classrooms where learning opportunities are differentiated, and *all* students have meaningful opportunities to achieve.

Crawford (2007) suggests that effective teachers do the following for successful differentiation in the adolescent classroom:

- Inquire about students' personal strengths, preferences, and interests and incorporate these into planning.
- Learn about students' families and cultural backgrounds and honor these within the curriculum.

- Find out what students know or remember and help them relate to new learning by building connections.
- Look for broad themes in the content to include a wider range of students' ideas.
- Help students make a bridge between content and real life.
- Vary tasks to accommodate individual learning strengths and preferences.
- Structure groups that are flexible to validate interests and a range of learning abilities.
- Give assignments that differentiate for students' varying learning abilities.
- Allow students to discuss, explore, wonder, and question.
- Listen, guide, encourage, expect, push, facilitate, and challenge.
- Celebrate students' individuality by letting their thoughts be heard and their creativity flourish.
- Allow students to work, talk, and question collaboratively.
- Permit all students to delve into and better understand content through direct, meaningful, and relevant involvement.
- Challenge students to use knowledge in ways that make sense and a difference in their lives and others.
- Trust and guide students as they take ownership of their own learning.
- Respect and value students' differences and build on them so that they become more competent and confident in personal learning management.
- Enable students to expand the horizons of learning by interacting with resources in the local and global community.

DIFFERENTIATION DESIGN PRINCIPLES

Differentiation for adolescent learning capitalizes on the developmental and personal strengths these students bring to the classroom. It incorporates these six design principles.

Principle 1: Evaluation. Seek to know students' developmental and individual learning needs, strengths, interests, and preferences through initial, multiple, and ongoing assessment.

Principle 2: Expectation. Use assessment knowledge strategically to design meaningful curriculum and appropriately challenging learning opportunities for a range of learners.

Principle 3: Engagement. Use varied, multiple, and engaging instructional strategies for students to learn and demonstrate understanding.

Principle 4: Exploration. Organize flexible opportunities for students to collaborate, explore, and practice under guidance and feedback.

Principle 5: Extension. Promote learning management by making cognitive strategies explicit and structuring time for reflection and metacognitive extension.

Principle 6: Environment. Create and maintain a learning environment that is supportive for adolescents' intellectual, social, physical, and emotional development.

Figure 1.1 shows a visual of these six design principles. It is important to remember that these elements do not function in a linear manner. They are interrelated and interactive. Evaluation—in terms of the assessment of adolescents' interest, readiness, content knowledge, and learning preferences—is an ongoing process as teachers modify and adjust curriculum and instruction responsively. Expectation sets the curricular context of important disciplinary content that is differentiated through flexible access and cognitive supports. Engagement of adolescents' emotions, curiosity, and thinking is important throughout the learning experience. Exploration sets the mindset for intellectual inquiry and collaborative construction of meaning and understanding. Extension is likewise ongoing as teachers model cognitive strategies and coach students to reflect metacognitively and to transfer learning to other contexts. Critical to all learning experiences is a supportive learning environment in which students feel accepted and valued and where they have equitable opportunities to thrive personally and intellectually.

Figure 1.1   Adolescent-Centered Differentiation

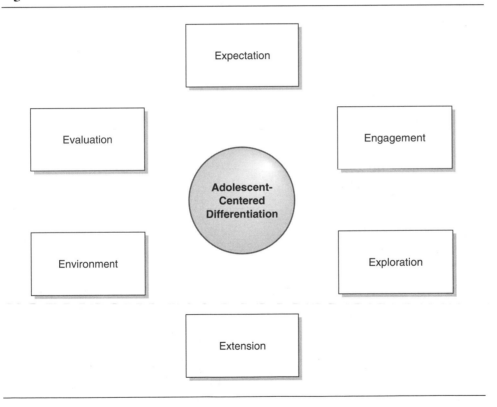

SUMMARY AND LOOKING AHEAD

Chapter 1 approaches the many and varied learning differences among adolescents that are contingent on hereditary and background experiences. It addresses brain research related to the differing ways adolescents' learning brains receive, process, and relate to content and classroom conditions. It defines differentiation as a strategic approach to curriculum design and instruction that builds meaningfully and responsively on adolescents' developmental needs and learning strengths. It also, importantly, identifies six design principles that support adolescent-centered differentiation. It then introduces the language of differentiation through examples of content, process, and product and illustrates the differentiation strategy, tiered assignments, as used in student research. Other noted strategies that differentiate for adolescents' readiness, interests, and learning profiles follow. Many of these are illustrated in the following chapters.

- Varied complexity of reading levels
- Highlighted text and translation as scaffolding
- Varied supplemental materials for learning styles
- Varied questioning strategies
- Digests of key concepts
- Interest centers
- Use of examples and illustrations based on student interest and knowledge
- Mini-lectures based on students' questions
- Multiple Intelligences in products
- Reading partners
- Reteaching
- Alternate/multiple presentation modes
- Choice in activities and products based on Multiple Intelligences
- Cultural sensitivity and diversity
- Process partners
- Interactive response journals
- Thinking maps or graphic organizers
- Collaborative learning groups
- Cooperative controversy
- Guided note taking
- Tiered assignments or parallel tasks
- Interactive technology

Chapter 2 explores the relationship between adolescents' unique intellectual, personal, and social learning needs and how their brains generally function during the learning process. It illustrates with examples for classroom practice. It also examines pivotal findings from the field of neuroscience that shed light on the developing adolescent brain and associated cognitive and emotional maturity.

2

Differentiation and Adolescent Development

Chapter 1 defined differentiation as the strategic approach to curriculum design and instruction that builds meaningfully and responsively on students' developmental needs and learning strengths. Box 2.1, "Adolescent-Centered Design Principles," identifies six Es that are key principles for adolescent-centered differentiation.

❖ BOX 2.1 Adolescent-Centered Design Principles

Principle 1: Evaluation. Seek to know students' developmental and individual learning needs, strengths, interests, and preferences through initial, multiple, and ongoing assessments.

Principle 2: Expectation. Use assessment knowledge strategically to design meaningful curriculum and appropriately challenging learning opportunities for a range of learners.

Principle 3: Engagement. Use varied, multiple, and engaging instructional strategies for students to learn and demonstrate understanding.

Principle 4: Exploration. Organize flexible opportunities for students to collaborate, explore, and practice under guidance and feedback.

Principle 5: Extension. Promote learning management by making cognitive strategies explicit and structuring time for reflection and metacognitive extension.

Principle 6: Environment. Create and maintain a learning environment that is supportive for adolescents' intellectual, social, physical, and emotional development.

Adolescent-centered differentiation additionally requires an understanding of the ever-changing developmental nature that defines adolescents as learners. Chapter 2 explores the relationship between adolescents' unique intellectual, personal, and social learning needs and the way their brains generally function during the learning process. It draws parallels between adolescent learning needs and the six differentiation design principles and illustrates these with implications for classroom practice. The chapter also reveals pivotal findings from the field of neuroscience associated with adolescents' intellectual and emotional maturity.

ADOLESCENT DEVELOPMENT

Adolescence is a developmental time of erratic physical growth, social exploration, and unfolding intellectual capacity. It is a time of awakening, realization, anticipation, confusion, awkwardness, transition, change, identity defining, and self discovery. As a unique population, adolescents share distinguishing developmental tendencies. Although there is great variation in intellectual capability and learning strengths, culture and language, and interests and experiences, several inter-related generalizations can be made that have implications for adolescent learning (Crawford, 2007).

Adolescence
The transitional time between late childhood and young adulthood characterized by rapid changes in physical, social, emotional, and intellectual development.

Adolescents' expanding cognitive capacity, for example, enables them to think abstractly and conceptually about more sophisticated content. Their capacity for intellectual reasoning and reflection is emerging faster than their ability to make rational decisions about personal health and lifestyle. They are eager to tackle relevant problems, discuss and share viewpoints about critical issues, and talk about ethical choices that impact their actions. They are also developing the capacity to reflect upon and regulate their own learning. Academically, adolescents are more self-motivated and push to direct their own learning, yet they may become easily discouraged if they fail to accomplish their goals.

Physically, adolescents' bodies are developing adult features and sexuality; personally they yearn for independence and autonomy. On a personal level, they crave normalcy and tend to obsess about appearance, physical differences, and perceived self-inadequacies. They frequently measure their personal worth and define self-identity by what they believe others think and feel about them. This self-identity is in a state of tentative and precarious negotiation as they move into who they are becoming.

Socially, adolescents crave acceptance and validation. They are entering a "brave new world" of peer negotiation and peer pressure, yet emotionally, they may lack the judgment to contain their feelings or to make healthy or appropriate decisions. Table 2.1, "Adolescent Developmental Tendencies, Implications for Learning," aligns adolescents' personal, intellectual, and social developmental inclinations with associated learning needs.

Table 2.1   Adolescent Developmental Tendencies, Implications for Learning

Adolescent Developmental Tendencies	Implications for Learning
Personal	Learning Needs
Anxious for developmental normality	Climate of acceptance, tolerance
Easily angered, slow to recover	Emotional safety, guidance
Push for independence, autonomy	Choice, responsibility, accountability
Easily discouraged if do not achieve	Appropriate challenge, relative success
Intellectual	Learning Needs
Have diverse knowledge, interests, abilities	Opportunities to develop range of skill and to pursue variety of content areas
Can see relationships among similar concepts, ideas, and experiences	Complex subject matter, relevant issues
Capable of inferential thinking, reasoning	Higher-level, analytical questioning
Capable of critical evaluation, extended focus	Time and opportunity for critical thinking
Reflective, metacognitive, self-motivated	Self-evaluation, choice
Social	Learning Needs
Can be indifferent to adult figures	Opportunity to interact with knowledgeable adults in collaborative projects
Concerned about self-presentation to peers	Emphasis on cooperation, inclusiveness, group contribution
Strive to conform for peer acceptance	Structured, positive student interaction

ADOLESCENTS AS LEARNERS

Adolescent learning is an intellectual process highly influenced by social interaction, situational context, personal beliefs, dispositions, and emotions (Bransford, Brown, & Cocking, 2000; Vygotsky, 1978). Teaching that capitalizes on adolescents' developmental tendencies is responsive to their associated developmental learning needs (Crawford, 2007). These developmental learning needs are identified and described below.

- **Personal connection**. Adolescents need to connect learning with prior knowledge, personal experience and interests, and mode of learning. They respond to relevance and authenticity in learning experiences that enable them to make meaningful personal connections and relate learning to the larger world of their experience.
- **Appropriate intellectual challenge**. Adolescents need to be cognitively engaged within the reach of their capabilities. Their developing cognitive capacities enable them to think about, question, and grapple with the pertinent issues and problems found in substantive content.
- **Emotional engagement**. Adolescents need to be motivated by relevant experiences that intrigue, activate their emotions, and actively involve

them—physically, intellectually, and socially. They are captivated by multi-sensory engagement, and they thrive on the opportunity for choice based on personal interests, strengths, and preferences.

- **Purposeful social interaction**. Adolescents need guided and meaningful collaboration with peers and others in the learning community. This interaction allows them to explore, experiment, and socially construct knowledge and learning.
- **Metacognitive development**. Adolescents are developing the capacity to think about, reflect on, and take ownership of their own learning. They need opportunities to acquire the cognitive and metacognitive skills and strategies to manage their learning and to extend it to other learning situations in and beyond the school.
- **Supportive learning environment**. Adolescents need a safe, structured, and supportive learning space where they can express and shape ideas, articulate developing thinking without fear of embarrassment, and feel included, accepted, and valued. In this space they can develop naturally, intellectually, socially, personally, and emotionally; be successful; and gain both competence and self-efficacy.

These six categories of adolescent developmental learning needs are supported by current research in learning, cognition, and brain development and functioning, as discussed in the following sections. This classification aligns with the six adolescent-centered differentiation principles identified in Chapter 1. Table 2.2, "Adolescent-Centered Differentiation," indicates this alignment.

Table 2.2   Adolescent-Centered Differentiation

Differentiation Principle	Brain-Based/Developmental Learning Needs
Knowledge of students through multiple and ongoing assessments	Personal connection, or the need to connect learning with prior knowledge, experience, interests, and learning preference
Design of consequential content and intellectually motivating instruction	Appropriate challenge, or the need to be cognitively engaged within the reach of personal capability
Varied, multiple, and engaging instructional strategies	Emotional engagement, or the need to be motivated by multisensory experiences that intrigue and actively involve
Flexible opportunities for guided collaboration, exploration, and practice with feedback	Purposeful social interaction, or the need for guided and meaningful collaboration with peers and others in the learning community
Strategy instruction for reflection and metacognitive extension	Learning ownership, or the need to acquire the metacognitive cognitive strategies for personal learning management and extension
Supportive learning environment that is emotionally and intellectually safe for adolescent thinking, learning, and development	Supportive learning environment, or the need to feel supported, valued, accepted, and protected in a community of learners.

PERSONAL CONNECTION

Learning is internally mediated, controlled primarily by the learner, and dependent on the knowledge, skills, and experiences that the learner brings to the learning experience (Bransford, Brown, & Cocking, 2000). Learning occurs when students actively construct personal meaning based on how they relate to or make sense of what they are trying to know or understand. Since adolescents bring a diverse range of knowledge and interests that are shaped by varying biological, cultural, and experiential factors, the challenge for teachers is to find a point of connection with what students know, believe, and feel (Crawford, 2007). When teachers pay attention to the knowledge and beliefs that learners bring to the learning task and use this knowledge as a starting point for new instruction, learning is enhanced (Bransford, Brown, & Cocking, 2000). Making personal connections with adolescents not only facilitates learning, but also validates who they are and what they can contribute as learners.

Supporting Brain-Based Research

Learning is a brain-based function that similarly relies on the need for personal connection. The brain is a pattern-seeking organ that chunks together, organizes, and integrates pieces of new information with what is familiar. It works like a sieve to filter out incoming sensory information that it cannot associate within its memory structure (Wolfe, 2001).The brain's key "sorter" is the internal perception of whether or not incoming information can connect with existing, related neural structures. The brain's filtering activity is thus directly linked to what it selects to pay attention (Sylwester, 2004).

The brain's active and dynamic nature enables adolescents to construct and reconstruct knowledge over time as they interact within learning environments. Even before adolescents are born, their brains rapidly develop complex, interrelated networks of neural structures that form the basis for memory and association (Caine, Caine, McClintic &, Klimek 2005; Diamond & Hopson, 1998; Sousa, 2001, 2003; Sylwester, 2003; Willis, 2006; Wolfe, 2001). These neural structures are influenced and shaped by the factors in the external environmental, including home life, culture, hobbies, interests, and level and amount of stimulation. All adolescents are capable of learning; yet the way their individual brains are structurally "wired" to learn differs. As a result of varying environmental and biological factors, what each brings to the learning situation varies.

Implications for Practice

The implication for teachers is to design instruction that enables adolescents' brains to make personally relevant connections. "Whenever new material is presented in such a way that students see relationships, they generate greater brain cell activity (forming new neural connections) and achieve more successful long-term memory storage and retrieval" (Willis & Horch, 2002, p. 15). As adolescents increase the quantity and quality of neural connections, they expand the ability to recognize, use, and communicate these connections.

In other words, they have a stronger capacity for executive functioning, or personal learning management.

Wolfe (2001) suggests that teachers "hook the unfamiliar with something familiar" by comparing a new concept with one known or by using analogies, similes, and metaphors (p. 104). The mathematical concept of parallel lines is illustrated by the tracks of a railroad or sides of a sheet of paper, for example. Prior knowledge of the circulatory system in the human body is useful when adolescents learn to dissect frogs. The ecosystem of a neighborhood creek is a stepping stone for them to understand the delicate balance of plant and fish life in saltwater marshes. Adolescents' interest in music can be connected to research about culture and traditions of ancient civilizations. The challenge for teachers is to activate what is stored in the long-term memory by making learning experiences relevant to prior knowledge. Accordingly, adolescents connect to and form new mental associations.

Teachers have access to a range of strategies that capture the brain's attention and help adolescents make relevant connections with new learning (Beamon, 2001; Caine & Caine, 1997; Caine, Caine, McClintic, & Klimik, 2005; Jensen, 2000; LaDoux, 1996; Sousa, 2001, 2003; Sprenger, 1999; Sylwester, 2003, 2004; Willis, 2006; Wolfe, 2001). These strategies are varied, hands-on, multisensory, active, and interactive. They also connect with students' visual, verbal, kinesthetic, and other intelligence strengths (Gardner, 2006). Helping adolescents make personal connections magnifies their cognitive response capability and enhances their memory. Ways to practice making these connections in the classroom include:

- Music, art, dance, and sensory enhancements that enable hands-on learning.
- Visuals and graphic organizers that help organize and "chunk" information.
- Physical movement for its interactive and kinesthetic value.
- Periodic processing time, in small discussion groups and individually, that gives opportunity for consolidation and internalization of new learning.
- Humor to heighten emotional response and promote relaxation.
- Other sensory-engaging experiences such as pantomime, simulations and role plays, real-life problems, field trips, mock trials or debates related to historical and current issues, experiments, model building, and mind mapping.

EMOTIONAL ENGAGEMENT

Emotional engagement is closely linked with adolescents' learning and thinking. Gardner (1999) explains the importance of emotions in the learning process: "[If] one wants something to be attended to, mastered, and subsequently used, one must be sure to wrap it in a context that engages the emotions" (p. 76). He further observes that students are "more likely to learn, remember, and make subsequent use of those experiences with respect to which they had strong—and one hopes—positive emotional reactions" (p. 77). Introducing a problem-based learning unit, for example, with the arrival of a mysterious telegram immediately stirs adolescents' curiosity. Students who engage in debate over current issues and events, such as immigration policy, digital privacy, censorship, or global warming, grapple with matters of high emotional investment. Reading and discussing adolescent literature related to the teen issues of friendship, death, peer pressure, and cultural identity rouse emotions related to who they are as young people.

Emotional engagement is also closely linked to the quality of classroom relationships. When adolescents feel marginalized because of differences in race, ethnicity, capabilities, or economic advantages, they may be angry or sad, and these emotions can directly interfere with learning (Jensen, 1998). Conversely, when students feel affirmed and purposeful, they are more likely to find emotional joy in learning.

Supporting Brain-Based Research

Current neuroscience technology confirms that emotions play a critical role in learning (Damasio, 1994; Feinstein, 2004). Unlike feelings, which are conscious expressions, emotions are beneath the level of conscious and are deeply rooted in memory. Wolfe (2001) notes that emotion is a primary catalyst in the learning process. She likens emotional response to a biological thermostat that alerts the brain and body to something in the environment that warrants attention. "The brain is programmed to attend first to information that has strong emotional content" (p. 88). Whether the determination is potentially dangerous or not, emotions capture attention and "get a privileged treatment in our brain's memory system" (p. 108).

Jensen (1998) writes that "emotions give us a more activated and chemically stimulated brain, which helps us recall things better" (p. 79). Emotional arousal stimulates the *amygdala*, the area in the middle brain that processes emotions, and starts a chain of physiological responses that determine the emotional relevance (i.e., is it harmful or something I'll like? Should I engage or should I withdraw?). A fraction of a second later, the incoming information goes from the thalamus, another sensory relay station, to the prefrontal cortex, the part of the brain that enables a more rational response and memory recall (i.e., have I confronted this before? How should I respond or act? How can I solve this problem?)

Amygdala
The area in the middle brain that is stimulated by emotional arousal and processes incoming information based on emotional relevance. Incoming information subsequently travels to the thalamus, another sensory relay station, and on to the prefrontal cortex where rational responses are made. In stressful situations, emotions dominate the ability for higher-level cognitive processing.

In stressful situations where the brain perceives threat, such as instances of humiliation or alienation, embarrassment or physical harm, such as bullying or boredom, emotions can dominant cognition and the rational/thinking part of the brain is less efficient (Beamon, 1997). When teaching engages adolescents' interests, stress is reduced and they are, as

Willis (2006) describes, "more successful and happier learners" (p. 59). Willis continues:

> The common theme to the brain research about stress and knowledge acquisition is that superior learning takes place when stress is lowered and learning experiences are relevant to students' lives, interests, and experiences. Lessons must be stimulating and challenging, without being intimidating. . . . Otherwise the stress, anxiety, boredom, and alienation that students experience block the neuronal transmission, synaptic connections, and dendrite growth that are the physical and now visible manifestations of learning. (p. 59)

Implications for Practice

Learning experiences that positively stimulate adolescents' curiosity and activate their senses are more likely to engage them emotionally (Crawford, 2007). Novelty, intrigue, and humor "hook" adolescents' interests. Teachers can introduce a problem scenario that is authentic and urgent; stage a mystery to solve by selectively bringing in clues; rearrange a room to simulate a coffee house for a poetry reading; bring in real props related to the lesson for background effect, dress in costume, or wear a hat for a role play (Kaufeldt, 2005).

Feinstein (2004) notes that emotional experiences affect what adolescents pay attention to, their motivation, reasoning strategies, and their ability to remember. She recommends music, played softly to welcome students to class or to accompany a content area, for example, Gustav Holst's *The Planets* during a science lesson. She writes of a physics teacher who skates into a classroom to demonstrate force and speed with two different masses. Another teacher turns cartwheels to simulate molecular rotation.

Willis (2006) determines several low-stress strategies that captivate students' attention and improve the brain's receiving, encoding, storing, and retrieval capacities. These are staging an element of surprise through unexpected classroom events; showing dynamic videos; creating a state of positive anticipation to stir students' curiosity; using humor and unique visuals, such as illusions; asking intriguing open-ended questions followed by quick writes or think-pair-share; and designing enriched and varied sensory learning experiences that are student centered and include choice. Engaging and holding students' attention enhances their readiness to use higher-order thinking. She suggests one strategy called "popcorn" reading, which is a read-aloud technique where students "jump in" and read at any time (p. 21). Crawford (2007) lists other emotionally engaging experiences, all presented in a physically safe and inviting classroom climate, as follows:

- drama, role play, and debate
- problem-based learning, problem solving
- games and simulations
- classroom celebrations
- seminars and class discussions

- cooperative learning and team events
- storytelling, personal expression, and journal writing
- mock trials, experiments, and projects
- field-based projects and service learning
- interactive technology

APPROPRIATE INTELLECTUAL CHALLENGE

In a period when rapid growth appears in the prefrontal cortex, or thinking part of the brain, cognitive capacity is unfolding and adolescents are intellectually primed for inquiry, critical thinking, and problem solving (Beamon, 1997). Adolescents thrive on challenge that is meaningful, appropriate, and relevant. "They love to play with words, to write limericks, to delve into science fiction, to debate political and environmental issues (the more controversial the better), to give opinions, to solve real life problems—the possibilities are endless" (p. 23). Intellectual challenge is not passively receiving information; it rather "gives adolescents the freedom to experiment with their imaginations, to release their passion for make-believe, to explore their fascination for fantasy, and to use developing psychomotor skills" (p. 24).

Adolescents are increasingly capable of abstract thinking and moral reasoning, which makes them responsive to ethical problems that impact them personally. They can consider hypothetical questions, analyze complex situations, and make reflective conclusions (Feinstein, 2004). Topics such as stem cell research, immigration regulations, deforestation of rain forests, genetic sequencing, human and civil rights, animal protection, and issues related to war justification and world peace generate engaging discussion and debate. Appropriate challenge brings novelty, interaction, movement, and emotional engagement to the learning experience.

Since all adolescents do not develop a capacity for abstraction simultaneously, teachers can reduce failure and frustration by providing hands-on, concrete learning strategies (Feinstein, 2004). Dissecting frogs helps adolescents understand the complex circulatory system, and manipulatives assist in the study of geometry. Vygotsky's (1978) concept of *zone of proximal development* contends that students are able to navigate challenge that is set one step above their readiness levels if they have adequate supports (Bransford, Brown, & Cocking, 2000). These supports, or *scaffolding*, can be human, such as the teacher, other students, and other adults, or symbolic, such as computers or graphing calculators, or graphic organizers and thinking maps that help students retrieve, manipulate, and organize new information in meaningful ways.

> **Zone of Proximal Development**
>
> Vygotsky's (1978) concept that students can navigate challenge that is one step above their readiness levels with adequate supports, or scaffolding.

Supporting Brain-Based Research

Challenge within a stimulating environment changes the brain's structure, density, and size (Kaufeldt, 2005). The brain is incredibly malleable, referred to as *brain plasticity*, and responsive to challenging experiences within the

Scaffolding
Supports in the learning environment that are human, such as the teacher, peers, or other adults, or symbolic, such as computers, graphing calculators, or graphic organizers.

learning environment (Diamond, 1967). On a cellular level, the adolescent brain's 30 billion intricate nerve cells connect with trillions of dendrites in an elaborate information-processing system (Beamon, 1997). Axons extend from cell bodies and transmit chemical signals across connective pathways to neighboring neurons. These synapses literally "fire" with conductive electrochemical transmissions as adolescents' brains process incoming stimuli and make connections with previously-learned knowledge in the long-term memory (Willis, 2006). With repeated practice and activation, the brain constructs more permanent and complex circuits of axons and dendrites, and neural associations become faster, richer, and more efficient.

As neural structures form, change, and alter, a fatty tissue of white glial cells called myelin forms around, stabilizes, and thus strengthen axons. This myelin sheath aids in the transmission of information between neurons and among brain regions and facilitates more integrated brain functioning. When the adolescent brain is actively engaged with new information—such as through questioning, discussion, problem solving, small group activities, and processing and application—cognitive connections are reinforced and new learning more potentially moves into long-term memory (Wolfe, 2001). Within an enriched environment, the brain can literally grow new and increasingly complex synaptic connections.

Brain Plasticity
The brain's responsiveness to a challenging learning environment by the development of dendrites and new, increasingly synaptic connectivity, which facilitates more integrated brain functioning.

Implications for Practice

When teachers present new material to be learned in multiple and multisensory ways, and allow time for practice, process, and review, neural connections become more numerous and more interrelated (Willis, 2006). In learning about the abstract concept of acceleration, for example, eighth graders learn a formula, visualize the process in small groups by conducting a series of lab trials with rulers, wind-up toys, and clock watchers, then discuss observations, analyze collected data, calculate speed and negative acceleration, figure in velocity, are reminded of the distinction between average velocity and final velocity through a graph the teacher draws on the board, write up the lab results in interactive notebook, share findings, and discuss evidences of acceleration in the real world (i.e., How can we determine the negative acceleration of the skateboard you are riding across the school parking lot?). With each activity, different parts of the brain are connecting and making associations with the new concept. The new information is thus stored in multiple brain regions, connected through memory circuits, and more easily accessed.

PURPOSEFUL SOCIAL INTERACTION

Adolescent learning is socially motivated through a natural inclination to interact with peers and a cognitive need to collaboratively construct knowledge and new learning.

Cognitive psychologists have contended for some time that learning is a social process that is supported by meaningful interaction with resources, human and symbolic, in the learning environment (Perkins, 1992; Resnick, 1987). Socially shared interaction, or *shared cognition*, makes internal conversations visible so that knowledge can be built upon, strengthened, or reshaped. Others (Pea, 1993; Gardner, 1999) assert that knowledge and intelligence are distributed among humans and supported by technology. When adolescents are able to interact with peers, whether solving a problem, conducting an investigation, creating a play, or planning for a debate, they benefit socially and cognitively from shared perspectives and shared resources.

> **Shared Cognition**
>
> The theory that learning and knowledge construction is supported by meaningful social interaction with resources in the learning environment, human and symbolic.

Similarly, the constructivist approach promotes the value of social interaction and shared knowledge within a local or global community of learners (Bransford, Brown, & Cocking, 2000; Perkins, 1999). Constructivism is a view of learning based on the belief that adolescents adjust prior knowledge to accommodate new experiences as their brains actively seek connections with what is already known and make meaning (Brooks & Brooks, 1993). This view supports the purposeful design of instruction that relates to adolescents' prior learning and experiences and that emphasizes hands-on problem solving. A key tenet of constructivism is that knowledge and understanding are socially constructed in dialogue with others.

As social as adolescents naturally are, however, they are not readily adept in social and personal skills to work together in a group toward a common academic goal. Social interaction is meaningful if it is well planned and if teachers instill in students the skills for purposeful collaboration. When structure and accountability are apparent through specific guidelines for learning tasks, when expectations for behavior and demonstration are clearly communicated, and when procedures for evaluation and reflection are organized, social interaction is more likely to work (Crawford, 2007).

Supporting Brain-Based Research

Brain research gives further credibility to the importance of social interaction. Renate Caine, one expert in brain-compatible learning, stresses the social dimension of the brain (Caine as cited in Franklin, 2005). "Remember, the mind is social . . . You're embedding this knowledge in their experiences and everyday worlds" (p. 3). Siegal (1999), author of *The Developing Mind*, suggests that the social interactions among people—within families, classrooms, cultures, or the larger world culture via the Internet—enhance the flow of energy and information into the brain where it is processed actively by the mind.

Sylwester (2006) explains the brain's maturation during late childhood and early adolescence ("the tween brain") as a progression from "childhood acceptance of dependence" to "an adolescent reach for independence' (p. 1). As the frontal lobes mature during the preteen years, thinking and actions shift from reactive to proactive thinking and behavior. As young children, adolescents depended on adults to make executive decisions; however, with maturation in the frontal cortex, adolescents begin to expect to make their own decisions and solve their own problems. With this cognitive shift, they crave exploration, peer interaction, and personal autonomy.

Implications for Practice

Instructional strategies abound that enable adolescents to work collaboratively to explore problems (Crawford, 2007). Problem- or project-based learning, service learning, simulations, cooperative learning structures, literature circles, and other grouping strategies provide opportunities for students to communicate ideas and learn collaboratively. Through interpersonal connections adolescents' "brain energy" is shared and the cognitive potential of thinking and learning is enhanced. Teachers accordingly can select among numerous available strategies to incorporate peer grouping into instruction. For adolescents, purposeful, shared interaction can promote positive self-concept, academic achievement, critical thinking, peer relationship, positive social behavior, and motivation to learn (Johnson, 1979; Johnson &, Johnson, 1988).

For social interaction to be successful, instruction, practice, and feedback must be purposeful, and the teacher's interactive role is essential. Ongoing assessment that supplies constructive feedback can help adolescents direct a learning activity productively and positively manage their actions toward one another. Interactive group work, implemented effectively, can benefit adolescents socially, personally, and intellectually.

METACOGNITIVE DEVELOPMENT

A critical goal of learning is to help adolescents to become responsible managers of their own cognition (Bransford, Brown, & Cocking, 2000). Important to this goal is that students develop the strategic competence for metacognition and self-regulation. "In order to develop strategic competence in learning, children need to understand what it means to learn, who they are as learners, and how to go about planning, monitoring, revising, and reflecting upon their learning and that of others" (p. 100). For self-management to be realized, however, guidance and structure from others more expert in learning is necessary. This relationship between teachers and adolescent learners is known as *cognitive apprenticeship* (Collins, Brown, & Newman, 1989). Under a teacher's guidance, adolescents become increasingly more competent and self-directed over time.

> **Cognitive Apprenticeship**
>
> Also referred to as metacognitive coaching, the process by which teachers model strategic thinking and guide as students practice and obtain the cognitive strategies for self-directed learning. Teacher assistance gradually decreases and student strategic competence increases.

Adolescents' emerging ability for metacognitive thinking enables them to think more strategically about personal learning. A powerful phenomenon, metacognition enables adolescents to set goals, plan, problem solve, and monitor and evaluate learning progress. Through ongoing feedback from teachers or more expert others in the learning context, adolescents can make adjustments and increasingly develop competence. In the final stage, the teacher gives less assistance, referred to as fading, and students assume more responsibility and a sense of ownership over their own learning. The goal of metacognitive coaching is to help adolescents think strategically about knowledge while they progressively strengthen cognitive skills.

Supporting Brain-Based Research

Similar to the teacher's role in the cognitive apprenticeship model is the brain-based strategy of elaborate rehearsal (Wolfe, 2001). *Elaborate rehearsal strategies* help adolescents interact with and process new information until it is learned. Repeated associations of pieces of information enable long-term memory circuits to form (Martin & Morris, 2002). Elaborate rehearsal strategies motivate adolescents through movement, emotion, multisensory engagement, social interaction, and intellectual challenge. They activate a new dendrite network and increase the probability that new information will be retained. Another benefit for the adolescent brain is more efficient neural processing. This increase in the speed of synaptic activity enables the brain to process information and make connections between previous and current learning more readily.

> **Elaborate Rehearsal Strategies**
>
> Strategies that activate the brain's natural capacity to build long-term memory circuits through repeated association. They motivate through movement, emotional stimulation, multisensory engagement, social interaction, and intellectual challenge.

Implications for Practice

The brain-based literature identifies many elaborate rehearsal strategies (Crawford, 2007; Caine & Caine, 1994; Jensen, 1998; Sousa, 2001, 2003; Sylwester, 1999; Wolfe, 2001). They include the following:

- Writing activities across the curriculum, including journaling, poetry, stories, speeches, letters, newspaper eulogies, dialogues, and Quickwrite/Quickdraw diagrams or interactive notebooks
- Mneumonic devices, including music, rap, jingles, acronyms, rhymes, phrases, key word imagery, location association, and narrative chaining
- Peer teaching and other cooperative learning structures that enable summarization, discussion, analysis, and evaluation
- Reciprocal teaching
- Active review, including student presentations and game format
- Reading punctuated with intervals of note taking, discussion, and reflection
- Thinking maps, including webs, graphic organizers, story-plots, diagrams, data organization charts, matrixes, and t-charts
- Physical movement, including role play, simulations, and reenactment

A SUPPORTIVE LEARNING ENVIRONMENT

Learning environments are multidimensional entities of physical space, structure, and time; social interaction and intellectual interplay; and emotional, affective interchange (Crawford, 2004). Teachers create learning environments when they make decisions about furniture arrangement and wall displays, routines and procedure, expectations for student behavior, materials and resources, student grouping, curriculum development and instruction, and teacher-student and student-student relationships. Learning environments comprise visible and invisible classroom structures and processes that are designed to benefit individual students and the whole class (Tomlinson & Eidson, 2003).

A learning environment that is conducive to adolescent thinking and learning is responsive to their personal, intellectual, and social needs (Crawford, 2007). Adolescents learn and think better in a flexible, yet structured community-oriented environment where they move, talk, and interact. They thrive in a learning environment where they are motivated personally, challenged intellectively, and supported intentionally; where they engage in relevant and meaningful learning activities; and where they can accomplish and experience academic success.

Supporting Brain-Based Research

In a physically, social-emotionally, and intellectually safe classroom environment, the brain operates at maximum capacity. In her book, *Differentiation Through Learning Styles and Memory*, Sprenger (2003) writes that physical characteristics such as natural lighting, cooler temperatures, natural colors, music, water, orderliness, and safety are linked to attention, learning, and retention. A learning environment that helps students understand and manage emotions, develop empathy toward the feelings of others, and build skills for interpersonal relationships is important for the brain's social-emotional development. A brain-compatible cognitive environment includes "predictability, feedback, novelty, choice, challenge, and reflection" (p. 18). Predictability reduces stress; continuous, interactive feedback enables the brain to learn; appropriate levels of novelty stimulate attention; and opportunities for choice appeal to the brain's emotional amygdala and motivate the capacity for decision making, planning, and critical thinking. Appropriate challenge and opportunity for reflection enable deeper processing and long-term memory.

Implications for Practice

Chapters 4 and 5 provide an extensive discussion of the developmentally appropriate learning environment and how the physical, affective, and cognitive dimensions can be differentiated to meet the varying needs of adolescents. They address interrelated research-based practices for structuring and managing an adolescent-centered environment for learning.

A PRIME TIME FOR LEARNING

Sophisticated neuroimaging and brain-mapping studies in neuroscience yield insight into adolescent brain development associated with learning and behavior (Giedd et al., 2004; Strauss, 2003; Willis, 2006). These findings are imminent in understanding the relationship among brain functioning, development, and instructional practice. Educators who write about *brain-compatible instruction* caution against a simplistic and causal interpretation (Caine, Caine, McClintic, & Klimik, 2005; Crawford, 2007; Jensen, 2000; Sylwester, 2005; Wolfe, 2001), yet they do agree that understanding how the brain learns is "an essential element in the foundation on which we should base educational decisions" (Wolfe, 2001, p. 191). Several new adolescent brain discoveries follow.

Scanned Exuberance

Important to teaching and learning is neural imaging documenting that the adolescent brain is still growing, maturing, and evolving. Strauss (2003), author of *The Primal Teen: What the New Discoveries about the Teenage Brain Tell Us About Our Kids,* explains the phenomena in this way:

> The teenage brain, it's now becoming clear, is still very much a work in progress, a giant construction project. Millions of connections are being hooked up; millions more are swept away. Neurochemicals wash over the teenage brain, giving it a new paint job, a new look, a new chance at life. The teenage brain is raw, vulnerable. It's a brain that's still becoming what it will be. (p. 8)

The adolescent brain's gray matter thickens as neurons grow more and more synaptic connections, or new pathways for nerve-cell communication. This overproduction, or *neural exuberance,* occurs just prior to puberty in the frontal lobes of the cerebral cortex (Strauss, 2003). Gray matter in this outer area of the cerebrum, associated with reasoning, metacognition, planning, problem solving, attention focusing, emotional self-regulation, and language specialization, actually thickens "as tiny branches [dendrites] of brain cells bloom madly . . ." (p. 15). This region of the adolescent brain is the last to mature and does not fully develop until early adulthood. As mentioned earlier, the brain's white matter, the fatty myelin sheaths that insulates the axons and carry information away from the neurons, additionally thickens. This myelin coating makes the nerve signals between cellular neurons transmit faster and more efficiently (Willis, 2006).

Brain growth in the prefrontal cortex is associated with adolescents' development of executive functioning, or the ability to plan and organize thinking, use reason, access working memory, engage in risk assessment, moderate emotions, and reflect on personal strengths and weaknesses (Caine, Caine, McClintic, & Klimek, 2005). While adolescents eventually become capable of executive functioning, it does not happen instantaneously. What remains "under construction," at times to the dismay of teachers and parents, is the adolescent brain's ability to resist impulses, to control emotions, to think out decisions, and to plan ahead (Strauss, 2003).

Brain-Compatible Instruction

Teaching that is responsive to the way the human brain receives and organizes new information through association with prior knowledge, processes information in long-term memory, and retrieves information previously learned. Conditions conducive for brain-compatible instruction include emotional stimulation and cognitive engagement within a supportive and safe learning environment.

Neural Exuberance

The overproduction of neurons and synaptic connections in the frontal lobes of the cerebral cortex just prior to the onset of puberty as the adolescent brain matures.

Neural Sculpting

Another relevant discovery is that between the ages of thirteen and fifteen, following the phase of neural overproduction, the adolescent brain goes through a "pruning back" phase known as *neural sculpting.* A small percentage of synaptic connections are actually lost. Neuroscientist Jay Giedd, in an interview for Frontline's *Inside the Teenage Brain* (Spinks, 2002) notes that "there is a fierce, competitive elimination, in which brain cells and connections fight it out for survival" (p. 2). Adolescent brains appear to go through a period of circuit refinement when synapses that are more frequently activated are strengthened at the expense of those less used (Wilson & Horch, 2002). Brain maturation thus involves a fine tuning of neural connections as the brain consolidates, focuses, and prepares for the adult years.

Neural Sculpting
The phase of circuit refinement following neural exuberance when neural connections that are used frequently strengthen and those less used are lost. Neural sculpting is susceptible to experiences as the adolescent brain matures.

Interestingly, the experiences in which adolescents are involved can play a role in determining which neural structures survive the pruning process (Spinks, 2002) As adolescents explore and shape their identities, what they do in their social, personal, and academic experiences factors into the brain's maturation. Those who engage actively in music, sports, or academics, for example, potentially strengthen and sustain synaptic connections in the associated brain areas. An associated and cruel irony, however, is that the maturing teen brain is highly susceptible to drug, alcohol, and nutrition abuse during a time when experimentation, need for social acceptance, and personal perceptions of infallibility are developmentally characteristic. These functional changes in the adolescent brain carry both potential and risk.

Crazy by Design

For years, the erratic, unpredictable behaviors of adolescents have been dismissed as the by-product of an oversupply of hormones. Recent brain research, however, may explain why teens make impulsive decisions or act out in reckless ways. The emotional turmoil associated with adolescence has less to do with raging hormones than the "complex interplay of body chemistry, brain development, and cognitive development" (Price, 2005, p. 22). The area of the brain associated with impulse control and self-regulation is still undergoing change. As Strauss (2003) humorously writes, "[t]he teenage brain may, in fact, be briefly insane. But, scientists say, it is crazy by design. The teenage brain is in flux, maddening and muddled. And that's how it's supposed to be" (p. 8).

An adolescent's underdeveloped prefrontal cortex is linked to an inability to regulate and refrain from certain behaviors. Feinstein (2004) notes that "[s]erotonin, the neurotransmitter that makes us feel calm and at peace, is at a natural low during adolescence" (p. 108). Not thinking of consequences for potentially harmful decisions and actions, adolescents are more prone to sensation-seeking or risky behavior that includes sexual engagement, cigarette smoking, and substance use (Caine, Caine, McClintic, & Klimek, 2005). Even a cognitive awareness of the associated dangers of thrill-seeking behavior does not appear to control adolescents' impulsive actions.

Although neuroscientists are wary to draw a direct relationship between brain functioning and teen behavior, they do speculate that brain development explains why adolescents at times have trouble regulating their emotional responses (Thompson, Giedd, & Woods, 2000). In emotion-inducing situations, adolescents tend to respond more on the "gut responses" of the amygdala, as mentioned earlier. than to the executive or regulating function of the prefrontal cortex. As teens grow older, however, the brain activity shifts to the frontal lobes, and emotional responses are more reasoned and justifiable. With support and structure, adolescents can develop the skills for responsible decision making and personal management.

A Physically Responsive Entity

Two other regions are of interest in the adolescent developing brain: the *cerebellum* and the mid-brain. A small area located above the brain stem, the cerebellum is responsible for balance, posture, muscle coordination, and physical movement (Jensen, 2000; Sylwester, 2006). Current brain research associates the cerebellum with cognitive functions, including the coordination of thinking processes (Wilson & Horsch, 2002). Neuroscientists speculate that growth in the cerebellum during adolescence is not genetically controlled and thus is susceptible to environmental influence. The traditional classroom where adolescents sit passively and memorize discrete, minimally relevant information is not an environment that primes cognitive development.

The association of the adolescent brain and physical activity is not new to brain research. Jensen (1998), who calls the brain a physically-responsive entity, writes of the connection of movement with learning. The cerebellum, according to Jensen, may be the brain's "sleeping giant because it is so neurologically connected to the frontal cortex" (p. 83). The cerebellum consists of approximately one-tenth of the brain's volume, yet contains over half of its neurons.

Multiple studies have linked physical movement and kinesthetic activity such as sculpture and design to enhanced visual thinking, problem solving, language development, and creativity (Greenfield, 1995; Silverman, 1992; Simmons, 1995). Physical exercise, including recess, sports, and in-class activities, fuel the brain with a high amount of food, called neurotropins, which enhance growth and connectivity among neurons. Movement associated with neural development includes physical activities such as a "living" graphic organizers, body sculpture, human bingo, summary ball toss, in-school field trips, and simple stretching exercises.

> **Cerebellum**
>
> The small area located above the brain stem responsible for balance, posture, muscle coordination, physical movement, and coordination of thinking processes. The cerebellum is responsive to conditions in the learning environment.

BRAIN-COMPATIBLE INSTRUCTION: A SUMMARY

Crawford (2007) highlights several brain-compatible instructional strategies that are appropriate for adolescent learning and development. These are recommended in the professional literature and have been implemented in middle and high school classrooms (Caine, Caine, McClintic, & Klimek, 2005; Jensen, 1998; Nelson, 2001; Sousa, 2001, 2003; Sylwester, 2003; Wolfe, 2001). These include:

- **Integrated thematic units of study** that encourage adolescents to make thematic connections across disciplines related to social issues and personal concerns

- **Problem/project-based units of study** that engage adolescents as stakeholders in investigation and critical analysis of authentic problems
- **Academic service-learning units of study** that promote collaborative inquiry, civic action, and community outreach
- **Real-life apprenticeships** that involve adolescents in internships with adults in jobs related to the curriculum or based on their personal interests
- **Simulations and games** that cast adolescents in roles where they consider alternate perspectives and pertinent ethical issues
- **Music and arts integration** that heightens emotion through sensori-motor stimulation and thus enhance memory
- **Peer collaboration and cooperative learning structures** that give adolescents the opportunity to share and construct knowledge, problem solve, and hone social and interpersonal skills
- **Thinking maps** that provide a visual and tangible mechanism for adolescents to organize and analyze their thinking
- **Reflective writing** that offers a vehicle for adolescents to process, consolidate, and think metacognitively about personal learning
- **Puzzles and word problems** that serve as "brain teasers" for adolescents to improve thinking skills and strengthen synaptic connectivity
- **Physical movement and exercise** that keeps the brain alert and attending
- **Physical group challenges** that promote collaboration and problem solving
- **Internet activities** that open the world to adolescents as they research relevant and timely issues; collaborate with mentors, experts, and peers; and actively manipulate data and skills

SUMMARY AND LOOKING AHEAD

Chapter 2 discusses the interrelationship of adolescents' developmental tendencies, learning, and brain functioning. It aligns the six differentiated design elements with associated developmental, brain-based elements that support adolescent learning. These are personal connection, appropriate intellectual challenge, emotional engagement, purposeful social interaction, metacognitive development, and supportive learning environment. The chapter also examines pivotal research on the developing adolescent brain related to adolescent learning and emotional management and suggests responsive classroom practices.

Chapter 3 expands the discussion of adolescent-centered differentiation through elaboration and application of four of the six design principles: evaluation, expectation, engagement, and exploration. Subsequent chapters discuss extension and the learning environment. Chapter 3 also introduces and illustrates multiple differentiation strategies in the content areas of science, social studies, math, and English.

3

Adolescent-Centered Differentiation

Evaluation, Expectation, Engagement, and Exploration

Chapter 2 structured a framework for adolescent-centered differentiation based on six interrelated components. These elements are associated with adolescent learning and development and brain-compatible teaching. These are Evaluation, Expectation, Engagement, Exploration, Extension, and Environment. Chapter 3 broadens the discussion of adolescent-centered differentiation through elaboration and application of four of these design elements: Evaluation, Expectation, Engagement, and Exploration, within the disciplines of science, social studies, English/language arts, and mathematics. It builds on the differentiation strategies introduced in Chapter 1 and adds others that are appropriate in mixed-ability middle and high school classrooms.

START WITH THE STUDENTS

Principle 1: Evaluation, or the inquiry into students' developmental and individual learning needs, strengths, interests, and preferences through initial, multiple, and ongoing assessments (need for personal connection).

The first "E" in adolescent-centered differentiation, **Evaluation,** parallels adolescents' developmental need for personal connection. As discussed in Chapter 1, adolescents learn when they actively construct personal meaning based on prior knowledge, beliefs, and experiences. Learning is enhanced when teachers determine a point of connection and use this knowledge as a starting point for instruction. Evaluation calls for teachers to structure assessments that continually determine students' content knowledge, capabilities, interests, and learning preferences. Figure 3.1, "The Powerful Role of Assessment in the Differentiated Classroom," shows an overview of the components and purposes of Evaluation. Key associated questions for teachers are these:

- What does the adolescent bring to the learning experience in interests, learning styles, and learning preferences?
- What does the adolescent know about the content knowledge?
- What is the adolescent learning throughout the experience?
- What instructional adaptations and adjustments do I need to make to maximize adolescent learning?
- What has the adolescent learned about the content, its application, and personal learning?

Stevenson (2002) describes inquiry into students' preferences, interests, likes and dislikes, personal perceptions, priorities, and perspectives as a developmentally appropriate tool to "advance understanding, communication, and learning . . ." (p. 58). He suggests various inquiry techniques. These include questionnaire/ surveys, scenarios that invite reflection and speculation, interviews, discussions about current issues, journal writing, logs, letter writing, suggestion boxes, and portfolios. He notes that inquiry "allows us to gain a critical grasp of how our

Figure 3.1   The Powerful Role of Assessment in the Differentiated Classroom

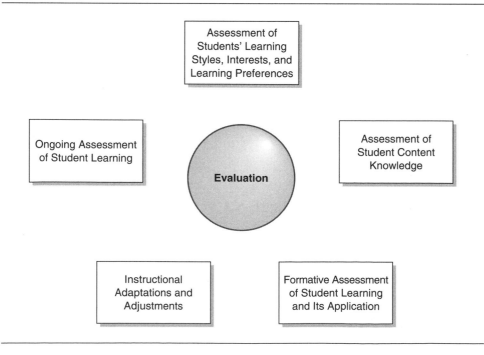

students comprehend their school experience . . . and is the most direct route for us to learn about our youngsters as individuals" (p. 70). Beyond the purpose of information gathering in developing curriculum and planning instruction, inquiries help adolescents learn more about their own strengths and preferences so that they will make corresponding choices in their own learning management.

Box 3.1, "Getting to Know Your Students," gives a sampling of queries that assess adolescents' interests and learning profiles (Kaufeldt, 2005; Northey, 2005; Stevenson, 2002). A free Learning Styles Inventory is also available at www.howtolearn.com. A Learning Channel Preference survey that helps students determine if they are auditory, kinesthetic, or visual learners can be accessed at www.way2go.com (Northey, 2005). Other inventories include the 4Mat System (McCarthy, 1981), the "Four Learning Styles" (Silver, Strong, & Perini (2000), multiple intelligences (see Northey, 2005, pp. 20–23), and emotional intelligence tests (see www.EQ.org and www.cqi.org). Assessment structures can be open-ended questions, multiple-choice items, rating scales, checklists, oral responses, and artistic or pictorial tasks, depending on the purpose of the inquiry (Tomlinson, 2005).

❖ BOX 3.1 Getting to Know Your Students

Interests	A letter or essay about what interests me. . . .
	Things I like to do most in my spare time. . . .
	Things I like to do with my friends outside of school. . . .
	Sports and hobbies I enjoy; my favorite books. . . .
	Societal or medical issues interesting to me. . . .
	Favorite subjects. . . .
	Things I'd like to learn more about. . . .
	Favorite things to do with my family. . . .
Learning Preferences	Ways I like to show what I have learned or can do. . . .
	Times of day/week/year when I learn best. . . .
	I do not learn well when I have to sit in rows.
	I do better with an assignment if I can listen to music.
	I prefer studying by myself.
Multiple Intelligences	I enjoy working crossword puzzles and playing Scrabble.
	I am good at strategy games such as chess or checkers.
	Geometry is easier for me than algebra.
	I need to touch things to learn more about them.
	I can hear when a musical note is off-key.
	I enjoy being involved in social activities.
	I keep a journal where I describe my feelings.
	I know how to identify most plants and animals.

Informal and formal strategies abound that enable teachers to assess, and thus evaluate, adolescents' prior knowledge, learning progress, and academic success. Tomlinson (2005) notes that pre-assessments do not have to be formal measures. They can consist of Know–Want to know–Learn (KWL) or other graphic organizers such as concept maps, small or whole group discussions, interviews, writing prompts/quick writes, demonstrations, drawings, or past work samples. Other formative measures for ongoing assessment include homework assignments, weekly recap letters, quizzes, checklists, dialectic journals, observation, threaded discussions, exit cards, clipboard notes, conferences, and questioning, among others. As discussed in Chapter 1, products of learning can be traditional and structured (such as a unit test) or authentic and performance-based (such as a presentation, a construction, a project, or a documentary, to name a few). Key in the design of assessments in the Evaluation component is that they inform instructional planning and modification, provide constructive feedback to adolescents on an ongoing basis, and help them to gauge their own learning progress.

Differentiation in Practice

A game format is a developmentally appropriate way to find out about adolescents' interests. Ms. Ciarfello and Ms. Gardner (M. Ciarfello, personal interview, 2006), sixth-grade teammates, use the bingo game as the structure for a student inquiry. On the first day of class, they distribute 4 × 4 bingo cards with the designated columns of sports, food, hobbies, and subjects. The sixth graders reproduce the card on notebook paper. On the board, they list the following items under each category;

Sports	Food	Hobbies	Subject
field hockey	fast food	traveling	language arts
football basketball	pizza	camping	math
soccer	seafood	reading	science
cheerleading	salad	drawing	foreign language
horseback riding	snack food	exercising	social studies

These words are also written on index cards divided between the two teachers. As the items are called out randomly, students identify an interest or favorite by drawing a symbol or coloring in a box under the corresponding heading on personal bingo cards. After multiple games are played (with candy prizes), the teachers collect the cards. An examination of the bingo cards not only indicates the adolescents' interests but also gives the teachers an idea of the students' unique style and creativity. Some students draw pictures of food or sports while other use multiple colors to indicate their choices. The activity gives the teachers valuable information about students' individuality and is engaging and enjoyable to the young adolescents.

Another differentiation strategy is a *personal learning profile assessment* (Tomlinson, 2005, p. 79). Teachers give adolescents a list of phrases related to how the students think they learn best. This self-assessment is simple to administer and renders useful information about students' learning preferences and intelligences. Box 3.2, "Personal Learning Profile," gives ideas for possible choices.

❖ BOX 3.2 Personal Learning Profile

Students respond by placing choices that *best* describe positive and negative conditions for personal learning, accordingly.

I learn best when I can. . . .   *But I don't learn as well when I am expected to.* . . .

Be artistic	Be a leader	Get out of my seat frequently
Doodle	Ask questions	Engage in hands-on activities
Act in a drama or skit	Discuss in small groups	Do something with my hands
Take notes	Role play	Work with a partner
Work in groups	Listen to music	Watch videos
Speak in front of a group	Follow a guide	Have something to eat/drink

Principle 1 of adolescent-centered differentiation is the intentional effort by teachers to understand the varying ways adolescents approach school and experience learning. A teacher who arrives in the classroom with a differentiated curriculum is more successful in teaching students of all types—those with advanced ability and those who need remediation, students who speak the "language of power" and those to whom that language is evolving, students who have bold aspirations and those who have few, students from homes of plenty and those who live in poverty, students who trust and students whose experiences have left them with little faith, students who learn by listening and those who learn through application, and students who are compliant and those who challenge authority.

As Tomlinson and McTighe (2006) aptly render, "[t]o pretend those differences do not matter in the teaching/learning process is to live an illusion" (p. 16). Being attuned to students' varied learning needs is as important in differentiated teaching, as is a well-designed curriculum. With the goal of maximizing the success of each learner, teachers in differentiated classrooms make modifications to ensure all students' access to important knowledge and skills. A responsive and meaningful curriculum is the expectation of Principle 2.

A CURRICULUM OF CONSEQUENCE

Principle 2: Expectation, or the strategic use of assessment knowledge to design meaningful curriculum and appropriately challenging learning experiences for a range of learners (need for appropriate intellectual challenge).

The teacher's challenge in differentiated classrooms is to design curriculum in ways that *all* students have an opportunity to learn important, thought-provoking, and relevant content. The second "E," setting the **Expectation** for learning in academically diverse classrooms, involves making decisions about what is important and essential for all students to know, understand, or be able to do (Tomlinson & McTighe, 2006). Perkins (1992) notes that when students encounter the "overarching mental image" that holds subject matter together, they begin to develop an understanding of important concepts, principles, and skills that shape the discipline (p. 17). The teacher's challenge is to use state and national standards as a starting point to identify "big ideas" or generalizations that have both enduring value and the potential to engage students' interests (Wiggins & McTighe, 1998). Figure 3.2, "A Curriculum of Consequence," provides a visual of the key components of Expectation. Key curriculum design questions are as follows:

- What are the essential understandings that emanate from content standards?
- What is relevant for adolescents to know, understand, and be able to do?
- What are the essential questions that all adolescents should explore?
- What do I want adolescents to remember and apply to their own lives?
- How can I use the evaluation data from student inquiries to design curriculum that is meaningful and supportive of adolescents' varied learning needs?

Curriculum based on the important concepts, themes, and generalizations of a discipline is more likely to engage students and link to their life experiences and interests (Tomlinson & McTighe, 2006). Curriculum based on *enduring understandings* is also more flexible than curriculum based on facts. Curricular goals that are relevant and consequential also provide an opportunity for students with varied backgrounds, strengths, and academic abilities to work with essential ideas at varying levels of complexity. These powerful learning goals become the "springboard from which differentiation ought to begin" (p. 41).

Figure 3.2   A Curriculum of Consequence

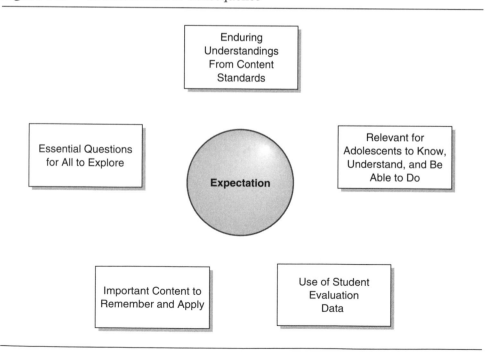

Essential questions are broad enough to be generalized across topics of study within a discipline (Crawford, 2007). They also serve as connections among themes and concepts. In a study of the bombing of Pearl Harbor in World War II, for example, an essential question is, "How does conflict shape history?" A study of the relationship among the strata of the rainforest in science is encompassed by the broad question, "How is interdependency reflected in the environment?" In a mathematical study of the Fibonacci sequence, the connective question is, "How is symmetrical patterning apparent in nature?" Similarly, in a study of the social, personal, and political factors that influenced Dali's artistic style, a question that extends the content to other content in the art field is, "How can nonconformity lead to creative expression?"

Thematic units designed around adolescents' developmental needs and social concerns are also effective ways to organize content. Adolescents are dealing with physical, social, and psychological changes as they negotiate identity and purpose. They are also fast developing the cognitive skills to think about abstract issues that affect their daily lives (Beamon, 1997). Beane (1992) identifies several age-relevant themes: culture, independence, exploration, conflict, interdependence, power, relationship, change, communication, expression, honor, and justice, among others. Themes provide a connective framework for the basic standards and skills of state and district-level curriculum guides (Beamon, 1997). "Basic content is mastered but in the more comprehensive framework of relevant problems, key issues, and abstract themes" (p. 114). Within this framework of more complex content, teachers can plan appropriately challenging learning experiences that meet the learning needs and interests of a variety of students.

Respectful Tasks

Once curricular expectations are delineated, the teacher's challenge is to (1) design quality learning experiences that *appropriately challenge* and (2) build in a *support system* that facilitates students' access to the content and helps them successfully achieve. Important to differentiation is that all students have what Tomlinson (2005) refers to as "respectful tasks" (p. 161). Although not all students are involved in identical tasks, each student's work is interesting, based on the targeted learning goals, and intellectually compelling. According to Tomlinson (2005), the best tasks are those that students find "a little too difficult to complete comfortably" (p. 184). With appropriate support, students can attain success. Tomlinson and Eidson (2003) write that "[o]nce the essential knowledge, understanding, and skills of a unit or topic are clear, the teacher also begins thinking about the second facet of content—how she will ensure student access to that essential knowledge, understanding and skill set" (p. 4).

The scenario that follows is an example of a differentiation strategy called *RAFT* (Santa, 1988) in which students grapple with meaningful content through differentiated tasks of varying levels of complexity. RAFT is an acronym that stands for the Role of the writer, the Audience that the writer will address, the varying Formats for writing, and the content Task.

- Role of the writer—Who are you as a writer? A conservationist? A homeless person? An endangered animal? A bacterium?

- Audience—To whom are you writing? The French people? A close friend? Readers of a newspaper?
- Format—What form will your writing take? A persuasive letter? An advertisement? An editorial? A poem?
- Topic and Task—What's the subject or the point of this piece? Is it to call for stricter regulations on logging? To tell a personal story? To persuade someone to choose a different lifestyle?

RAFT
A differentiation strategy that varies the complexity level of tasks. RAFT stands for the Role of the writer; the Audience that the writer will address, the varying Formats for writing, and the content Task.

RAFTs are generally written from a viewpoint different than the role of student, to an audience other than the teacher, and in a creative format. RAFTs help students improve their writing composition and are often used in association with content areas to apply and deepen understanding. RAFTs can be used at any appropriate point in a unit to differentiate so that all students have access to important content. The following example shows how an eighth-grade science teacher uses the RAFT strategy as a final assessment for a unit on microbiology.

A Differentiation Example

Ms. Rickard's eighth-grade science class is heterogeneous, ranging from highly gifted to inclusion students. Her unit on microbiology is based on grade level standards from the state science and technology curriculum. The unit's learning goals for all students include:

- Students will use technologies and information systems to research, gather, and analyze data.
- Students will analyze and evaluate information from a scientifically literate viewpoint by reading, hearing, and/or viewing.
- Students will use written and oral language to communicate findings.
- Students will describe diseases caused by microscopic biological hazards, including viruses, bacteria, and parasites.
- Students will analyze data to determine trends related to how infectious disease spreads, including carrier, vectors, and conditions conducive to disease.

Ms. Rickard then decides on the following essential understandings to frame the study:

Infectious disease is caused by the spread of microscopic biological hazards, including viruses, bacteria, and parasites.

The scientific analysis of data related to the spread of infectious disease is useful in its control and prevention.

During the unit, students study the structure and functions of many types of microbes and the transmission of diseases. As a final assessment of content knowledge, she uses the RAFTs in Table 3.1, "Microbe Project

Table 3.1   Microbe Project RAFTs

Read the directions for your RAFT below. This project is independent and will require much of the work to be done at home. Please be accurate, thorough, and creative.

Role	Audience	Format	Topic and Task
Virus	Other viruses and microbes	Autobiography	In first person narrative, explain your life story. Include details on how you gain energy, your environment, reproduction, and effects on your host. Please also give information about the hardships you have faced in your life—-attacks against you. Expected length is at least 1 ½ pages. Include a book jacket for your autobiography.
Helpful bacterium	Harmful bacteria	Persuasive dialogue between the two bacteria	Do research on one helpful bacterium to find specific details on the benefits of being a helpful bacterium. In your dialogue, share information on your scientific name, environment, method of reproduction, and preferred environment, and anything else interesting to you. Of course, you will need to elaborate on your benefits to your host. Be persuasive but honest. Expected length is 2 pages.
Harmful bacterium	Judge	Confession	Do research on one helpful bacterium. Tell the story of your life of crime. Include details on how you get needed materials, reproduce, and your preferred target. Of course, you will need to include details on your crimes. Be specific and explain how your victims fight back. Expected length is 1½ pages. Include a picture of yourself in action.
Protist rock star or rapper	Protist fans	Song lyrics	Choose a protist and research characteristics of its environment, structure, energy requirements, and reproduction. Incorporate these details into a song that has at least two verses and a chorus. Include a cover to the song's CD case that includes a picture of the star.

All work must be typed, original, and good quality.

Due date: _____

Please review the rubric below.

	Excellent	Acceptable	Needs Work	Unacceptable
Role	20 has voice, personality, and creativity	17 uses first person pronouns	14 switches person	0 no first person present at all
Audience	10 grabs attention, uses audience-appropriate vocabulary	7 uses appropriate vocabulary	4 uses incorrect audience	0 doesn't address audience at all

(Continued)

Table 3.1 (Continued)

	Excellent	Acceptable	Needs Work	Unacceptable
Format	30 free of errors, creatively presented	25 no spelling errors, 1–2 grammatical errors	20 1–2 spelling errors, more than 2 grammatical errors	0 not typed, more than 3 spelling errors, no paragraphs
Task	40 information is highly detailed and may include humor, satire, irony, or other creative devices	35 information is complete, accurate, and original	30 minor information is missing, or minor inaccuracies are present	0 information is significantly lacking or incorrect or has been plagiarized

Source: Used with permission from Melaine Rickard, Turrentine Middle School, Burlington, NC.

RAFTs." Each task requires the use of research skills, encourages creativity, and appropriately challenges the varying ability levels within the class. Each choice is slightly different and increasingly complex, yet students work with comparable content. Ms. Rickard selects the roles for individual student in order to differentiate for ability, learning preference, and interest. She assigns the harmful bacterium or parasite rapper role to the gifted and talented (GT) students, the helpful bacterium to the advanced students, and the virus autobiography to the grade-level students who also receive more teacher guidance. She also assigns the parasite rapper role to some other grade-level students who are creative or musically talented. Ms. Rickard has one student who wants to be a lawyer, so she assigns the persuasive role (helpful bacterium) to him. "I really thought about each student's strengths and tried to tailor the assignment according" (M. Rickard, personal interview, 2006). She uses the same rubric for all student products.

Ms. Rickard further differentiates the task for the exceptional (inclusion) children (EC) in her science class. Keeping the RAFT on a knowledge level, she asks these students to make a poster about a virus that includes these criteria:

Name of disease

Name of microbe causing it

Picture of the disease

Symptoms of disease

Treatments

How the disease is transmitted

When the disease was first discovered

Anything else they find interesting

She compiles a list of well known diseases, writes these on slips of paper for the EC students to draw from a hat. All projects are then shared with the class.

The following links provide more information about and samples of RAFTs:

- Getting Your Ideas Across on a RAFT:
  http://www.earth.uni.edu/EECP/mid/mod3_la.html
- Reading Comprehension—RAFT Papers:
  http://www.readingquest.org/strat/raft.html
- Ideas for designing RAFTs:
  http://olc.spsd.sk.ca/DE/PD/instr/strats/raft/index.html

Principle 1 of adolescent-centered differentiation stresses the importance of the ongoing evaluation of students' interests, readiness, and learning preferences. Principle 2 places value on a responsive curriculum that ensures all adolescents have the opportunity to learn curriculum that is relevant, substantive, and appropriately challenging. Connecting adolescents to the curriculum through varied and engaging instructional strategies is the thrust of Principle 3 of adolescent-centered differentiation.

GETTING AND KEEPING THEIR ATTENTION

Principle 3: Engagement, or the use of varied, multiple, and engaging instructional strategies for students to learn and demonstrate understanding (need for emotional engagement).

As noted in Chapter 2, positive emotional **Engagement,** the third "E" of adolescent-centered differentiation, plays an important role in the learning process for adolescents. Learning experiences that stimulate curiosity and activate students' senses engage them emotionally (Crawford, 2007). Multisensory experiences that connect and build on personal interests, abilities, and prior knowledge motivate adolescents to engage, learn, and remember. When teachers incorporate novelty, intrigue, variety, or humor into lessons, they are more likely to catch and maintain adolescents' attention. Adolescents are also engaged through active learning experiences that are student-centered and include choice. These might include drama, role play, debate, problem-based learning, games, simulations, mock trials, storytelling, seminars, and projects, among others.

Engagement is also a brain-compatible strategy. When emotional relevance is attached to a task, the brain is more focused and alert. Neurons transmit, synapses connect, and dendrites grow as a result of positive emotional stimulation (Feinstein, 2004; Jensen, 1998; Wolfe, 2001). Figure 1.3, "Motivation

Through Positive Engagement," shows elements of the Engagement component. Key questions for teachers are as follows:

- What will intrigue, motivate, and connect with my students' interests and knowledge?
- What will be the learning "hook" that captures their attention?
- What will stimulate the students' curiosity?
- What is relevant in the learning experience to adolescents' lives and experiences?
- What will make students want to "find out"?

Tomlinson and Eidson (2003) write about the importance of positive emotional engagement in the differentiated classroom. Students, as human beings, need to feel that they belong, have value and importance, and can contribute and participate legitimately within the classroom community. They note the inextricable link between affective competence and cognitive competence, and suggest that teachers promote both by building on students' strengths and helping them to feel included and efficacious. They suggest that teachers repeatedly ask themselves these questions:

- What can I do to ensure that students of all readiness levels feel safe, integrated, affirmed, valued, challenged, and supported?
- What can I do to ensure that students know their interests and strengths are important to me as a person, important to their peers, and important to our success as a class?

Figure 3.3   Motivation Through Positive Engagement

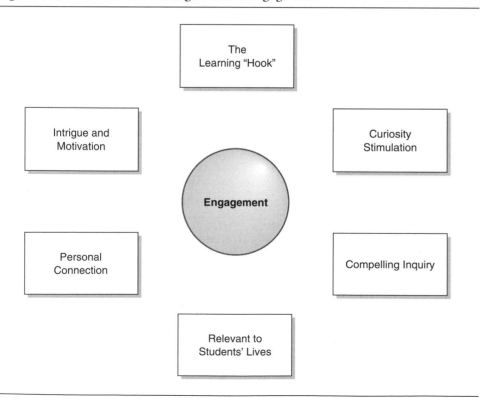

- How can I increase the likelihood that each student comes to a better understanding of his or her particular learning patterns, finds opportunities to work in ways that are comfortable and effective, and respects the learning needs of others? (p. 10)

In the following scenario, a high school social studies teacher engages adolescents emotionally in multiple ways through a popular unit on the 1960s. Through music, period dress, and interest-based research, he guides students through a multisensory, student-centered learning experience differentiated by readiness, intelligence preference, and choice.

A Differentiation Example

Students hear the Beatles' music playing before they walk through the door of Mr. Beamon's classroom. Sporting polyester pants, a tie-dye tee shirt, a fringed vest, hippie-style necklaces, and a bandana, Mr. Beamon welcomes the eleventh graders to the life and culture of the 1960s. Surrounded by posters of Martin Luther King, Jr., Malcolm X, Andy Warhol, and Elvis Presley; peace symbols and war protest signs; and high school yearbooks from the 1960s decade, students are immersed in the memorable era of the Civil Rights Movement, the Vietnam War, the Feminine Mystique, space travel, the Black Power Movement, and integration. Over the next few weeks they will read about this era in their history books; view a documentary on Malcolm X; watch movie clips about integration; complete timelines and cause-effect thinking maps on critical events of the decade; fill in bubble map organizers of key concepts; hear first-hand accounts about the Vietnam War from parent guests; make tie-dye tee shirts; and read and discuss *Black Coach* (Jordan, 1971), a novel about the first black coach at their school in Burlington, North Carolina.

Mr. Beamon's engaging unit is based on state curriculum standards. Learning goals for the students are:

- Students will trace and evaluate the impact of major events of the Civil Rights Movement in United States history.
- Students will identify and evaluate the impact of major social movements involving women, young people, and the environment in United States society.
- Students will identify the causes of the U.S. involvement in Vietnam and determine the effect of the war on U.S. society.
- Students will examine the effect of technological innovations during the 1960s decade on American life.

The overarching essential understanding is that economic, political, and social developments have significant effect on the lives of a country's people.

Through a variety of multisensory strategies, Mr. Beamon differentiates for the range of learning styles in his ninety-minute block of thirty students. Through lectures, videos, music, graphic organizers, visual displays, collaborative group work, read-alouds, and class discussion, he provides multiple ways to interactively engage the adolescents and learn meaningful content. "Education can't be static," he notes (M. Beamon, personal interview, 2006). "Students need to move around and interact. They need to be involved in a variety of activities." He admits to being a little "wacky" to keep learning novel and fun. He rearranges desks each day, for example, and works to establish a genuine rapport with all of his students. Early in the year, he determines what the students' best learning styles are and tries to vary his instruction accordingly.

The hallmark differentiation strategy of Mr. Beamon's unit on the sixties is the culminating project. Adolescents have a choice of topics for a research paper and class presentation. They choose to work individually or in small groups. Other expectations for the project are that students use three sources, with at least one book, and include a supporting visual, either from the Internet or hand illustrated. They have free choice of presentation format. He collaborates with the media specialist who prepares a variety of books, fiction and nonfiction, on varying reading levels for students to use in their research. Mr. Beamon also encourages students to look in their parents' high school yearbooks, "raid" home attics, and dress in appropriate fashion on presentation day. Samples of the variety of inventive products created by his students are:

- One group who researched the 1969 moon landing and walk made aluminum foil helmets and a rocket ship.
- A student who researched Woodstock videotaped himself while playing an original song on his guitar.
- Two students dressed in suits and staged a civil rights debate between Martin Luther King, Jr., and Malcolm X.
- One student dressed up as Jimmy Hendricks and sang; another made up and sang an original rap song related to sixties events.
- Several students staged a fashion show with original sixties clothing.
- One boy who researched the Rocky Horror Picture Show and pop culture of the decade dressed up with painted black fingernails and a boa, showed excerpts from the movie, and explained the film's satire.
- A group of girls dressed up like the Supremes and sang original hits.
- Another student studied the Cuban Missile Crisis and made a board game.
- Other students made hand puppets and acted out a "sixties show."
- Another group played "Name That Tune" with snippets from Beatles' music; another used the Jeopardy format with Beatles' trivia.
- Another who researched the Vietnam War made hot cross buns decorated with a peace symbol.
- Another who researched Vietnam interviewed her grandfather, who had served, and made a scrapbook.

On presentation day, most students dress the part, from the Afros and sunglasses of the Black Panther Party to the characteristic garb of the hippie generation. They also travel to other classrooms in the school and pose for photographs.

Mr. Beamon attributes the success of this popular unit to high interest and choice. He sets the expectation that all members of groups contribute and encourages them to take advantage of one another's strengths, such as artistic talent or speaking ability. Mr. Beamon also helps students relate their learning to their own lives by returning to the unit's essential understanding, "economic, political, and social developments have significant effect on the lives of a country's people." Afterwards, he asks these metacognitive questions to extend their content knowledge:

- Are there problems today related to social class?
- How does economic status affect social class in today's society?
- Is there a dominant social class? How is it determined?
- Are there groups who are currently targeted because of beliefs, religion, or economic status?

Unit Menus

One variation of Mr. Beamon's product differentiation is the strategy *unit menus*. Unit menus provide an array of project choices that demonstrates content knowledge mastery (Benjamin, 2005). The project choices are generally performance-based, offering authentic, alternative ways for adolescents to demonstrate their understanding. Unit menus build on students' knowledge, learning strengths and style, and interests. As in Mr. Beamon's high school classroom, students generate many varied projects that are shared with the rest of the class to reinforce the learning of all members. Another benefit of the unit menus strategy is that the process of producing the product extends the learning of core content and encourages creativity.

> **Unit Menus**
>
> A differentiation strategy in which teachers give adolescents an array of creative choices for final performance-based products to extend learning and prepare for traditional testing.

Benjamin (2005) suggests that well-designed unit menus offer increased opportunities for adolescents to actively use and apply content knowledge. She offers these design suggestions: (1) plan around essential and thematic unit questions; (2) design projects that require language and improved reading and writing; (3) promote interdisciplinary connections; (4) encourage personal connections; (5) require technology; (6) use products as a means to learn content for traditional testing; (7) consider project suggestions that can be presented or displayed; and (8) develop a simple rubric. She also suggests that teachers limit choices from four to six, at most. On the other hand, unit menu projects should not consume an inordinate amount of class time, replace traditional testing, or be so overly complex that parents need to get involved.

Project choices on unit menus might include videos and multimedia productions; WebQuests, Scavenger hunts, or other web-based research projects; skits and scenarios; panel discussions and debates; exhibits and simulated museums; threaded online discussions; or community-based projects that involve interviews, surveys, or research, to name a few of Benjamin's (2005) suggestions.

As the past sections promote, principle 3 of adolescent-centered differentiation embraces the need to motivate and engage adolescents through multiple and varied instructional strategies that capture their interest and respect their individual learning needs and preferences. Structured, purposeful social interaction enables adolescents to explore and collaborate as they share ideas and construct knowledge. Principle 4, Exploration, nurtures adolescents' developmental disposition for guided social investigation.

FLEXIBLE OPPORTUNITIES FOR INTERACTION

Principle 4: Exploration, or the organization of flexible opportunities for students to collaborate, explore, and practice under guidance and feedback (need for purposeful social interaction).

Adolescents enjoy opportunities for social interaction. Developmentally, they are beginning to perceive and consider the differing perspectives on issues. They are intrigued by problems that allow them to use their newfound capacities for analysis and speculation. They are eager to express ideas, and their learning is enhanced when they can discuss, bounce ideas off others, and construct knowledge collaboratively with peers. They also need intentional and sustained interaction with supporting resources in the environment (Crawford, 2007). In short, adolescents need opportunity for guided, purposeful, interactive **Exploration**, the fourth "E" of the differentiated classroom. Figure 3.4, "Flexible Opportunities for Interaction," provides the important elements of Exploration in the differentiated classroom. Key questions are as follows:

- How can teachers purposefully and flexibly structure small groups of learners?
- How can teachers guide the social interaction of multiple groups?
- How will students be held accountable academically and behaviorally?
- How can teachers share the ownership for students' learning?

Figure 3.4 Flexible Opportunities for Interaction

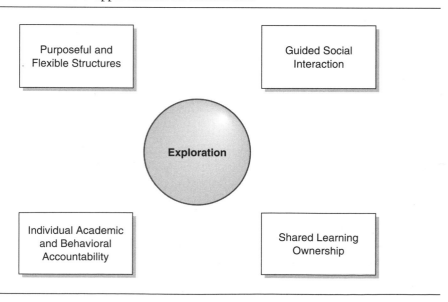

In a differentiated classroom, student grouping is flexible rather than static. Groups are formed and changed according to students' interests, readiness levels, and learning profiles (Tomlinson, 2001). "Teachers may create skills-based or interest-based groups that are heterogeneous or homogenous in readiness level. Sometimes students select work groups, and sometimes teachers select them" (p. 102). *Flexible grouping* is a differentiation strategy that keeps adolescents from being labeled as advanced or struggling and allows them to work with a range of peers.

Flexible grouping also encourages teachers to "try out" students in a variety of grouping configurations. Box 3.3, "Purposeful Social Interaction," gives several ideas for focused collaborative activity based on the work of Daniels and Bizar (1998); Johnson and Johnson (1988); Kagan (1990); and Sharan and Sharan (1976).

> **Flexible Grouping**
>
> Heterogeneous and homogenous student groupings determined flexible by student readiness, interests, learning styles, and skills level. At times, students select work groups and at other times, the teacher determines the configuration based on pre-assessment knowledge. Groups may be purposeful or random.

❖ BOX 3.3 Purposeful Social Interaction

When Discussion Is Needed

- Literature Circles—Student-led discussion groups that meet regularly to talk about books or other literary works.
- Classroom Workshops—From literacy to mathematics, students go through a set schedule of mini-lessons, work time interaction, feedback, and sharing.
- Focus Groups—Each group is given a facet of a problem or an element of a piece of literature. Topics can also be selected according to interests. A set of thought questions helps to guide this seminar-modeled discussion.

Mainly For Partners

- Dialogue Journals—Pairs of students write and exchange "conversations" on a regular basis about content, such as a story, a scientific concept, or a historical event.
- Paired for Action—Students are paired and given interlocking assignments that require joint activity for experimentation, observation, or reading. Partners can also be used to clarify ideas about concepts, for "think-alouds" during problem solving, for "think-pair-share" dyads, or to "punctuate" a lecture, reading, or film, as in "turn to your partner and share."

Grouped for Inquiry

- Student Survey Teams—Adolescents choose a social issue (such as freedom of speech, gun control, drug control, and prejudice), design, and send surveys to a targeted population, analyze results, exhibit findings, and respond personally to the issue through writing and discussion.
- Group Investigation Models—A jigsaw method used for more sophisticated inquiry. Each student is responsible for a part of information that must be reassembled or synthesized to complete the whole "puzzle."
- Problem-Based Learning (PBL)—Students solve ill-structured problems or research problem situations by posing questions, gathering information, analyzing results, and often presenting findings in a creative way.
- WebQuests—Structured project-based inquiry into a real-world problem with research mainly through web sites. Final products are often posted on the Web.

Differentiation Through Literature Circles

Literature circles (Daniels, 1994; Northey, 2005; Tomlinson, 2001) constitute one versatile differentiation strategy that supports flexible grouping by interest or readiness level.

Small groups of three to four students choose or are assigned a common text, fiction or nonfiction, to read. The books provided by the teacher might be connected thematically, such as overcoming adversity or multicultural diversity. The students read independently and meet on a regular schedule to discuss the reading. They keep journals where they define key vocabulary words and respond to open-ended questions and topics in preparation for discussion. Students determine reading goals for the week and rotate roles within the literature circles. Northey (2005) suggests the following role options:

- *Discussion Leader,* who initiates, ends, and keeps the discussion going. He asks prepared questions and determines the next reading assignment and role rotation.
- *Literary Illustrator,* who draws a representative picture of an important aspect in the text, which is graded for neatness, organization, and higher level thinking.
- *Vocabulary Highlighter,* or *Word Wizard,* who chooses key words which must be understood in order to understand the book's meaning. She writes the page number, rationale for choosing the word, and the word's meaning.
- *Page Illuminator,* who chooses a passage for the group to discuss based on critical, confusing, or well-written information. He decides whether the passage will be read silently or aloud and provides the page number in the text.
- *Summarizer,* who summarizes the text and notes important events or concepts.
- *Connection Maker,* who connects the text with personal self and real events in life or other readings.
- *Globe Trotter,* who provides information about locations or settings in the book. She uses maps or globes for visualization.
- *Investigator,* who uses research to broaden understanding of events in the text.

The teacher's role in literature circles is that of facilitator, allowing students to explore within the provided structure (Northey, 2005). To introduce the book selections, the teacher gives a book talk and sets up stations with copies of each book. Students read the back cover or book jacket, look at cover illustrations, read the first page, count unknown vocabulary (five words means it's too difficult), consider why the book might be interesting, and rank by preference on a selection sheet. The teacher assigns groups based on students' top choices, gives a timeline for reading the book, monitors as students determine roles, and circulates continuously during group meetings. Roles are evaluated on a per meeting basis to ensure accountability, and each group is expected to extend their learning through a culminating project.

Literature Circles

A differentiation strategy in which small groups of students meet regularly to talk about books or other literary works. Students assume assigned roles and keep response journals. Literature circles are generally followed by an extension project that demonstrates understanding.

Literature circles work well in widely diverse classrooms. Students generally select books and form groups at their own reading level. Sometimes students pick easier or harder books, depending on interest in certain topics, authors, or genres. Through teacher support and the flexibility of discussion roles, each student can contribute successfully. According to Daniels (1994):

> . . . a student who isn't strong on verbal analysis may still offer her group an illustration that surprises and enriches the conversation. Or a special education student who needs to have the novel read aloud at home can still come to a discussion group and make arresting connections between the characters and his own life. In other words, literature circles, when done well, help make ability grouping unnecessary. They show how heterogeneous, diverse student groups—including mainstreamed special education kids—can work together effectively. (p. 37)

For more information on literature circles, role forms and response journal guidelines, and illustrated extension products, these Internet sites are useful: http://fac-staff.seattleu.edu/kschlnoe/LitCircles and www.literaturecircles.com.

Literature Circles in Action

Ms. Logan is ready to implement literature circles in her seventh-grade mixed-ability classroom. Based on thematic topic of "overcoming cultural adversity," she selects several books in which the protagonists struggle with the challenges of adolescence and cultural identity. Box 3.4, "Ideas for Thematic Literature Circles," shows her book choices with annotations. Ms. Logan talks about each novel, describes some captivating aspects, and gives students an idea of number of pages and difficulty level. She then places copies of the books at different stations around the room for students to explore and make choices. Ms. Logan then forms six groups of four each, in most cases trying to honor students' choices but also giving thought to personalities, gender, and abilities. She assigns the roles of word wizard, discussion leader, literary illustrator, and creative connector based on students' strengths.

❖ **BOX 3.4 Ideas for Thematic Literature Circles**

Thematic Topic: Overcoming Cultural Adversity

Crew, L. (1989). *Children of the river.* New York: Bantam Doubleday Dell Books for Young Readers.

The story of Sundara who flees to the United States from Cambodia during the Vietnam War. Constantly worrying about the continuing troubles at home, she wonders each day whether she would be reunited with her family and friends.

Ryan, P. M. (2000). *Esperanza rising.* New York: Scholastic Books.

Esperanza, a wealthy young girl living in Mexico, experiences her life turn upside down when she and her mother must flee their comfortable lifestyle after her father dies. Subsequently, they make a new life in a migrant camp in California.

(Continued)

(Continued)

Lowry, L. (1989). *Number the stars*. Boston: Houghton Mifflin Company.

The story of Anne-Marie, a Danish girl whose family helps a Jewish family escape from the Nazis during World War II. Anne-Marie befriends Ellen and learns the value of strength and courage in the face of adversity.

Paulsen, G. (1993). *Nightjohn*. New York: Bantam Doubleday Dell Publishing Group, Inc.

The tale of Sarny, a young African American slave who is drawn to Nightjohn, a renegade and rebellious man who takes the daring risk to teach her to read.

Park, L. S. (2002). *A single shard*. Boston: Clarion Books.

Set in 12th century Korea, this is the story of Tree-ear who lives under a bridge with his disabled older friend Crane-man. Tree-ear becomes fascinated with the potter's craft and longs to create celadon ceramics. He works hard hoping to become an apprentice.

Houston, J., & Houston, J. (1973). *Farewell to Manzanar*. New York: Random House, Inc.

After she and her family are ordered to the Manzanar internment camp, Jeanne Wakatsuki tells a compelling story of love, cooperation, and perseverance behind the barbed wires of a Japanese internment camp.

To give students guidance about good discussion techniques, Ms. Logan assigns a "practice" reading of the short story, *Charles*, by Shirley Jackson (1951) for the next day. She additionally asks four students to come to class prepared to model a discussion. The rest of the class listens and observes this fishbowl demonstration (Schlick, Noe, & Johnson, 1999). When the discussion is over, students identify good discussion techniques, which Ms. Logan records on chart paper to display as the "ground rules" for literature circles. To give students practice in exploring the assigned roles, Ms. Logan uses a jigsaw format to assemble them by role groups to discuss what each role entails.

Ms. Logan determines a weekly literature schedule in which two of the six groups meet on Tuesday, Wednesday, or Thursday, respectively, for twenty minutes. During this twenty-minute time slot, other students in the class work independently on *anchor activities* that include reading silently, writing in journals, preparing for literature discussion logs, or working on role tasks. This schedule enables Ms. Logan to observe and monitor the literature circles that are in session. On Mondays, students meet briefly to set reading goals, and on Fridays, students have free reading. During the week, Ms. Logan interjects mini-lessons, as needed, and cues students' written responses with open-ended questions and prompts such as, "What did you like about this character? What do you think will happen next and why?" She also encourages students to creatively assume a character's viewpoint, write a character a letter, or sketch a drawing.

> **Anchor Activity**
>
> A differentiation strategy in which most of the class works independently on an activity such as silent reading, journaling, literature discussion logs preparation, or role task work. Anchor activities enable teachers to observe and monitor the small groups, such as literature circles, which are in session.

Since most literature circles culminate with an extension project, Ms. Logan additionally differentiates by giving students choice in how they express their interpretation of the book in an artistic from for others groups to see. These projects provide students an opportunity to revisit the readings, continue the conversations, and use personal talents in a creative and meaningful way. A good culminating project keeps student thinking and responses alive while enhancing learning. They also give students a chance to use personal intelligences. A few ideas for extension projects for middle school students follow. Other ideas and descriptions are available at the Literature Circles Resource Center, K. L. Schlick Noe, 2004, http://www.litcircles.org/Extension/extension.html.

- A **CD cover** with the front and back designed to capture the theme or spirit of the book. The cover includes the name of the book, the title of the hit single, and an appealing sketch or design. On the back, students list the other songs from the CD that creatively relate to the book and its characters' experiences.
- A **board game** based on the characters, events, or theme of the book. The game must be playable and participants must rely on knowledge of the book to succeed.
- A **commemorative stamp** that focuses on a character, scene, or theme from the book. Students include a picture, a selected phrase, and the stamp's value.
- A **map** that depicts a character's journey, whether physical, psychological, spiritual, or emotional. Students illustrate significant events, setting, and/or themes in the character's journey.
- A **bookmark** that features either a favorite character or the character considered to be most significant in the book. Students include the book title, author, and the character's name and "portrait" or illustration. On the back of the bookmark, students describe the character and explain his or her importance in the book.
- A **setting pamphlet** that uses a pamphlet or brochure format. Students select four or five key settings for significant events in the book, or places that had major impact on character development. Each panel of the pamphlet represents a different setting with illustration and short written explanation for selection.
- A **jackdaw** is a bird that scavenges material to build its nest. Students collect artifacts that represent ideas, events, characters, and themes from the book and prepare a display with labels and brief explanations of the importance of each.
- **Literary weaving** that uses strips of adding machine tape onto which students design visuals using symbols, colors, and words to capture significant ideas or themes. The strips can then be woven together, either as a temporary artistic installation on the floor or more permanently as attached to a colored border.

Other ideas include collages with representative scenes and symbols, A-B-C books, and illustrated accordion-shaped books with significant words about events and characters.

High School Examples of Literature Circles

Daniels (1994) writes of the successful implementation of literature circles in which high school teachers differentiate for student ability and interest. One teacher, for example, uses this technique with *The Canterbury Tales* (Chaucer,

1957) in an advanced senior English class. The entire class reads and discusses the "Prologue" to learn techniques for good discussion. The literature circles begin with the assignment to read "The Knight's Tale." The teacher assigns roles, giving the strongest students that of discussion director. She provides fifteen to twenty minutes in the role-alike groups so that students understand the expectation, and then has the students move into heterogeneous circles for discussion. Assessment takes the form of grading student role sheets for thoroughness, observed participation, tests, and other associated writing assignments.

Another high school teacher uses literature circles effectively to differentiate for a culminating assessment that served as a final exam in a senior English course (N. McMahon, personal interview, 2001). Adolescents divide into small groups of four or five based on their common preference of a book from a recommended reading list supplied by the teacher. They are expected to read and discuss the book's theme, symbolism, characterization, and style and to plan a creative extension project that conveys the group's interpretation of these literacy elements. The teacher monitors as groups determine discussion days and encourages students to be creative by integrating the arts or using technology enhancement.

The final extension presentations are evaluated by a three-level rubric that is collaboratively developed by teacher and students according to the criteria of literary elements and use of literary enhancements. Students also evaluate each others' social skills according to group participation, contribution of new ideas, and prompting others to question (Crawford, 2007). A debriefing time follows the presentations in which the adolescents reflect on the process of book analysis and their group's interpretive and decision-making strategies.

Other Differentiation Applications

Ms. Phelps's sixth-grade mathematics students learn about fractions in an exploratory way. They pretend they are teaching fourth graders how to add and subtract like and unlike fractions using manipulatives and paper and pencil examples. They work in small groups to create a notes sheet and ten homework problems with an answer key. A first-year teacher, Ms. Phelps plans to take the project to the next level of real-world tutoring at a nearby elementary school with another year's experience.

Ms. Phelps's students also engage in an enjoyable mini-cookbook Thanksgiving project. Each sixth grader brings in a favorite holiday or fall recipe, which they scale to smaller and larger amounts. Ms. Phelps also plans a project on percents and decimals that involves sports statistics and holiday shopping percentages, depending on students' choice. For review sheets, Ms. Phelps designs number stories using math problems that the students have worked on as blanks in the story so students can practice their skills. Her students enjoy the opportunity to interact socially on many projects.

Ms. Phelps has found grouping strategies to be very effective with sixth graders—they really respond to incentive programs and games. Her class is now set up in groups, and in two of her classes, the students have a target behavior for the week, such as time on task, class participation, and homework completion. As a group amasses points, they get to go to the prize box. "The students really enjoy it, and the grouping gives them a sense of both competition with other groups and unity within the group" (M. Phelps, personal communication, 2006).

Whether in pairs, small discussion groups, or more elaborate projects such as WebQuests or problem-based learning, adolescents respond positively to the opportunity to share ideas and interact socially and purposefully. The differentiation principle Exploration, the fourth "E," invites multiple, flexible possibilities for grouping adolescents for collaboration and learning.

SUMMARY AND LOOKING AHEAD

Chapter 3 broadens the discussion of adolescent-centered differentiation through elaboration of four of the six design elements, Evaluation, Expectation, Engagement, and Exploration, with application in the disciplines of science, social studies, English/language arts, and mathematics. It suggests ideas for evaluating adolescents' interests, abilities, and learning preferences and in setting expectations that all adolescents, with pertinent support, have access to meaningful, relevant, and appropriately challenging curriculum. It also describes instructional approaches that motivate and engage adolescent learners and enable them to interact collaboratively in structured exploration and inquiry.

Chapter 3 features the differentiation strategy, RAFT, in which the complexity of a task is differentiated based on students' readiness while maintaining appropriate challenge and content expectations. It further illustrates ways to engage students' interests and build upon these through choice in the selection of culminating products. The chapter also showcases literature circles as a means of flexible grouping in which teachers differentiate for readiness and interest. It introduces the differentiation concept of anchor activity, a management strategy that enables teachers to monitor group discussion while other students work independently.

Chapter 4 focuses on the fourth "E," **Extension,** as the component of adolescent-centered differentiation that promotes learning management through explicit strategy development and structured time for reflection and metacognitive extension. The chapter features problem-based learning (PBL) as a prime instructional strategy for Extension. Involvement in PBLs enables adolescents to take ownership of their own learning as they acquire the cognitive strategies necessary to solve relevant and authentic problems. The chapter also illustrates the instructional advantage of interactive technology for student inquiry and the attainment and use of pertinent cognitive strategies.

4

Metacognitive Extension in Adolescent-Centered Differentiation

Chapter 3 focused on the adolescent-centered differentiation design principles Evaluation, Expectation, and Exploration. It illustrated RAFT, student product selection, anchor activities, literature circles, and flexible grouping as instructional strategies to differentiate for interest, readiness, and/or learning preference. Chapter 4 elaborates on the fourth "E," **Extension**, by exploring ways adolescents can attain cognitive strategies that enable them to take ownership over and to manage their own learning. The chapter showcases two integrated, technology-enhanced problem-based learning (PBL) units that incorporate cognitive strategy development, guided reflection, and metacognition extension. Each additionally incorporates the differentiation principles of Universal Design for Learning (UDL).

THE POWER OF ADOLESCENT METACOGNITION

Principle 5: Extension, or the promotion of learning management by making cognitive strategies explicit and structuring time for reflection and metacognitive extension (need for learning ownership).

A critical goal of teaching is that *all* adolescents become responsible managers of their own cognition. *Metacognition*, or "cognition about cognition," refers to the deliberate conscious control of one's cognitive activity (Flavell, 1985). Adolescents' emerging ability for metacognitive thinking enables them to think strategically about their own thinking as they set goals, plan, problem solve, and monitor their learning progress, and subsequently evaluate the effectiveness of their thinking direction. Metacognitive skills are believed to play a key role in many learning-related cognitive activities, including communication, comprehension, attention, memory, and problem solving. Many researchers propose that ineffective strategy use is a source of students' learning disabilities (Deshler, Ellis, & Lenz, 1996).

> **Metacognition**
>
> The deliberate and conscious control of one's cognitive activity, "cognition about cognition." Adolescents' emerging ability for metacognitive thinking enables them to think strategically about their own thinking as they set goals, plan, problem solve, and monitor their learning progress, and subsequently evaluate the effectiveness of their thinking direction.

Metacognitive skill development begins with an understanding of which strategies and resources are best used to accomplish a particular task (Flavell, 1985). Adolescents might use a mnemonic, for example, to learn the distance sequence of the planets or the order of mathematical computations in an algebra problem. Once the appropriate cognitive strategy is chosen, the second skill in metacognitive development is how to use it. A Punnett square is of little use in determining the probability of inherited genetic traits in humans, for example, without the knowledge of how to fill the individual cells. Thirdly, adolescents need to know when to use a specific strategy. To solve a brain puzzler, how many adolescents would automatically know to create a matrix or to use a KWL chart to investigate a challenge in problem-based learning?

The fourth "E," Extension, proposes instructional techniques that help adolescents acquire and know how to use cognitive strategies that help them to direct and manage their own learning. Figure 4.1, "The Power of Adolescent Metacognition," gives important elements related to Extension. Key questions are:

- How can teachers help students identify the cognitive strategies that will be most effective in acquiring information or solving a problem?
- How can teachers model cognitive strategies to make them explicit for students?
- How can teachers guide students to think back and assess the effectiveness of the cognitive strategies they use?
- How can teachers motivate students to inquire further on their own?
- How can teachers help students see parallels in other disciplines or situations?
- What instructional strategies promote transfer?

COGNITIVE MODELING

The goal of metacognitive coaching is for teachers to help students think strategically about knowledge as they develop and progressively strengthen personal

Figure 4.1   The Power of Adolescent Metacognition

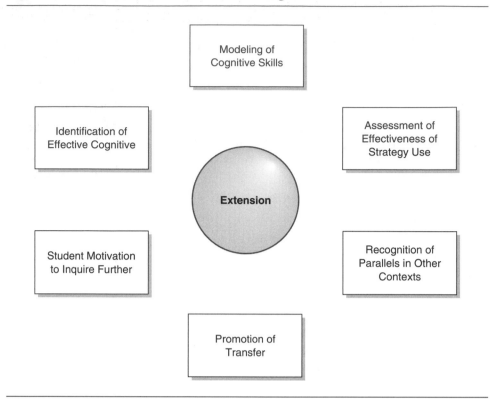

cognitive skills (Collins, Beranek, & Newman, 1991; Collins, Brown, & Newman, 1989). The first step in the process is for the teacher to demonstrate, or model, a thinking strategy by verbalizing it aloud. Referred to as *cognitive modeling,* this instructional strategy has the teacher express out loud about what he or she is thinking as a strategy is used (Meichenbaum, 1977). Through this technique, teachers model their thinking and reasoning about how and when to use a certain cognitive strategy (Howard, 2004c). In a class of mixed ability, students need to be exposed to multiple strategies so that they can begin to understand and internalize those strategies that are appropriate for a particular situation *and* begin to recognize which strategies work best for their individual needs.

Cognitive modeling is a form of scaffolding in itself, as teachers "talk through" a given strategy while students listen. For adolescents to become more self-directing in their thinking and its management, they need this guidance and structure. Howard (2004c) illustrates cognitive modeling through the use of language of effective problem solvers. She expands on the classic problem-solving operations of Polya (1945) through a series of inquiry-based questions. Box 4.1, "Cognitive Modeling Through Questioning," shows the questions a teacher might ask to mentally "walk" adolescents through the problem-solving process in a problem-based learning (PBL) unit.

> **Cognitive Modeling**
>
> A scaffolding tool by which teachers talk aloud about their thinking as they demonstrate the use of a cognitive strategy. They guide and give feedback as students practice and internalize the new strategy.

❖ **BOX 4.1 Cognitive Modeling Through Questioning**

Understand the problem situation	What is going on here?
	How might I summarize it? Visualize it?
	Who expects what?
Set goals	What is my goal?
	What am I trying to accomplish?
	What subgoals should I set?
Identify helps and hindrances	What resources are available to help?
	What barriers might be encountered?
Devise a plan	What needs to be done?
	Who (on my team) can do these things?
Carry out the plan	How should I sequence these tasks?
Monitor and evaluate	Am I making progress toward my goal?
	How well am I accomplishing my goals?

Source: Shared with permission from Howard, J. B. (2004c), Director of Project T2. *Metacognitive inquiry*. Elon University, NC Project T2. Retrieved November 20, 2006 from http://org.elon.edu/t2project/index.htm

METACOGNITIVE COACHING

The teacher's role in *metacognitive coaching,* often referred to as *cognitive apprenticeship,* is to model, guide, and assist as students think about and use cognitive strategies and, through practice and over time, gain a level of proficiency (Collins, Beranek, & Newman, 1991; Collins, Brown, & Newman, 1989). Metacognitive coaching typically includes these features (Beamon, 2001):

- Modeling—students observe and listen while the teacher demonstrates and explains a task.
- Coaching—students perform the task while the teacher supports and makes suggestions through constructive feedback.
- Sequencing—students engage in more challenging and diverse tasks as proficiency is gained.
- Externalizing—students explain aloud their knowledge, thinking, and reasoning.
- Reflecting—students compare their thinking and performance with that of experts.
- Exploring—students are helped to apply, expand, and refine their skills independently. (pp. 115–116)

The focus in metacognitive coaching is on adolescents' mental processes as compared to experts in the discipline for the purpose of solving a complex problem or working though a challenging task (Crawford, 2007). As illustrated in the problem-solving questioning in the previous box, the expert's thinking becomes the standard that students thrive to emulate. A math teacher, after

Metacognitive Coaching

The process by which teachers model strategic thinking and guide as students practice and obtain the cognitive strategies for self-directed learning. Also referred to as cognitive apprenticeship. Teacher assistance gradually decreases and student strategic competence increases.

verbally modeling the steps to solve a word problem, asks students to record and explain their own reasoning strategies with a similar problem. An English teacher, in order to help adolescents understand and internalize the strategies for stronger writing skills used by accomplished writers, models and encourages students to ask, "Do I need a better word choice to convey my meaning? Is this transition strong enough between paragraphs? Do I have sufficient reasons to justify my point of view?"

The support and reinforcement afforded through metacognitive coaching also supports the brain-based strategy, elaborate rehearsal, as discussed in Chapter 2 (Wolfe, 2001). Elaborate rehearsal strategies help adolescents interact with and process new information repeatedly as long-term memory circuits form (Martin & Morris, 2002). These strategies help to activate new dendrite networks and increase the probability that new information will be retained; these strategies also increase the speed that information can be later accessed.

Jackson and Davis (2000), authors of *Turning Points 2000: Educating Adolescents in the 21st Century,* note that one characteristic of differentiated classrooms is that teachers and students collaborate in the learning process. "Together, teachers and students plan, set goals, and try to learn both from what went well and from what did not" (p. 79). Through ongoing feedback and support from the teacher and others in the learning environment, adolescents self-assess, make adjustments, and progressively develop personal competence. In the final stage, the teacher "fades" by giving less assistance as students assume greater responsibility and gain a *sense of ownership* over their own learning management. Figure 4.2 depicts this progression from a dependence on the teacher's structured guidance to a more independent relationship in which adolescents rely with greater confidence and capability on their own self-regulating metacognitive "power."

Figure 4.2   Guiding Toward Metacognitive Management

The Teacher's Role

verbalizes thinking	guides, questions	becomes less directive (fades)
asks questions	helps with resources	connects to other situations
helps define task	monitors progress	facilitates reflection
structures groups	assists as resource	evaluates learning
helps shape strategy		

METACOGNITIVE GROWTH
The Adolescent's Role

watches, listens	designs inquiry	evaluates learning
verbalizes conceptions	implements strategy	reflects on process
poses questions	checks personal progress	makes learning connections
suggests strategy	reconsiders strategy	assumes future responsibility

GUIDED METACOGNITIVE INQUIRY

Beyer (1987) suggests that teachers ask purposeful cueing questions to prompt adolescents' metacognitive thinking and inquiry, known as *guided metacognitive inquiry*. Adolescents need guidance in knowing what it means to extend the experience of reading a book in literature circles, for example. Exemplary extension projects supplement and deepen what students have gained through reading, circle discussion, and journaling. Students also need to consider how their extension projects may be perceived by others. Schlick Noe and Johnson (1999) suggest these guiding metacognitive questions for literature circle extension projects:

- How does our project show what we have learned from the book?
- In what ways does our project reflect important information from the book?
- When others in the class view our project, what will they learn about the book?

The explicit use of metacognitive extension questions additionally helps adolescents to think about their own learning as it develops and to extend this learning to the larger world of personal experiences (Crawford, 2007). Guided metacognitive inquiry ultimately enables adolescents to identify strategies, know how to use them, and understand when a certain strategy is appropriate. A few examples of metacognitive questions are as follows:

> **Guided Metacognitive Inquiry**
>
> The prompting of adolescent metacognitive thinking and inquiry through metacognitive extension questions that guide students to think about their learning as it develops.

- What are you trying to do? (elicits the purpose for a chosen approach when students are engaged in an academic task)
- Why are you doing it? (shifts the student's thinking to the rationale)
- Is there another way you might do it? (encourages a consideration of alternate strategies and supports flexible thinking)
- How well did it work? or Is there a better way? (promotes metacognitive reflection and evaluation at the end of a task)
- How can you help someone else do it? (reinforces learning and challenges the student to discuss possible strategies with another)

Other examples of metacognitive extension questions help adolescents to think about specific content concepts, the use of resources, human and symbolic, the process of collaborative learning, and their own personal contribution (Crawford, 2007). These examples include:

- Why is it important to consider historical and cultural context when critiquing seminal documents?
- How do graphing tools assist your thinking and learning?
- What have you learned about the value of working in groups to solve problems?
- What other ways can you engage in meaningful community service?

TEACHING FOR TRANSFER

Teaching for *transfer* involves helping students to make learning connections from one context to another. The process is relatively simple if the transfer is straightforward, such as the use of math calculations to figure a tip or the application of map reading skills to determine the best route for a family road trip. For less obvious situations, the pathway is not as explicit. Beamon (2001) describes the challenge:

> A history teacher, however, might wonder why students do not see any parallel between the atrocities in Albania and Hitler's attempt to annihilate a Jewish population. The drama teacher might be surprised that students make no apparent link between the satirical content of a play and its historical context, and the language teacher might be surprised that students do not recognize the theme of 'pride and prejudice' in their own relationships. (p. 164)

Because learning situations in schools are generally contextualized, adolescents have difficulty in transferring skills and knowledge from one situation to another. Beamon (2001) offers several teaching suggestions that help students think explicitly and metacognitively about where learning might connect, apply, or extend as follows:

- **Don't shortchange content.** Select broad curricular themes, understandings, concepts, and principles that can be connected across content areas. Teach for understanding.
- **Consider context.** Structure learning experiences that are active, collaborative, personally meaningful, motivational, and relevant. Provide a wide range of examples, analogies, comparative, and contrasting examples. Ideas include simulations, role play, debates, problem-based and project-based learning.
- **Don't leave transfer to chance.** Be deliberate in coaching adolescents to generalize, apply, and adapt learning to other pertinent situations. Provide a structured opportunity for reflection and assessment. Ask questions that push for and prompt connection. Extend and generalize to other appropriate contexts.
- **Model strategies** that scaffold learning. Use KWL charts and other graphic organizers to help students visualize ideas and understand criteria.
- **Verbalize thinking** to demonstrate reasoning skills or different kinds of thinking.
- **Alter situations or problems** to encourage flexible and adaptive thinking. Ask "what if" questions that stretch and extend thinking creatively. (pp. 165–166)

Howard (2006c) stresses that modeled behaviors by teachers have limited transferability unless they are used repeatedly and in many different situations. Metacognitive inquiry, in the form of teacher questioning and guided student reflection, needs to occur throughout a problem-solving situation and be made explicit again during the final debriefing stage when students think back over the cognitive strategies used during the problem-solving process. Debriefing, a critical phase in problem-based learning, helps promote transfer, as illustrated in the examples below.

The Metacognitive Power of Problem-Based Learning

Problem-based learning (PBL) is an effective instructional strategy that invites differentiation and encourages metacognitive development in adolescents (Crawford, 2007). PBLs are designed to build on adolescents' interests and concerns; they also enable students to be actively involved in investigation groups that can be differentiated for readiness, interest, or learning preference. Students take on the persona of adult roles in authentic, ethical situations that are intriguing, perplexing, compelling, and open-ended (Barell; 1995; Howard, 2003; Stepien & Gallagher, 1997; Torp & Sage, 2002). They hypothesize about missing information, determine resources and strategies for data collection, gather information from a variety of sources, consider multiple perspectives, and generate thoughtful solutions (Crawford, 2007). Involvement in PBLs also enables adolescents to retain content and transfer problem-solving strategies to new situations.

Lambros (2004) suggests that problem scenarios be designed for relevance in adolescents' frame of reference. Younger adolescents in middle school, for example, may respond to fantasy and futuristic problem scenarios such as space exploration or underwater research; older students in high school relate to more realistic situations with career-oriented roles, such as engineer or landscape artist. Lambros also recommends that teachers consider small groups and roles that differentiate for, and thus complement, the learning needs and strengths of individual students. PBLs generally consist of these stages (Torp & Sage, 1998):

> **Transfer**
>
> The ability to make learning connections from one context to another. Because learning is so situated, or contextualized, teachers have to make adolescents explicitly aware of pertinent connections through questioning, coaching, and modeling.

> **Problem-Based Learning**
>
> An effective instructional strategy that invites differentiation and encourages metacognitive development. Adolescents assume the persona of authentic roles and interact in investigation teams differentiated for readiness, interest, or learning preference to solve intriguing, open-ended problems.

Engagement Stage. Students' interests and motivation are aroused through an intriguing scenario ("the hook") followed by guided questioning and discussion.

Investigation/Exploration Stage. Students acquire, organize, and analyze information in response to the problem scenario.

Resolution/Refinement Stage. Students analyze options, agree on solutions, and communicate these solutions to the appropriate audience in a realistic manner.

Debriefing Stage. Students reflect and generalize. They think metacognitively about the content and process of the PBL, and, through the teachers' extension questions, are encouraged to apply, extend, and transfer beyond the immediate problem situation.

The benefit of problem-based learning for adolescents goes beyond the academic acquisition and retention of content knowledge. Involvement in a well-designed PBL leads to the achievement of skills for lifelong learning, such as the ability to work in functional relationships, to communicate and problem solve, to decide what is needed to know to solve the problem, to think critically, and to find and use this information to make an informed decision (Gallagher, 1997; Howard, 2003; Lambros, 2004). As students work through a PBL, they gradually assume ownership and responsibility over their own learning and its management.

DIFFERENTIATION IN PBL: TWO EXAMPLES

Differentiation by Universal Design for Learning (UDL)

The PBL units described in the ensuing discussion were designed by teachers, educators, and teacher candidates and sponsored by the Preparing Tomorrow's Teachers to Use Technology (PT3) initiative. (See http://org.elon.edu/t2project/index.htm.) Each unit incorporates the differentiation principles of UDL in order to make challenging curriculum accessible to all learners. Each unit, for example, is built around an essential understanding. According to Howard (2004d):

> Having one essential understanding ("big idea") that serves to relate the information in the unit is probably the single most important adaptation that can be made for students with learning disabilities. Since it encourages abstract, relational thinking and encourages transfer to a variety of situations, it is good for all students, but it is critical for students with learning disabilities. The focus on a central point or feature provides an organizer for large amounts of information, thus providing an organizational tool and a memory aid. (pp. 1–2)

Each unit is also designed for equitable access by incorporating the conspicuous, or explicit, use of cognitive strategies, content enhancements, and peer mediation. The units also incorporate the metacognitive coaching/ cognitive apprenticeship stages (model-coach-fade) through the instructional sequence of teacher demonstration (think-aloud modeling) of what the strategy is, how it is used, and when it is used appropriately. The teachers coach and assist, as needed, as students use the cognitive strategies. "As students become more proficient in strategy use, the teacher gradually withdraws guidance until students are using the strategy independently" (Howard, 2004d, p. 3).

Howard (2004d) encourages teachers to differentiate for learning needs by selecting students who need instruction in the use of cognitive strategies. Explicit strategy instruction, as a scaffolding tool, gives a wider range of students more equitable access to important content. It encourages adolescents to think metacognitively about their own learning. The goal of this cognitive modeling is to enable students to realize what they need and to ask for or seek it independently.

Equitable access is further promoted in these PBLs through a variety of content enhancements available on the PT3 web site for students to use as needed. Each PBL features two types of content enhancements: (1) structural graphic organizers and (2) diagrams, charts, and tables. Structural graphic organizers resemble the structure they represent. Figure 4.3, "Structural Graphic Organizers for Problem-Based Learning," shows three commonly used information organizers—cause-effect (the fishbone), sequence, and compare-contrast. (For others, see Ed Ellis, *Makes Sense Strategies—The Works*, available at www.Graphic.Organizers.com.) The diagrams, charts, and tables include the Learning Issues Board (similar to a KWL chart) and the Decision Matrix, a visual for listing decision alternatives in order to organize and clarify the decision process. Figure 4.4, "Graphic Organizers for Problem-Based Learning," gives a representation of each.

The illustrative PBLs also feature numerous differentiation tools that include problem logs, QD4R Research Guides, concept maps, cause-effect organizers, compare-contrast structural organizers, force field analyses, and presentation guidelines, to name a few. A definition of each of these scaffolding tools is found on the PBL sites. Teachers are encouraged to select the content enhancements for those students who need them. "The goal is for students to recognize what they need and ask for it—or proceed without assistance if, in fact, they need none" (Howard, 2004d, p. 5).

Additionally, the PBL units provide strategies and structures for flexible grouping and team collaboration, such as Jigsaw and Reciprocal Teaching. Chapters 6 and 7 discuss these differentiation strategies in detail with practical examples. Each PBL builds on student interest by incorporating a variety of topics for research and allowing flexibility in the way students represent and express their learning. Information can be gathered through visual media, print, personal interview, and electronic format, for example. Each PBL unit is interdisciplinary, technology-enhanced, aligned with state and national curriculum standards, and spans approximately two weeks. Each site contains a Professional Information Center with research-based scaffolding tools and inquiry strategies for differentiation, online resources, assessment tools, sample interviews with content experts, and professional literature about problem-based learning and UDL. The Student Investigation Center contains all materials needed for the student investigations.

PBLs and Adolescent-Centered Differentiation

The two PBL units described in the following sections are appropriate for middle or high school students. Each unit is summarized, and the differentiation principles are specified. Links to the URLs provide fuller detail. The PBLs illustrate the adolescent-centered differentiation principles discussed thus far. Adolescents are **engaged** through authentic, challenging, and high-interest problem scenarios that invite inquiry and resolution. Curriculum standards and essential content understandings are identified and **expectations** for learning are clearly communicated. Guided by the teacher, students form investigative teams (**exploration**) that can be differentiated for interest or learning preference, depending on students' learning needs. Student progress is continually **evaluated** through checkpoints, quizzes, concept maps, teacher questioning, and other assessments. Teachers are also encouraged to learn about and differentiate for students' interests, abilities, and learning preferences.

What is highlighted for the purpose of this chapter is the differentiation design principle, **Extension**. Through cognitive modeling, guided reflection,

Figure 4.3 Structural Graphic Organizers for Problem-Based Learning

Cause and Effect (the Fishbone)

Graphically depicts information that depicts a number of items, with accompanying details, which lead to an event, for example a war. Subsequent events can also be shown.

Sequence

Graphically represents sequential information that has a starting and ending point, for example, processing steps or historical events. These graphs may be linear or cyclical, such as a depiction of the water cycle.

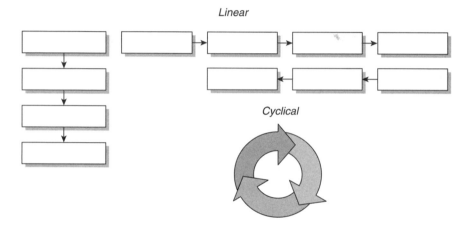

Linear

Cyclical

Compare-Contrast

Graphically represents information about likenesses and differences between two items, such as the comparison of mitosis and meiosis or two forms of government.

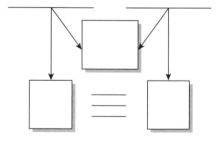

Source: Shared with permission from Howard, J. B. (2004d), Director of Project T2. *Problem-based learning.* Elon University, NC: Project T2. Retrieved November 20, 2006 from http://org.elon.edu/t2project/index.htm

and metacognitive coaching, a teacher potentially facilitates the students' cognitive strategy attainment. Teachers assist as needed resources are determined to solve the problem and through the modeling of cognitive processes. The metacognitive questions in the debriefing section extend adolescent thinking and are designed to promote learning transfer. The PBL units demonstrate how teachers, as metacognitive coaches, help adolescents take ownership of personal thinking and learning management.

Figure 4.4   Graphic Organizers for Problem-Based Learning

Learning Issues Board

LEARNING ISSUES BOARD		
What do we Know?	*What do we need to know?*	*How can we find out?*

Decision Matrix

Graphically reflects the decision-making process. Criteria are noted along the vertical axis and alternatives along the horizontal axis,

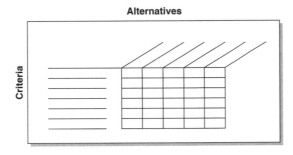

Source: Shared with permission from Howard, J. B. (2004d), Director of Project T2. *Problem-based learning.* Elon University, NC: Project T2. Retrieved November 20, 2006 from http://org.elon.edu/t2project/index.htm

The Malaria Mission

"The Malaria Mission" is a PBL appropriate for middle or high school that integrates science, social studies, and English/communication skills. Adolescents become members of a team of professional experts, geographers, economists, biologists, and public relations personnel who embark on a timely mission to Mozambique, Africa. Their charge (Engagement) is to determine where and how vaccination trials for malaria can be conducted. They must construct convincing arguments to gain the cooperation of reluctant government officials and illiterate rural villagers. Students hypothesize about missing information, determine resources and strategies for data collection (Investigation/Exploration), and generate a solution that is presented to an appropriate audience (Resolution/Refinement.) The teacher, as metacognitive coach, guides and directs the students through questioning, available scaffolding tools, and online resources.

The essential understanding for this unit is, "Systems interact, and the effects of interaction can be limiting or enabling." The learning goals are these:

- Students will develop inquiry, problem-solving, and decision-making skills by engaging in an authentic problem experience, the Malaria Mission.
- Students will acquire content knowledge about the causes and treatment of malaria through research and interviews with experts in the field.

- Students will conceptualize the complex interactions of science, politics, economics, cultural beliefs, and traditions through their selection of countries for clinical trials and their plan for the delivery of the malaria vaccine.

Guided Metacognitive Inquiry

Adolescents have access to substantive content through multiple visual organizers that serve as scaffolding tools to differentiate for individual learning needs. To initiate the problem investigation, the teacher poses these suggested questions:

- What do we know about this problem?
- What do we know about Africa? About malaria?
- What do we need to know?
- How shall we order/sequence our investigation? Are there things that need to be done before we do other things?
- Are any pieces of information especially important?
- What questions should be answered first?
- Where might we find the answers?
- How should we divide the questions among us?

Students discuss the situation and formulate a Learning Issues Board on chart paper as a visual organizer for "What we know," "What we need to know," and "How we will find out." Students update this Learning Issues Board throughout the investigation as new information is gained.

- Other suggested questions guide adolescents in their selection of the four countries for the clinical trials. These include:
- What characteristics would make a country a good place in which to conduct this clinical trial?
- Should the four countries we select have the same characteristics, or should they be different? Why?
- Are some of these criteria more important than others?

Additional suggested teacher queries help students identify personal assumptions, recognize relevant issues, and plan the investigation. Some examples are:

- Why would the Gates Foundation give all that money to fight malaria in Africa?
- Malaria is not a problem here in the United States. Why is it such a problem there?
- What are we being asked to do about this problem?
- Where is Mozambique? Why would we be going there?
- What would experts advise?
- How can we record and organize all of the information we will need to consider in our decision?
- How can we distribute all the research work that must be done to enable us to make good judgments?

The teacher also guides as students create a database to organize information about the countries and as students form country teams. Authentic roles are designated based on interest or learning preference. The teacher further facilitates as the teams explore selected Internet sites to gather data, enter information into a database, narrow the selection of clinical trials to four countries, determine location of vaccination centers, designate transportation routes, and decide on communication systems. A Decision Matrix, as illustrated in Figure 4.4, serves as a graphic organizer to help students narrow their thinking and make the selection. These guiding questions help the students prepare a justification rationale for the project staff:

- What will you say to government agencies and organizations to gain support and assistance?
- What educational materials will you use in the campaign to get as many people as possible to come to the vaccination centers and be vaccinated?

At the end of the first phase of the PBL, teachers ask these metacognitive extension questions to help adolescents think about the essential understanding, "Systems interact, and the effects of interaction can be limiting or enabling." Questions are as follows:

- Were some of the interactions limiting? Were some enabling? How?
- How did our understanding of these interactions help us to make our decision and devise our vaccination strategy?
- How has an understanding of the interaction systems helped us to solve this problem?
- How might this understanding of interactions help us to solve other problems?

Sample guided reflection questions on *decision-making* and *problem-solving processes* include:

- What are the advantages of our country selection? The disadvantages?
- What influenced us most in our decision?
- What values or ethical issues influenced our decision?

Sample guided reflection questions on *product development* include:

- What are the advantages of our vaccination plan? The disadvantages?
- What led us to choose that particular approach? Are there other things we should have considered?
- Is it important to respect tradition and culture, even in issues of health and well-being?
- How did the audience affect how we presented our plan?

Other Available Scaffolding Tools for Metacognitive Inquiry

Numerous visual organizers are available on "The Malaria Mission" site to assist teachers and adolescents as they work collaboratively through the investigation and as they plan presentations. These include strategies for problem solving, research investigation, and presentation preparation; visual organizers, such as a blank Learning Issues Board, problem logs, QD4R Research Guides, concept maps, decision matrices, cause-effect organizers, compare-contrast structural organizers, force field analyses, and presentation guidelines. The site also includes rubrics for participation, team collaboration, and presentation evaluation.

The complete PBL, The Malaria Mission, is accessed at the URL http://org.elon.edu/t2project/article0003/index.htm.

The Alhambra Restoration

"The Alhambra Restoration" is a PBL for middle or high school students that integrates mathematics, social studies, and the visual arts. Students are placed in the role of art restoration experts who are asked to come to Granada, Spain, to investigate the restoration of the historic Alhambra Palace that has been struck by a mild earthquake (Engagement). Students are asked to prepare an economically feasible proposal to replace a portion of the Palace's damaged mosaic tiles. Through the inquiry, students learn about the Alhambra and a portion of Spanish history, explore geometric shapes and tessellating patterns, and deal firsthand with economic issues and constraints. In addition, they become acquainted with 14th century Moorish art and the work of the Dutch artist, M.C. Escher (Investigation/Exploration). Their proposals are presented to the Granada Municipal Council (Resolution/Refinement). As in The Malaria Mission, the teacher, as the metacognitive coach, guides and directs the students through questioning, available scaffolding tools, and online resources. During the debriefing stage, time is dedicated for metacognitive reflection.

The essential understanding for this unit is, "Pattern recognition is fundamental to problem solving." The learning goals are briefly summarized here:

- Students will use problem solving, decision making, and planning skills by engaging in an authentic problem experience, the damage of Alhambra Palace.
- Students will assess the influence of major religions, ethical beliefs, and aesthetic values on life in Europe, Africa, and Asia by researching the historical context of the Alhambra Palace.
- Students will use economic reasoning to make decisions about allocation and use of resources through investigation of financial implications for the Palace tile restoration.
- Students will perceive the connections between visual arts and historical context by researching the time period of 14th century Moorish art.
- Students will understand patterns, relations, and functions by applying transformations and using symmetry to analyze mathematical problems.

Guided Metacognitive Inquiry

As in The Malaria Mission, adolescents have access to substantive content through multiple visual organizers that serve as scaffolding tools to differentiate for their learning needs. To initiate the problem investigation, the teacher poses these suggested questions:

- What is this all about?
- What are we being asked to do as art restoration professionals?

- What is an art restoration professional?
- What do you suppose those panels looked like?
- How would we find out?

Suggested guiding questions for the Learning Issues Board include:

- What do we know about the Alhambra situation?
- How do we know that?
- What do we need to know?
- Why is that important to find out?
- Can any of these items that we've listed be grouped together or combined in some way?
- How shall we order/sequence our investigation?
- Are any pieces of information especially important?
- Are there questions we should answer first?
- Where might we find the answers?
- Should we divide the questions among us?
- Who is interested in finding out ___?

The PBL encourages the student investigation of several topics that can be differentiated for interest. These include the location, description, history, culture, religion, and art of the Alhambra Palace and the appearance and design of mosaics. Students learn about geometric patterns and tessellations and economic issues, such as availability, cost of materials, and expense of different mosaic designs. Content enhancements, such as spreadsheets and graphic organizers, and strategy reminders, accompany each task and afford students the flexibility to use them as needed or as encouraged by the teacher. Other available instructional activities include mini-lessons, demonstrations, interviews with experts, supplementary readings, and videos that help adolescents acquire necessary information during the investigation stage.

Teachers are additionally encouraged to ask questions periodically during the inquiry for students to "stop and think" metacognitively about the ongoing investigation. Suggested questions are in Box 4.2 below.

❖ BOX 4.2 "Stop and Think" Questions

- How has the history affected the culture of Granada?
- How has history and culture affected the appearance and design of the Alhambra?
- Why is authenticity of design important? What makes a design authentic?
- How will the tourist business influence this problem/solution?
- How does the location of Granada affect the problem/solution?
- What patterns are we beginning to see? In the panel designs? In the cost of panel replacement?
- How has your thinking about the situation changed?
- How is this information relevant to our situation?
- What forces are operating on this problem? What are the real issues here?
- What more do we need to know? How can we find out?

As the inquiry continues, similar to The Malaria Mission, teachers are encouraged to ask other metacognitive questions that guide students through the decision-making and product-development process. At the end of the first phase of the PBL, teachers ask these suggested metacognitive extension questions to help adolescents think about the essential understanding, "Systems interact, and the effects of interaction can be limiting or enabling," as follows:

- Were some of the interactions limiting? Were some enabling? How?
- How did our understanding of these interactions help us to make our decision and devise our vaccination strategy?
- How has an understanding of the interaction systems helped us to solve this problem?
- How might this understanding of interactions help us to solve other problems?

Similar to The Malaria Mission, numerous scaffolding and other visual organizers are available to assist teachers and adolescents as they work collaboratively through the investigation and plan presentations. Teachers are encouraged to allow students flexibility and choice in the format of the final proposals.

The complete PBL, The Alhambra Restoration, is accessed at the URL: http://org.elon.edu/t2project/article0001/index.htm.

Source: Howard, J. B. (2004a). *The Alhambra restoration*. Elon University, NC: Project T2. Retrieved November 20, 2006 from http://org.elon.edu/t2project/article0001index.htm

SUMMARY AND LOOKING AHEAD

This chapter elaborates on the Extension component of adolescent-centered differentiation with discussion of metacognition, cognitive modeling, metacognitive coaching, and teaching for transfer, each of which manifests in the problem-based learning (PBL) units that are featured for illustration. These units differentiate based on interest, readiness, and learning preferences, and each encourages strong student engagement and self-directed learning. They also provide teachers and adolescents with multiple cognitive strategies and resources that are interactive, equitable, and accessible through the technology-based format. Through guided inquiry, adolescent thinking becomes more productive and the cognitive skills for problem solving are more likely to be transferred to other contexts.

Chapters 5 and 6 address the sixth and final "E" in the adolescent-centered differentiation approach, the learning **Environment**. The creation and maintenance of a learning environment that is supportive of adolescents' intellectual, social, physical, and emotional development is critical for their healthy development. An environment that is responsive to adolescents' individual learning needs differentiates accordingly.

A Differentiated Learning Environment

The Affective, Social-Emotional, and Physical Dimensions

Alearning environment is a multidimensional entity of emotional interchange, social interaction, physical space, and intellectual interplay (Crawford, 2004). It consists of visible and invisible structures and processes that are designed to benefit individual students and the whole class (Tomlinson & Eidson, 2003). Teachers create learning environments when they make decisions about furniture arrangement and wall displays, establish routines and procedures, set expectations for student behavior, select materials and resources, assign students in groups, design curriculum development and instruction, and ascertain teacher-student and student-student relationships. An environment conducive to adolescent learning *anticipates* and *is responsive to* students' personal, social-emotional, and intellectual needs (Crawford, 2007). Chapters 5 and 6 describe the interrelated affective, social-emotional, physical, and intellectual dimensions of the adolescent-centered learning **Environment**, the sixth "E" in the differentiation framework.

Chapter 5 focuses on the *affective, social-emotional,* and *physical* dimensions of the differentiated learning environment. Adolescents learn and think better in a *flexible,* yet *structured, community-oriented* environment where they move, talk, act, and interact. They thrive in a learning environment where they are motivated personally, guided socially, challenged intellectually, and supported intentionally as they engage in relevant and meaningful learning experiences. Adolescents also need a safe learning environment that is defined by respect for and acceptance of students as individuals, however diverse. A safe classroom is a risk-free setting that invites trust and open communication and supports adolescents' developmental needs.

Essential to the social dimension is instructional use of flexible grouping that enables adolescents to interact with peers on a variety of engaging, appropriately complex tasks. Adolescents also learn better in a physical setting characterized by order, cleanliness, movement, and structure. The physical dimension encompasses the teacher's organization of time, space, and resources. Chapter 5 also offers several research-based strategies for managing the differentiated adolescent classroom.

Figure 5.1, "The Affective, Social-Emotional, and Physical Dimensions," denotes the affective, social-emotional, and physical elements of the adolescent-centered learning environment. Key questions are:

- How might teachers create an affective learning environment that is community-oriented and mutually respectful?
- How can teachers create a safe learning environment that accommodates adolescents' developmental needs?
- How can teachers construct an environment that is socially-emotionally supportive?
- How might teachers structure an orderly physical environment where adolescents interact meaningfully in flexible groupings?
- How do teachers manage an environment that differentiates for adolescent learning?

Figure 5.1   The Affective, Social-Emotional, and Physical Dimensions

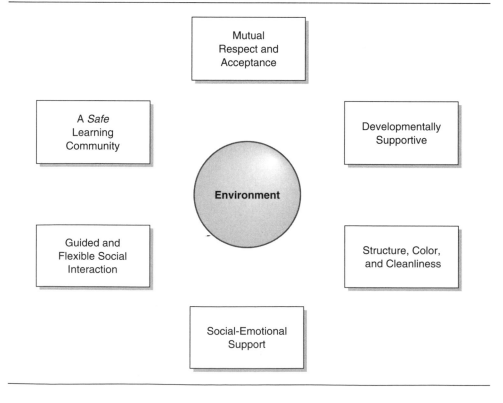

INVITATIONS TO LEARN

The affective elements of the learning environment are revealed in the climate of a classroom. The inferences that teachers make about students' abilities, the expectations they convey to students through interactions, and the opportunities they extend that help students be successful and feel competent are all factors that affect students' attitudes toward learning (Beamon, 1997). Adolescents, as human beings, share the common need to belong and feel that they are an integral part of classroom life. Tomlinson (2002) notes five factors in the classroom environment that extend invitations to learn to all students. These elements parallel adolescents' developmental needs as learners and are described as follows:

- **Affirmation**, or the need to feel accepted, safe, cared about, listened to, and acknowledged.
- **Contribution**, or the need to make a difference, bring unique perspectives, collaborate mutually on common goals, and help others succeed.
- **Purpose**, or the need to understand the significance of learning and how it impacts and makes a difference personally and with the extended community.
- **Power**, or the need to make choices, create quality work, and have dependable support.
- **Challenge**, or the need for work that complements and stretches strengths and, through personal effort, leads to success and accomplishment. (pp. 236–238)

Tomlinson and Eidson (2003) suggest several teacher strategies that support a positive classroom environment. These include modeling and teaching respect and empathy, helping students examine multiple perspectives on critical issues, ensuring consistent and equitable participation, providing scaffolding to help students achieve, seeking legitimate opportunities to affirm all students, helping students become reflective decision makers and problem solvers, celebrating progress and growth, establishing benchmarks for success at appropriate levels, and helping students appreciate and value individual differences (p. 10). Sustaining a positive affective environment requires teachers to reflect upon and respond continually to the many ways students' differ in readiness, interests, learning styles, intelligence preferences, culture, gender, background experiences, home life, and economic status.

A Safe Environment for Learning

Beamon (1997) describes a safe learning environment as one that "reflects a profound respect for individual students, regardless of ability, an acceptance of student's ideas, however diverse, and an active involvement in the thinking-learning process" (p. 14). The creation of an environment that is safe for thinking and learning lies in the teacher's ability to generate trust and open communication, encourage individual differences, and engage students in meaningful and challenging learning experiences. This classroom is a risk-free, yet structured and expectant setting where adolescents' personal, intellectual, social, and physical needs are met.

A *safe* learning environment is one that is purposefully created by the teacher on the assumption that adolescent learning and thinking are "interactive, progressive, and developmental processes" (Beamon, 1997, p. 2). The climate of a safe classroom is based on the belief that, given trust, opportunity, and encouragement, most adolescents will try to do what is expected and appropriate (Crawford 2004). Adolescents thrive in a nonthreatening setting where they feel emotionally safe to test ideas, to use their diverse talents, and to negotiate and reflect upon how others perceive them and who they are becoming as human beings. A safe classroom is free of bullying, embarrassment, confusion, ridicule, frustration, boredom, and social exclusion.

A sense of physical and emotional security is also a brain-based precursor to effective adolescent learning. As discussed in Chapter 2, when adolescents feel marginalized because of differences in race, ethnicity, capabilities, or economic advantages, their emotions directly interfere with learning (Jensen, 1998). Under stressful conditions when the brain perceives threat, the emotion-bound limbic area overrides the thinking and memory capacity of the frontal cortex (Sprenger, 1999). Instead of sending incoming information to the prefrontal cortex for rational processing, the amygdala in the middle brain sends "danger" signals to the thalamus to prepare for mental "flight." As Willis (2006) explains, "stress, anxiety, boredom, and alienation . . . block the neuronal transmission, synaptic connections, and dendrite growth that are the physical and now visible manifestations of learning" (p. 59). In this situation, adolescent learning suffers.

Conversely, when adolescents feel accepted, valued, and affirmed as contributing members of a classroom culture, they are more likely to find emotional joy in learning. As Beamon (2001) writes, [a]dolescents need a learning context where personal competence is nurtured, emotions are positively stimulated, and social interaction is carefully structured" (p. 93). Box 5.1, "A Safe Environment for Learning," synthesizes ideas for fostering a classroom climate where adolescents feel safe to learn and thrive. Many of these instructional strategies appear in other sections of this chapter.

[handwritten margin note: Maslow's Hierarchy of needs]

❖ BOX 5.1 A Safe Environment for Learning

1. **Personalize Learning Opportunities**

   Differentiate curriculum for varying abilities and interests.

   Permit choice on topics, projects, and resources.

   Assess understanding through multiple avenues.

   Design authentic and developmentally challenging experiences.

   Allow for creativity and originality.

   Integrate music, art, and drama to promote individual expression.

   Give adolescents opportunities to "shine."

2. **Build Relationships**

   Provide opportunities for peer interaction.

   Structure collaborative tasks and monitor group dynamics.

   Teach interpersonal skills (e.g., team and consensus building).

   Provide opportunity for community connections and social action.

   Connect with students' families and cultural communities.

3. **Promote Inner Management**

   Build in metacognitive time (e.g., reflection, discussion, response writing, self-evaluation).

   Foster empathy (e.g., perspective-taking, debate, role playing).

   Encourage moral development (e.g., decision making, discussion, inquiry projects).

   Treat mistakes as learning experiences and emphasize personal progress.

   Provide opportunities for learning responsibility and ownership.

   Involve classroom management planning and conflict negotiation.

   Downplay extrinsic motivation and promote the value of learning.

4. **Create Emotional Security**

   Promote a climate of caring, respect, inclusiveness, and acceptance.

   Create an atmosphere of expectancy, challenge, and limited stress.

   Listen to and help them believe in the power of their ideas.

   Encourage efforts to understand and to be understood.

   Celebrate classroom cultures and discourage prejudice.

   Incorporate humor and playfulness.

5. **Teach Well**

   Capture curiosity through a challenging curriculum (e.g., concepts, issues, problems).

   Help adolescents to see the practicality of what they are learning.

   Expect adolescents to be active participants, not passive listeners.

   Foster thoughtful learning and understanding.

   Expand the "walls" of the classroom through technology and external resources.

Creating a Community of Learners

A positive affective environment is also the product of the teacher's intentional effort to create and sustain a community of learners. The reality that adolescents bring differing knowledge, skills, attitudes, and beliefs to the educational setting challenges teachers to ask, "What can I do to ensure that students of all readiness levels feel safe, integrated, challenged, valued, affirmed, and supported? How can I communicate to students that their interests and strengths are important to me and to their peers? How can I increase the likelihood that all students better understand their particular learning strengths, use them effectively, and respect the learning needs of others?" (Tomlinson & Eidson, 2003). In successful learning communities, teachers work continually to build connections between learning and the world of the learner.

Tomlinson (2001) delineates several characteristics that define community-oriented learning environments:

- **Each student feels welcomed, and each extends this welcome to all members of the class**. Teachers make a genuine and sustained effort to get to know and understand each student. They include all students in classroom discussions, display student work on bulletin boards, and make certain that each learner has a voice in small group tasks.

- **Mutual respect is intentionally cultivated**. Regardless of culture, language, gender, personal appearance, or personality, all human beings experience the feelings of disappointment, joy, doubt, and triumph. In differentiated classrooms, teachers help students distinguish between someone's actions and value as a person. Respect is modeled and expected.

- **Students feel emotional and physical safety**. Students feel safe to ask questions, express ideas, be creative, and make mistakes without the fear of being ridiculed or thought inept or foolish. The classroom is an orderly yet interactive place where emphasis is placed on achievement and success. Students have a clear sense of expectations, understand the relevance of an assignment, and have sufficient time to complete and reflect upon the task.

- **Personal growth is a source for celebration**. In differentiated classrooms, every learner is expected to achieve in relation to personal learning goals. One student's understanding of literary point of view, for example, is just as important to celebrate as another's insight into the more complex element of symbolism.

- **Teachers challenge and scaffold for success**. Each student is pushed slightly further and faster than is comfortable and is given the necessary assistance to reach expected learning goals. Scaffolding tools include, as needed, the use of manipulatives, study guides, graphic organizers, reading buddies, tape recorders, and appropriate reading level materials. Teachers may give more or less structure in directions, communicate criteria for success clearly, model, reteach, and present information through multiple modes.

- **Fairness is redefined**. In differentiated classrooms, teachers and students understand that fairness means ensuring that each student is given what he or she needs to succeed.

- **All students work toward increasing responsibility and independence as learners and members of a learning community**. The culture of the classroom is one in which students help develop routines, contribute in problem solving, assist one another, and keep track of personal learning progress. (pp. 21–24)

Beamon (2001) writes that "a community of learners is created when adolescents and teachers share ideas as they work together to expand what they know and improve how they think" (p. 73). Purposeful involvement in meaningful collaboration builds a sense of relationship among class members that is characterized by sharing, support, and respect. Adolescents' affective competence is explicably linked to their cognitive competence (Tomlinson & Eidson, 2003). In a differentiated learning environment, teachers are as persistently attuned to students' feelings as they are to their knowledge, skills, and understanding. They realize that, while adolescents may experience learning in different ways, they all need to perceive themselves as valued and active participants in the daily life of the classroom.

THE SOCIAL DIMENSION OF THE LEARNING ENVIRONMENT

The discussion in Chapter 3 of Exploration, the fourth "E" in the differentiation framework, assigns significance to adolescent learning through *purposeful* and *guided* social interaction. Adolescents are eager to express ideas, give opinions, and share perspectives. Structured opportunities to collaborate teach adolescents that shared knowledge has instructive value. Kaufeldt (2005) writes that "[w]hen we consider differentiating instruction in the classroom, some of the most important tools we have available to us—for free—are the other students. Knowing one can ask questions of peers, feeling supported by classmates, and having opportunities to get feedback from other students are all benefits to students who work with one another" (p. 45). She suggests a differentiation strategy called *tribes* as a grouping technique that builds community, social skills, and a sense of belonging.

> **Tribes**
>
> Social groupings balanced by such factors as gender, ability, leadership, problem solving, creative or artistic talent, cognitive abilities, backgrounds and languages, and energy levels. Tribes are base groups that help with classroom management and instruction.

More appropriate for young adolescents, tribes are social groupings that distribute students by choice, gender, ability, and peer acceptance for the purpose of motivating active participation and relationship (Kaufeldt, 2005). Tribes also comprise a balance of leadership, problem solving, creative or artistic talent, gender, cognitive abilities, backgrounds and languages, and energy levels. Teachers use tribes for both management and instructional purposes: attendance taking, collection and distribution of homework and other materials; assistance in makeup tasks and homework for absentees; buddies for field trips, carpools arrangements and assembly seating; and various collaborative learning tasks.

Kaufeldt (2005) notes that when students feel *connected* to multiple groups and partners, they will begin working much more quickly when they are asked. By establishing tribes as base groups, teachers give all students a circle of peers and a sense of belonging. The feeling of inclusion among students in the classroom maximizes learning. To save instructional time, Kaufeldt suggests the preset formations in Box 5.2, "Prearranged Partners and Small Groups." She also proposes the differentiation strategy, learning clubs, in which students cluster for skills review and tutorials, literature and novel study, or research and inquiry.

❖ **BOX 5.2 Prearranged Partners and Small Groups**

- **Process partners**: Students sitting close to each other discuss or work together.
- **Peer edition partners**: Students work with the same partner over a period of time to allow rapport and continuous feedback.
- **Clock partners**: Students collaborate to write each others' names on the numeral of a paper clock face. Upon a time cued by the teacher, they meet with that person.
- **Compass partners**: As variation to the clock partners, students record names on the points of a compass rose.
- **Three's a charm**: For conflict resolution processing, students form groups of three with one student as moderator.
- **Numbered heads**: Each student at a table, cluster of desks, or row has a permanently assigned number. The teacher assigns procedures for activities or designates roles and responsibilities, such as timekeeper, summarizer, recorder, and encourager. Numbered heads can also be used for materials distribution, assignment collection, or other classroom duties and needs.
- **That's my color**: Each student is assigned both a number and color (though not the same number and color to any, for example, number 1s are not also all blue). Color designation can be through sticky dots on name badges or handouts. This grouping works well with jigsaw activities, discussed later in the chapter, and paired color partners.
- **Peer helpers**: The teacher asks students to serve as advisors or peer helpers. They wear a badge such as "Math Master" or "Writing Helper." (pp. 46–50)

Flexible Social Grouping

Tomlinson and Eidson (2003) encourage teachers to be judicious with the use of grouping. Depending on the activity, they suggest that student groupings be varied according to readiness and mixed-ability, common and varied interests, similar and mixed learning preferences, teacher- or student-choice, and randomly. These *flexible* configurations help students to see themselves in different roles and increase their awareness of differing modes of learning. As discussed in Chapter 3, flexible grouping allows students to work with a variety of peers and prevents any students from being "pegged" as an advanced or challenged learner. Tomlinson (2001) suggests these guidelines for the use of flexible grouping in the mixed-ability classrooms:

- Ensure that students work both with peers similar and dissimilar to themselves in readiness and interest.
- Assign groups tasks that match individual readiness or interest based on pre-assessment knowledge.
- Allow students to select groups when the task is well-suited for peer selection; at other times, assign groups to ensure students work with a variety of classmates.
- Make certain students work cooperatively, collaboratively, and independently.
- Teach clear guidelines about group functioning in advance and reinforce consistently.
- Allow students to work also as a class and independently. (p. 102)

Jigsaw as a Differentiation Strategy

Cooperative learning promotes positive self-concept, academic achievement, critical thinking, peer relationship, social behavior, and motivation of students at any age (Johnson, 1979; Johnson et al., 1981; Johnson & Johnson, 1988). Collaborative learning, implemented well, is especially beneficial for adolescents' social, personal, and cognitive development (Crawford, 2007). Chapter 3 categorizes several grouping structures based on the work of Daniels and Bizer (1998); Johnson and Johnson (1988); Kagan (1990); and Sharan and Sharan (1976). These include discussion groups (literature circles, class-room workshops, and focus groups); partner work (think-pair-share dyads and dialogue journals); and group inquiry (survey teams, group investigation models, WebQuests, and problem-based learning).

This section illustrates the cooperative learning structure *jigsaw*, which groups students for task specialization (Howard, 2004a). Jigsaw is a powerful differentiation strategy because it gives all students the opportunity to contribute in a meaningful way. Originally designed by Aronson (1978) and varied by Kagan (1994), jigsaw places students on home teams of three to five members. Each home team is responsible for learning a complex subject or performing a challenging task. In order to learn about one aspect of the subject or task, students leave their home teams and form expert groups with members of other home teams. Each expert group learns a designated "piece" of the larger task. After a set time, members of the experts groups disband and return to their home team to teach their part to fellow team members. In this way, the home teams collaborate to learn a subject or task by assembling various parts of the original task.

> **Jigsaw**
>
> A cooperative learning structure that groups students for task specialization. Jigsaw is a powerful differentiation strategy because it gives all students opportunity to contribute in meaningful ways.

Figure 5.2 shows the jigsaw design.

Figure 5.2   Cooperative Learning Structure: Jigsaw

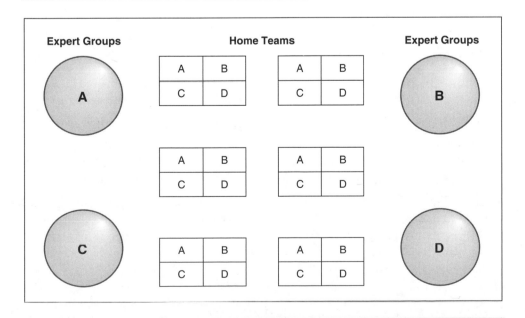

Source: Shared with permission from Howard, J. B. (2004a), Director of Project T2. *The Alhambra restoration.* Elon University, NC: Project T2. Retrieved November 20, 2006 from http://org.elon.edu/t2project/article0001index.htm

A Differentiation Example of Jigsaw

Chapter 4 gives two examples of technology-enhanced, problem-based learning units from Project T2 (http://org.elon.edu/t2project/index.htm) to illustrate metacognitive inquiry, development, and extension: The Alhambra Restoration and The Malaria Mission. Each PBL involves students working in investigative teams to explore and resolve an authentic problem. The designers of the PBLs suggest that teachers use jigsaw as a flexible grouping strategy for any of the learning tasks they deem appropriate. Students could jigsaw to investigate questions raised through the Learning Issues Board, for example, to listen to the taped interviews with content experts, to assume a particular role in an inquiry, or to research special interest topics.

One possibility for the use of jigsaw is in "Learning Task #5: Panel Design," in The Alhambra Restoration. After students examine many patterns and learn about tessellation design, they are ready for the challenge of formulating possible panel designs to restore the damaged Alhambra structure. The task contains six options that differentiate for readiness and interest, as shown in Box 5.3, "Jigsaw Options and Scaffolding Tools for 'The Alhambra Restoration'." Resources link each design choice to optional scaffolding tools that assist student work. Additional Internet resources are also available to be used as needed in the varying designs.

❖ BOX 5.3 Jigsaw Options and Scaffolding Tools for "The Alhambra Restoration"

5a You decide to use a set of geometric blocks to assemble a possible panel design.
Scaffolding tool: A link to a site that uses activity pattern blocks in tessellation design.

5b You decide to use an Internet site you found to assemble a possible pattern design.
Scaffolding tool: A link to a pattern blocks program.

5c You decide to use geometry exploration software, such as Geometer's Sketchpad, to investigate transformations and tessellations and then to construct your design.
Scaffolding tool: Links to The Geometer's Sketchpad resources.

5d You know that only three regular polygons tessellate in the Euclidean plan. You decide to design your panel using just those three polygons.
Scaffolding tool: Link to polygon tessellations.

5e You become interested in the nibbling technique and want to use that in your design along with slides, rotations, and reflections.
Scaffolding tool: Link to tantalizing tessellations.

5f You learn that many of Escher's drawings were inspired by designs he saw in the Alhambra. You are very interested in his work. Maybe you could include a "modern" panel in the restoration. You decide to look more closely at Escher's work and see if you can discern the tessellating patterns and the techniques he used. You will try to design a panel using patterns and techniques like his.
Scaffolding tools: Link to Escher tessellations and suggestions for print resources.

Source: Shared with permission from Howard, J. B. (2004a), Director of Project T2. *The Alhambra restoration*. Elon University, NC: Project T2. Retrieved November 20, 2006 from http://org.elon.edu/t2project/article0001index.htm

In this jigsaw example, heterogeneous home teams divide and form expert teams to collaborate on one of the six design approaches. Upon completion and return to home groups, each designer shares his or her work. The next task in the PBL asks home teams to (1) create a rubric to assess each design's authenticity and (2) develop a spreadsheet to determine the cost of each design option based on tile expenses. During the resolution stage, the students use the economic and cultural considerations from the original problem to decide on the most desirable panel design. They prepare a presentation, with justification, to deliver to the municipal council. As additional differentiation, students may choose to draw the panels or construct models depending on the learning preference of students in the home groups. A rubric assesses each presentation.

Individual Accountability

As social as adolescents are, they may not have the personal skills for true collaboration. For collaborative grouping to work well, Daniels and Bizar (1998) recommend that explicit procedures for keeping groups productive be in place. Instruction, modeling, practice, and feedback are prerequisites. Structures for procedures, accountability, evaluation, and reflection are essential. Beamon (2001) poses five questions that are helpful in making collaboration work:

1. **Where is the challenge?** Adolescents need to be engaged in significant activity that stimulates their thinking. They feel a sense of concerted purpose when asked to solve a problem, create a project, construct a debate, or make a decision. They also need support through graphic organizers or other scaffolding tools to develop the skills for problem solving, decision making, persuasion, and consensus building.

2. **Where is the interdependence?** Adolescents need to be involved in a joint effort that requires all members to interact and contribute cooperatively toward a final goal, such as a solution, decision, project, or presentation.

3. **Where is the accountability?** Adolescents need to feel individually responsible for personal contribution through assigned roles, a contract, a personal response, an individual quiz, or a self/group evaluation form.

4. **Where is the interpersonal development?** Successful group interaction depends on and extends adolescents' social skills. They develop the dispositions to respect others' viewpoints, to contribute ideas, and to build consensus.

5. **Where is the reflection?** Following group interaction is a necessary time to debrief, or think about the collaborative process, to assess contributions of group members, and to evaluate the final product against expected criteria. (p. 143)

Study Groups for Engaging Older Adolescents

The instructional use of student *study groups* is an effective differentiation strategy for high school students. Lent (2006a) writes that study groups are a powerful form of learning that promote student collaboration, ownership, and reflective application. Popular in English, science, and social studies classrooms, in particular U. S. government, study groups engage adolescents in reading, writing, and thinking critically about a topic that leads to some kind of concrete *action.* Lent (2006a), author of *Engaging Adolescent Learners: A Guide for Content Area Teachers* (2006b), notes that in too many instances, students in high school "are disengaged from and even contemptuous of learning, as though learning were something inflicted on them rather than a joyful and natural part of life" (p. 69). Through study groups, adolescents become immersed in and intrigued by social exploration that has relevance to their lives.

> **Study Groups**
>
> A high interest instructional strategy in which older adolescents tackle a stimulating, personally relevant topic. Students read, write, and think critically about the topic and take some concrete action.

Through collaborative study groups, adolescents delve into high-interest content topics. For example, students may take an in-depth excursion into poetry, explore intriguing periods of history, analyze current events, such as the escalating threat of nuclear power in North Korea; or probe current areas of science such as water pollution, time travel, black holes, alternative fuel sources, astronomy, or new diseases (Lent, 2006a). In each instance, adolescent study teams read intensely, meet in discussion groups, maintain a group meeting log, interact with relevant people and agencies in the community, and take creative action. Several effective study group initiatives are as follows:

- Adolescents in a speech and debate class interested in the underlying causes of school shootings researched the topic, interviewed students, and met with local teachers and the education editor of the local newspaper. The newspaper editor wrote an article about the issue, a local TV reporter interviewed the group members about their findings, and a national Internet radio show asked the students to participate in an online program on school shootings.
- Adolescents in a history class formed a study group to explore the Vietnam War. They talked with local Vietnam veterans, participated in reenactments, watched movies dealing with the conflict, and examined newspaper clippings from the era. The end product was an oral history project of interviews with U.S. soldiers who served in Vietnam.
- Adolescents in an English class formed a book club in conjunction with a local bookstore and donated the profits to improve classroom libraries. Others formed poetry discussion groups, wrote their own, and organized a poetry coffeehouse in conjunction with the school's yearly academic fair.
- Adolescents in a biology class formed a science study group interested in environmental issues teamed with parents and a community biologist, attended a conference on composting, and partnered with the local zoo to create a composting program to combine animal waste with newspapers to make compost for gardens on the school grounds. (Lent, 2006a)

Lent (2006a) notes that one of the advantages of using study groups as an instructional strategy is that adolescents take responsibility for their own learning. To ensure accountability and promote metacognitive reflection, students keep group logs to monitor what they are learning. At each meeting, generally scheduled at a designated time each week, a student facilitator, with input from group members, fills out the meeting log and places it in a notebook. Groups respond to questions such as, "What were the major points addressed? What new learning occurred? What questions emerged? Who will attempt to answer these? What outside resources can assist with these questions? What will be the focus of the next meeting? What will members need to do to prepare for the next meeting?" to name a few (p. 70). Students also keep individual reflection logs, which they turn in to the appropriate teacher sponsor.

Lent's (2006a) assessment of the value of study groups for adolescents parallels this book's emphasis on interest-based differentiation, engaged learning, meaningful social interaction and inquiry, metacognitive development, and personal learning ownership.

If we hope to engage students in critical thinking, we must allow them the freedom and opportunity to get involved in socially constructed ongoing processes that require the use and application of knowledge. It is important to include students in their own learning by engaging them in activities that teach them how to think. (p. 72)

VARYING THE PHYSICAL ENVIRONMENT

Tomlinson and Eidson (2003) suggest that in planning for a differentiated learning environment, teachers consider the flexible use of classroom space, time, and materials. Could furniture be rearranged more efficiently or seating patterns be adjusted smoothly to accommodate for a variety of instructional strategies? Are there spaces to have room for both group discussion and independent concentration? How might students rearrange themselves if the furniture cannot be moved? Kaufeldt (2005) suggests that teachers think creatively as they structure alternative work areas within and out of the classroom. A chair, low bookcase, small tables, or floor cushions accommodate silent reading or groups meetings. Pairs of students working just outside the open classroom door, in a nearby commons area, or in the technology lab or media center are flexible options. She also recommends a "Take-Five" area, such as a rocker or beanbag chair, for students to take five-minute rests, no questions asked.

In selecting flexible materials, teachers consider what is needed for students to learn in preferred individual ways and as a whole class (Tomlinson & Eidsen, 2003). Some supplies are readily accessible while others may be stored. Students know which materials or supplies to use when, how these are retrieved, and about their proper care. Are cabinets and drawers labeled? Is there a color system for boxes of manipulatives or art materials? Is there a "no zone" area that only the teacher accesses? The excerpt from the following case study, "This Is Their Space . . . Not My Room" showcases a middle grades art teacher who puts the responsibility for retrieval and organization of individual work on the shoulders of adolescents.

Text continues on p. 99.

"This Is Their Space . . . Not My Room"

Case Study

When students enter Ms. Morris's art classroom, they know exactly what to do. Portfolio-sized work folders, each creatively decorated with block letter initials, await collection from a center table near the front whiteboard. Following several friendly "Good mornings," Ms. Morris's crisp voice can be heard: "If you need resource materials from the back, you have two minutes to get what you need and return to your seat." This class of eighth graders is working on drafts for thematic maze drawings. One girl has selected a Pooh Bear design, and several guys are using sports images. Ms. Morris instructs the students to take these drafts out of the work folders and continue. "Please take time with your mazes. Use your imagination," she reminds. She suggests adding a honey pot to the Pooh design.

Ms. Morris takes roll by checking the names on any folders remaining on the front table. At each student desk is a black plastic tray that holds common art supplies—colored pencils, crayons, glue sticks, and rulers. As the thirteen-year-olds get settled, light talk about football can be heard from two boys' tables near the long windows. Two of the students are in wheelchairs. Ms. Morris reminds the class that they will need to trace the drafts onto white paper for the final product. A couple of students get a sheet of this white paper from the back table and position it against the glass door by the teacher's desk for better tracing light. Ms. Morris tells another student to "please cap that glue stick."

The atmosphere in Ms. Morris's sun-filled art room is calm and relaxed on this morning in late September. The student work tables are arranged in groups of two in rows facing the whiteboard. On a counter that runs the length of the side wall near the door are boxes labeled "Yarn," "Letters for tracing," and "Scissors." Paint trays share space with large art books, pictures, and a vase of artificial flowers. Cabinets at the back of the room, each labeled with a grade and block number, open onto large shelves. On one of these shelves, Ms. Morris will deposit the stack of student work folders gathered at the end of this class. From another shelf, she will get another set for the next group's arrival. Several other shelves in the back are designated for construction paper and design sample storage.

Ms. Morris's classroom is located at the beginning of the sixth grade hall facing the central hub area of the Eastern Guilford Middle School in Greensboro, North Carolina. It is a relatively large room with the side door opening onto a patio area. Over the classroom door, just inside, is a poster conveying that "What we see depends mainly on what we're looking for." Another poster at the back reads, "The willingness to do creates the ability to do." Bulletin boards showcase colorful student-scaled drawings and multimedia art projects. A word wall of art terms rises above the whiteboard. On the board an agenda appears to be more of a list of cognitive objectives than the typically seen itemized activities:

Grade 6

Describe Roman Art.

Describe music. Define portrait.

Grade 7

What are three kinds of balance?

Explain complementary and analogous colors.

Define symmetry. Describe positive/negative.

Grade 8

Explain value scale.

Shadow? Reflection?

Define medium, mean.

All sixth, seventh, and eighth graders at Eastern Guilford take Ms. Morris's nine-week, forty-minute art elective during the course of the school year. Eighth graders, the veterans, are familiar with the classroom, the procedures, and Ms. Morris's expectations. When the sixth graders enter the art room for the first time, however, they need to be acclimated carefully to the physical layout of the room, the routines, and the anticipated flow of movement. Ms. Morris devotes a good amount of class time in the beginning making certain these expectations are communicated and understood. The activity in a sixth grade class as electives alternate is different, as the following scenario reveals.

It's mid-November and the first day of election rotation. The sixth graders, seated by pairs at the work tables, direct their attention to Ms. Morris at the front of the room. Placed on each desk is an empty, unnamed, unadorned blue folder. "Are you comfortable? Can you see the board? Can you see me?" questions Ms. Morris. The eleven-year-olds indicate their satisfaction in unison. "If you're comfortable, then this is your assigned seat from here on. This is where I expect to see you." Ms. Morris calls the roll orally, asking the students to forgive her beforehand for any mispronunciations. The class, representative of the school system's changing demographics, is nearly 25 percent Hispanic.

Referring to a list of Expectations posted beside the whiteboard, Ms. Morris begins her explanation of the class proceedings: "Be here every day and on time. That's the first. Class starts at 11:35, so I'd like to get started by 11:38 with pencils sharpened. Fair enough? Number 2 is to bring a pencil." Ms. Morris pauses to make sure the eleven-year-olds are listening, "What time should you be in your seat?" Following a correct response, she continues, "I expect that, even if I'm not here. I need to count on you to handle that." The third expectation is to sit in assigned seats, and the fourth is to show respect. "Talk nicely like coming into one of your own homes. Listen when I talk. I won't talk all of the time," she smiles. For the fourth expectation, "to work quietly," Ms. Morris clarifies, "You can talk but keep the volume down." For the last one, "clean up your work area," she simply adds, "Don't blame your partner."

The orientation continues with a tour of the classroom's physical space. Ms. Morris directs the sixth graders' attention to the side of the room near the door. "You can use the computer only after work is finished. The sink and paper towels are for cleaning the work areas. The paper cutter is not to be touched! The supplies are for your daily use," she directs, as she makes her way to the back of the classroom. Ms. Morris points to a cabinet that is labeled "6–3" (sixth grade, third period) as the location for this class's folder storage. Beside the windows near her desk, Ms. Morris pauses at the glass door opening onto the patio. She allows that the students may use the panes for tracing but is quick to add, "The door locks behind you, so don't fool around." At the front of the room, Ms. Morris warns that the "very warm" kiln room is for her use only, pointing to the nearby fire alarm to underline the restriction. When she calls for questions, only one boy asks, "Which way is the bathroom from this class?"

With the visual expedition around the classroom complete, Ms. Morris instructs the sixth graders to take out a sheet of paper. On the whiteboard she writes, "Art Note Page," and explains that art has basic vocabulary just as English. She refers to the word wall and begins an introduction to the seven elements of art, the first of which is line. With brisk pace, the students brainstorm different kinds of lines—curvy, broken, diagonal, zigzag, wide, thin, double, thick, parallel. Ms. Morris records these ideas on the whiteboard and the sixth graders take notes.

Next, the students are asked to put the notes in the blue folder for another activity. For application, Ms. Morris instructs them to trace the first initial of their names on a small sheet of white paper using the assorted sizes of block letters spread out on the back table. She calls the students back to the table by rows and requests that they pass the letters among each other as they are used. Each white letter tracing will be glued in the center of the blue folders, and the surrounding area decorated creatively with as many different kinds of lines as the students can incorporate. This task will individualize their work folders for the upcoming weeks of the elective.

While the sixth graders work, Ms. Morris circulates, collects, and passes letters, offers comments, and practices the students' names: "That looks neat, Jon. Very nice, Nadia. Who has used a wavy line? Try to use all kinds. It's OK to repeat the same line. Outline the letters so we can see them well. Be sure to glue the edges of the white paper down carefully." When one girl laments that she has "messed up," Ms. Morris gives her an eraser from a box on her desk. The students move back and forth freely, getting markers from the supply buckets and testing them. They use the glue sticks and pencils at their desks unless anything needs to be replenished.

(Continued)

(Continued)

When the large television monitor at the front right corner of the room indicates 12:17, Ms. Morris asks the students to stop, pass the work folders back to the person behind them, return all pencils, markers, and glue, and to clean up. A minute later, the work areas are surprisingly clean and the folders stacked on the center table. Ms. Morris, seated on the front stool, asks a few quick review questions about the seven design elements and her classroom expectations. As the monitor shows 12:20, Ms. Morris dismisses the class row by row. No bells ring at Eastern Guilford; however, all teachers and students maintain a close watch over time.

A graduate of East Carolina University, Ms. Morris holds a bachelor of science in art with a K–12 licensure. She has seventeen years of teaching experience at the elementary or middle school level. She attributes much of her classroom management effectiveness as "instinctive," or to use a term from a recent reading workshop she attended, "unconsciously competent." Instead of a laundry list of management strategies, she tries to determine what the students need to help them to learn. One year, for instance, she noticed that her art students were having difficulty staying on task for large blocks of time. In response, she began to break her instruction into ten- to fifteen-minute segments, cueing students ahead of the time when they would stop and move to the next activity. She knew that the students liked this change, though she didn't fully realize the value until she, as a mentor, observed a new teacher having difficulty with student on-task behavior. She suggested that the teacher think about the strategy.

Ms. Morris believes that young adolescents need freedom to explore and create in order to learn and grow. At the same time, she knows that they need limitations. She sees middle school as a time of transitional growth, when students stretch themselves and test these limits. "For most students, this is the way they learn. As they grow, they learn what is acceptable behavior and what is not," she explains. Her perception of her own classroom management style parallels these beliefs about young adolescents and their learning needs: "Sometimes I think my style is very relaxed. However, expectations are established at the beginning so the atmosphere is one of freedom with limitation. Everyone understands and accepts the limits," she indicates. She confesses that she doesn't like to repeat herself, so "I get it all out on the first day. Students hate lectures, so they don't mind."

As evident in the time Ms. Morris takes to introduce new students to the procedures unique to her art room, she genuinely wants them to feel they belong there. She starts building relationships with students from the first day by finding out who they are and what they enjoy. Ms. Morris is also willing to let her students relate to her as a person. On a small front table, among several interesting items for the students to sketch, is a pair of platform shoes. When a sixth grade boy asks about the shoes, Ms. Morris tells him that she wore them as homecoming queen. "That was a time when you weren't even born," she laughs.

Ms. Morris firmly believes that teachers should show respect for students as individuals and to treat them accordingly. She interacts with her young adolescents in art with verbal politeness, and in response to this attitude, their respect is reciprocated. At one point during a class, her back turned, she addresses a student behind her in a calm, matter-of-fact voice, "Anton, getting a lot done over there?" The boy's responds, "Yes, ma'am."

Ms. Morris understands young adolescents and their developmental challenges, and she admits that sometimes this requires a good deal of patience and forgiveness. She is adamant about giving second chances, and her policy for accepting late work is indicative. She issues computer-generated interim reports that update the students on the status of their work completed by the set due dates. These reports must be taken home and signed by parents. According to Ms. Morris, if the student is given a zero on an assignment on the interim report, it could mean one of several things: (a) They did not do it, (b) it's lost somewhere in the room, (c) it simply hasn't been turned in, or (d) it's Ms. Morris's mistake. Students are given the chance to change their status before leaving class or to bring in the completed work within a reasonable length of time. One student discovered that his perspective drawing had slipped out of his work folder in the cabinet. The zero was corrected.

Even with the strong physical organization, clear expectations, and opportunities for redemption, Ms. Morris recognizes realistically that young adolescents need to be watched and reminded. She notes that there will always be someone who will misbehave. Thus, teachers have to be physically and mentally ready for almost anything. The interim reports, for example, caused some stir one day when a few of the eighth grade boys began comparing notes and exchanging jibes. Ms. Morris quickly stepped in, "Excuse me. I don't have anybody in here called an idiot." She's also firm about the students' showing respect to her when she is talking, and will correct any student who is not following this expectation. Students are furthermore expected to be where they're expected to be. To an eighth grade boy who stopped at a peer's desk, Ms. Morris states, "I appreciate your working at your own desk. You'll get a chance to go through everybody's maze." To another she addresses, "Why are you back here? Are you getting anything done today?"

During the transitional time for cleanup and preparation to change classes, Ms. Morris can often be heard saying a simple chant-response: "If you hear my voice, clap once. If you hear my voice, clap twice." With this cue, the students get quiet, and she is able to give the final directions: "Push your chairs in and have a good day."

Ms. Morris's purposeful use of the physical space facilitates the young adolescents' movement, activity, and learning. Her art classroom, nevertheless, is much more than a system of work folders, accessible shelves, and ready supplies. Her class is a student-friendly environment, and students are trusted with its care. In forty-minute turnovers, Ms. Morris's sixth, seventh, and eighth graders come and go, opening and closing the short intervals of instructional time. She sincerely wants the numerous students she teaches each year to feel a personal sense of belonging, responsibility, and ownership as they enter and exit for the elective. According to Ms. Morris, "It's their space . . . not my classroom."

Ms. Morris believes that middle school students need freedom to explore and create in order to learn and grow (Crawford, 2004). At the same time, she knows that they need limitations. She establishes expectations early so that the atmosphere of her class is one of freedom with structure. Students understand and accept the limits. Ms. Morris purposefully uses the physical space of her classroom to facilitate student movement, activity, and learning. Her classroom, nevertheless, is more than a system of work folders, accessible shelves, and ready supplies: it is a student-friendly learning environment, and students are trusted with its care. She sincerely wants the numerous academically diverse students she teaches each year "to feel a sense of belonging, responsibility, and ownership as they enter and exit for the elective." According to Ms. Morris, "It's their space . . . not my classroom" (as cited in Crawford, p. 71).

The Organization of Time

In a successful differentiated classroom, students know what is expected of them and they are held to high standards of performance (Tomlinson & Eidson, 2003). Teachers make decisions about when to work with small groups, which students can work independently, and how to work with the entire class as a group. The flow of instruction appears seamless, nevertheless, because students know the following procedures:

- What to do when the teacher is working with other students
- How to manage without direct teacher supervision
- What rules and actions to follow when working at various places and for various tasks
- Which tasks to work on and where in the room
- What to do when they finish work
- When it is appropriate to move around the classroom
- What to do if more time is needed to complete a task
- How to know if they are successful or doing quality work
- How to keep track of goals, work, and accomplishments (pp. 12–13)

For adolescents who need to become self-managing and academically competent, the last two expectations in the preceding list are critical.

To address certain learner needs, Tomlinson and McTighe (2006) provide flexible differentiation options for the physical elements of time, space, and resources. The *negotiated delay* of due dates or time for tasks helps students who work hard but slowly or who have skill challenges. Advanced learners benefit from the compacting or exemption from work they have already mastered. Homework contracts and learning centers help students develop prerequisite skills and catch up on missing background knowledge. Regarding space, these writers advise to create quiet zones of minimal auditory or visual stimulation for students who are easily distracted or need "time-out." They also suggest to post and use varying room arrangement charts to facilitate student and teacher movement into small group, whole class, and independent work configurations. Additionally, the following strategies give options for the flexible use of resources:

- **Textbooks on different readability levels**. This strategy benefits all students through access to key and appropriately challenging reading materials.
- **Bookmarks for non-English Internet sites on key topics.** English language learners gain an understanding of essential material in their first language as support of their learning English.
- **Instructional video and audio tapes.** Students who struggle with print, have auditory or visual learning strengths, or need practical, alternate applications. (pp. 91–92)

Other Physical Considerations

In her book, *Differentiation Through Learning Styles and Memory*, Sprenger (2003) writes that certain physical characteristics in the learning environment, such as natural lighting, cooler temperatures, natural colors, music, water, orderliness, and safety, are linked to attention, learning, and retention. Kaufeldt (2005) notes that bright natural, full-spectrum light is more conducive to learning, while fluorescent lights tend to have adverse effects on students' concentration level, vision, and general health. Noisy learning environments have a negative impact on students with behavioral or attending issues. English language learners and students with hearing impairments need to be able to hear articulation clearly. Poor acoustics and white noise (computer monitors, fans, overhead projectors, air systems) potentially contribute to headaches or fatigue and may hamper language skills and vocabulary development (Jensen & Dabney, 2003).

Kaufeldt (2005) suggests several strategies to compensate for the distraction of noise in the learning environment:

- **Soften hard surfaces** by hanging wall tapestries or using area floor rugs to reduce acoustical reverberation.
- **Mask white noise** by playing soft background music or using a small fountain or fish tank to produce more natural, environmental sounds.

- Institute **school-wide quiet times** when intercom interruptions or outdoor maintenance (grass mowers or leaf blowers) are not allowed.
- Use **voice audio-enhancements** such a wireless microphone or speaker system. (p. 37)

Jenson and Dabney (2003) report that color affects students' moods and attitudes. Red and orange, for example, associate with creativity and energy but may induce tension whereas blues and greens tend to have a calming effect that increases alertness. A dimly lit, cluttered, and poorly organized classroom negatively affects student behavior and attentiveness. Kaufeldt (2005) suggests that teachers enhance visual stimuli by organizing shelves, materials, and displays and by adding color to handouts and presentations. Other factors, such as temperature that is too hot or too cold, and classrooms that are "stuffy," interfere with alertness, comprehension, and learning performance. Students need good air circulation, a constant room temperature of 68 to 72 degrees Fahrenheit, and pleasant smelling classrooms for maximal engagement and enhanced learning.

Lastly, the satisfaction of basic physical and psychological needs factor into classroom learning. Adolescents need water and food, bathroom privilege, and the freedom to move around and stretch, breathe in fresh air, and take a break after extended periods of learning. A beanbag chair or a rocker gives an alternative to a desk or table for independent reading or studying. Kaufeldt (2005) recommends that teachers find out how students react to various stimuli in the physical environment and investigate modifications before moving to more complex differentiation strategies, stating:

> What might at first appear to be an attentional disorder, a learning disability, or a behavioral problem might have its roots in where the student is expected to learn ... If modifying lighting, noise, and temperature can help even a handful of our students be more successful learners, then what is stopping us from giving it a try? (pp. 39, 42)

MANAGING THE DIFFERENTIATED LEARNING ENVIRONMENT

In her book, *Managing the Adolescent Classroom: Lessons From Outstanding Teachers*, Crawford (2004) defines classroom management in terms of three interrelated dimensions: physical, or the teacher's use of time, space, and structure; affective, or strategies to promote personal and interpersonal development; and cognitive, or the use of intellectual engagement to motivate appropriate behavioral and learning management (p. 2). She writes of the crucial connection between classroom management practices and adolescents' developmental nature and related learning needs:

> Because adolescents push for independence and autonomy, they need opportunities for choice, responsibility, and self-direction. Their tentative confidence is less vulnerable in a climate of acceptance and accomplishment. Intellectually, they need instructional relevance, content

complexity, and a high level of engagement. Their social concerns for peer acceptance and conformity bring additional need to work cooperatively and to contribute meaningfully within a group. (p. 130)

Similarly, Wormeli (2006) contends that most behavioral problems and disciplinary issues are associated with a disconnect between instructional practice and student needs.

Jackson and Davis (2000) cite three conditions that lead to intrinsic motivation toward learning and active engagement. These are (1) a sense of belonging and acceptance, (2) a sense of fairness and equitable treatment, and (3) a sense of personal accomplishment. These conditions are supported by current research on brain-compatible practice (Crawford, 2004). Sylwester (2003), for example, indicates that a collaborative, community-building classroom environment provides the opportunity for adolescents to master social and problem-solving skills. Biologically, as adolescents mature, they develop the capacity for self-managed behavior, although this development tends to be awkward and marked by impulsivity. As Crawford (2004) writes, adolescents "need a classroom where their tentative efforts to acquire the skills for intellectual and social competence are supported" (p. 132). A classroom management system that promotes this development is one that allows student the freedom to try, fail, reflect upon personal actions, and try again without harsh judgment or recrimination.

Managing the complex learning environment of an academically diverse classroom requires teachers to attend to multiple signals and juggle a variety of roles (Tomlinson, 2001). She offers several basic strategies to help teachers manage a differentiated classroom. These are summarized as follows:

- **Have a strong rationale for differentiation based on student readiness, interest, and learning preference**. Help students and parents understand why and how your classroom offers students many avenues to learning.
- **Use an anchor activity to allow management of multiple class activities**. Use specified activities, adjusted for readiness and interest, to which students go automatically after assigned work is completed. Anchor activities could be reading, journaling, portfolio work, or practice in vocabulary, spelling, or mathematical computation. When a portion of the class is engaged in predictable, self-directed work, teachers are free to guide others in differentiated content-based tasks.
- **Design and deliver instruction carefully**. Task cards or assignment sheets, tape-recorded directions, and student leaders can supplement and facilitate communication of expectations. Have clear directions for classroom movement and time limitation.
- **Assign students into groups or seating areas efficiently**. List names by color or indicate on an overhead transparency or wall chart to allow smooth movement.
- **Have a home base for students**. Assigned home base seats for the beginning and ending of lessons help students and materials stay better organized.

- **Have an understood plan for when you are unavailable**. Designate student "experts of the day" to assist students who need help or have other options when you are busy with another student or group.
- **Minimize noise**. Teach students to interact with peers quietly and have a signal to remind when conversations are too loud. Assign students in small groups to monitor noise level. Have quiet sections of the room, or headsets or earplugs, for students who are particularly distracted by noise.
- **Have a plan for students to turn in work**. Have an assigned student to look over students' work for completeness and quality. If the "expert" concurs, students place the work in a predesignated box or labeled file.
- **Teach students to rearrange furniture**. Draw three or four color-coded, named, or numbered floor plans for differing furniture arrangements and teach students to rearrange upon cue and in an orderly manner.
- **Minimize idle roaming**. Reduce the amount of unnecessary movement by designating an expert to assist one student at a time or appoint a "gopher" to gather pertinent materials for his or her group's task.
- **Promote on-task behavior.** Clarify expectations and give a daily check or minus on how well students are using time. Allow students to note patterns in concentration over time and use the information for assessment of task level difficulty or needed change of seating arrangements.
- **Have a plan for early finishers**. Students who consistently complete work early signals that the task is insufficiently challenging or that they have not achieved a level of quality. Involve students in compiling, recognizing, and applying indicators and characteristics of superior work.
- **Have a plan to signal closure**. Give students advance warnings (1 to 2 days) of approaching deadlines and, if needed, provide ways to complete unfinished work, such as alternate homework assignments, learning contracts, or anchor time.
- **Foster student responsibility for personal learning**. Help student become more self-sufficient by giving responsibility for distributing and collecting materials, moving furniture for group work, critiquing the work of peers, establishing goals, keeping records, and charting progress.
- **Help students take ownership in the classroom**. Have ongoing conversations with students about classroom procedures and group processes. Help students understand your expectations and the rationale for having them. Involve them in the solution of problems. (pp. 32–38)

Tomlinson (2001) also suggests that teachers begin at a comfortable pace. They might vary learning resources, such as multilevel text and supplementary materials, computer programs, peer tutors; differentiate activities to accommodate student pacing and understanding; vary products based on student interest or learning preference; or design small-group tiered tasks for differing learning needs. She recommends that teachers elect a few "low-prep" strategies to use consistently and one "high-prep" strategy per unit or semester. Low-preparation strategies include book selection, homework options, menus for tasks and assessment products, reading partners, or other open-ended activities in which students have personal choice. Other "low-prep" differentiation strategies include varying questioning levels and journal prompts; review games, such as Jeopardy; mini-workshops to reteach or extend student learning, cooperative learning structures, such a think-pair-share or jigsaw; and scaffolding through the use of graphic organizers or other thinking maps.

High-preparation strategies, on the other hand, may require more time to plan and implement. These include tiered or interest-based activities; labs, centers, or stations, which may include tape-recorded materials and assessment products; literature circles with varied book levels or supplementary materials; problem-based learning or group investigation; and curriculum compacting for more advanced students.

SUMMARY AND LOOKING AHEAD

Chapter 5 begins the two-part discussion of the interrelated affective, social-emotional, physical, and intellectual dimensions of the learning Environment, the sixth "E" in the adolescent-centered differentiation framework. The current chapter focuses on differentiation related to the affective, social-emotional, and physical dimensions. Differentiation is evident in the way teachers create a positive, community-oriented learning climate where all adolescents feel invited to learn. In this setting, adolescents feel accepted and valued as diverse individuals who make a significant contribution to classroom life and learning. These classrooms are safe havens for adolescents to develop personally, socially, and emotionally.

Adolescents also thrive in an environment of purposeful and guided social interaction that is differentiated through flexible grouping. Chapter 5 describes several strategies for student grouping based on interest, readiness, and learning preference. These include jigsaw, which enables task specialization, and study groups, in which older adolescents are actively engaged in high-interest, self-motivating, relevant inquiries that involve experts in the community and lead to pertinent social action.

Chapter 5 additionally explores the physical dimension of the adolescent-centered environment. Differentiation is evident in the way teachers structure an orderly, colorful, clean, well-organized physical environment that supports the physical need to move and the social need to interact. Other physical characteristics, such as natural lighting, cooler temperatures, natural colors, music, water, orderliness, and safety, link to students' ability to attend, learn, and retain new knowledge. The chapter also suggests management strategies that are conducive for a differentiated classroom.

Chapter 6 continues the discussion of the adolescent-centered learning environment with a focus on the intellectual dimensions. Adolescents thrive in an intellectually charged environment where they are appropriately challenged and intentionally supported. They also learn better when they feel they are important and contributing members of a classroom culture, and they are motivated through active involvement in respectful tasks. Through teacher feedback, scaffolding, and reflection, adolescents understand new knowledge, gain competence, and become self-directed learners. Chapter 6 also features instructional technology as a community-building and scaffolding tool to promote adolescent thinking and cognitive development.

6

The Intellectual Dimension in The Differentiated Learning Environment

Chapter 5 began the discussion of the interrelated affective, social-emotional, physical, and intellectual dimensions of the adolescent-centered learning **Environment**, the sixth "E" in the differentiation framework. With focus on the affective, social-emotional, and physical dimensions, the chapter stressed the importance of creating a setting for learning where adolescents feel *invited* to share ideas, express opinions, and contribute to classroom learning. These classrooms provide *safe* havens for adolescents to develop personally, socially, emotionally, and intellectually. The social environment enables adolescents to interact with peers on a variety of meaningful and engaging tasks in *flexible groups* based on interest, readiness, and learning preference. Adolescents also learn better in a physical setting characterized by order, cleanliness, movement, and structure. Other physical factors related to learning and retention include natural lighting, cooler temperatures, natural colors, music, water, and safety. Chapter 5 also suggested effective management strategies for the differentiated classroom that support adolescents' learning and developmental needs.

Chapter 6 continues the discussion of the adolescent-centered learning environment with its focus on the intellectual dimensions of classroom life. Adolescents thrive in an intellectually charged environment where they are appropriately challenged and intentionally supported. The chapter illustrates two key instructional strategies that differentiate for student readiness: *sequenced teacher questioning* using the "SAFE" framework and tiered *assessment*. This chapter stresses the critical connection between affective and cognitive competence and proposes research-based affective and cognitive interaction practices that differentiate through equitable response opportunities and cognitive support.

Chapter 6 also emphasizes the important interplay of knowledge acquisition, understanding, and meaningful assessment in shaping the intellectual dimension. It suggests grading principles that support adolescent-centered differentiation and intellectual growth and mastery. With teacher feedback, scaffolding, and reflection, adolescents have the opportunity to succeed, achieve, and gain competence. Chapter 6 further features instructional technology as a cognitive scaffolding tool for adolescent learning and intellectual development.

Figure 6.1, "The Intellectual Dimension of the Learning Environment," reflects the critical elements that form the intellectual dimension of the adolescent-centered learning environment. Key questions are these:

- How might teachers construct an intellectual learning environment in which all adolescents are cognitively engaged and appropriately challenged?
- What is the interplay of knowledge acquisition, understanding, and meaningful assessment?
- How can teachers use instructional technology to differentiate in an adolescent-centered learning environment?
- How might teachers use instructional technology as a "mindtool" to stimulate intellectual inquiry?
- How can technology be used as a scaffolding tool that promotes cognitive access to meaningful content and learning?

Figure 6.1   The Intellectual Dimension of the Learning Environment

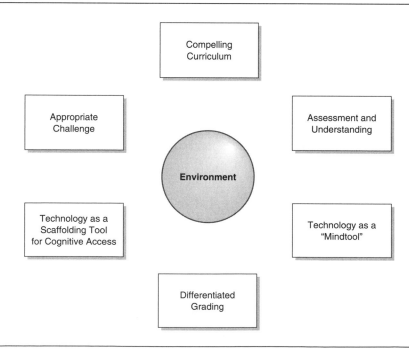

THE INTELLECTUAL DIMENSION OF THE LEARNING ENVIRONMENT

The intellectual challenge in differentiated classrooms is for teachers to help all learners become knowledgeable thinkers and problem solvers. As discussed in Chapter 3, *all* students deserve access to a coherent, compelling, dynamic, and relevant curriculum, one that focuses on the essential knowledge, understanding, and skills of the discipline (Tomlinson & Eidson, 2003). In this information era, the construction of knowledge and the acquisition of the cognitive strategies to process information and solve problems are critical (Crawford, 2007). A knowledge-centered learning environment gives students equitable opportunity to learn in ways that lead to understanding and transfer (Bransford, Brown, & Cocking, 2000). The challenge for the teacher is to find ways to build on students' strengths and scaffold in ways that support access to and mastery of important content.

One useful scaffolding strategy that helps teachers differentiate for varying readiness levels is *sequenced questioning*. Through the thoughtful sequencing of varying cognitive levels of questions, teachers connect with, build on, and extend students' thinking about important content knowledge. The "SAFE" Classification Model in Box 6.1, "Questioning to Challenge Adolescent Thinking: A 'SAFE' Classification Model," shows example questions constructed on four cognitive levels (Beamon, 1990, 1997, 2001). The first (S) level questions help adolescents "set up" the content knowledge base. These questions focus on basic comprehension and factual responses. The second (A) level questions are more analytical and require students to interpret knowledge through contextual clues. Questions on the third (F) level are more divergent and encourage students to hypothesize as they "focus" their thinking in a new direction. The fourth (E) level of questions elicits evaluative thinking and persuades students to appraise, assign value, and reflect. Box 6.1, "Questioning to Challenge Adolescent Thinking: A 'SAFE' Classification Model" illustrates the "SAFE" classification model through content examples.

> ### Sequenced Questioning
>
> The teacher's purposeful sequencing of questioning that varies cognitive levels in order to connect with, build on, and extend adolescents' thinking about important content. Cognitive levels include "Setting the Knowledge Base," "Analyzing the New Knowledge," "Focusing the New Knowledge," and "Evaluating the New Knowledge" (SAFE). Sequenced questioning also integrates follow-up questions, as appropriate.

❖ BOX 6.1 Questioning to Challenge Adolescent Thinking: A "SAFE" Classification Model

Setting the Knowledge Base

Students are asked to remember facts, relate personal experiences, and make meaningful connections with new knowledge. These questions are literal, with fairly apparent answers.

What are the basic steps in this process?

What is the formula to find this function?

What are the events that led to this occurrence?

What other story was set in this location?

What in your own experience helps you relate to this character?

Who are other artists who used this style?

(Continued)

(Continued)

Analyzing the New Knowledge

These questions ask students to make inferences, to interpret information based on contextual clues, to compare or explain, and to see new relationships in the knowledge. These questions require an analysis of meaning, and answers are interpretive.

What relationship do you see among these number properties?

What can you infer about this character's motive?

How could we classify these genetic characteristics?

How does this problem-solving method compare to the other one?

How can you differentiate this perspective from the others?

Why is the historical event pivotal?

Focusing the New Knowledge

These questions encourage divergent thinking. Students are asked to make predictions, to hypothesize, to extend knowledge to a new context, or to focus it in a new direction.

Based on what you've found, what hypothesis can you formulate?

If we change this angle, what will be the effect on the perimeter?

If the story took place in another time period, how might the ending change?

What is another way to view this decision?

If this composer could hear today's music, what might he say?

Evaluating the New Knowledge

These questions require students to evaluate, judge, appraise, critique, or give personal value to the new knowledge. They encourage personal reflection.

What is your perspective on the issue?

Which of the two methods worked more efficiently?

What criteria are you using to judge the value of the piece?

What argument could you present to verify your conclusion?

How can we determine the appropriateness of this decision?

Source: Beamon, G. W. (1990). *Classroom climate and teacher questioning strategies: Relationship to student cognitive development.* Unpublished doctoral dissertation, University of North Carolina at Greensboro.

The questioning levels in the "SAFE" framework elicit increasingly complex thinking in adolescents; however, the levels are not hierarchical in importance. What is important is a teacher's purposeful sequencing according to the cognitive needs of individual students (Beamon, 1997). A sequence that begins with one or two "S" questions, for example, helps a student think about content on a factual, more concrete level. For struggling readers these comprehension questions are critical building blocks before they can be expected to use more sophisticated thinking. An advanced reader may be able to respond more readily to a higher-level cognitive question, yet need a couple of lower-level follow-up questions in order to consider important details that could enrich a response. In both instances, the teacher uses sequenced questioning to scaffold and thus differentiate for student readiness. These sequencing examples from a class discussion of the familiar fairy tale, *Jack and the Beanstalk* (Johnson, 1976) illustrate:

Low to High Sequencing

- What was Jack's purpose for climbing up the beanstalk the first time? (S level)
- Did Jack plan to steal from the giant when he climbed the beanstalk the first time? (S level)
- Why does Jack go up the beanstalk a third time? (A level)
- Do you think Jack was wrong for going up the beanstalk a third time? (E level)

High to Low to High

- Do you think Jack is a bad person for going up the beanstalk for the third time? (E level)
- What was Jack's purpose for climbing up the beanstalk the first time? (S level)
- Why does Jack go up the beanstalk a third time? (A level)
- Do you think Jack is a greedy person for going up this last time? (E level)

Teachers also consciously integrate follow-up questions within the sequence to encourage adolescents to think metacognitively about their own thinking. Follow-up questions help students to "give more extensive responses, to clarify or strengthen the logic of their thinking by offering reasons, to substantiate thinking by providing details or examples, and to reflect on their own thinking" (Beamon, 1997, p. 69). Beamon suggests the following questions to encourage adolescents to think more deeply:

- What do you mean by. . . ?
- How did you arrive at your response?
- What clues in the story led you to think that?
- What ideas did you consider in forming your conclusion?
- Is there anything you could add to your answer?
- What makes your idea workable?
- What might be the consequence of your recommendation? The benefits?
- What might happen if we combined your idea with _____'s idea? (p. 70)

Question sequencing is thus most strategic when teachers integrate cognitive and process questions purposefully to facilitate student inquiry and metacognitive development. Box 6.2, "Sequencing Questions to Differentiate for Adolescent Thinking," illustrates four differing questioning sequences for the short story "Charles" (Jackson, 1951) during a Socratic seminar. The process questions are denoted with an asterisk (*).

❖ BOX 6.2 Sequencing Questions to Differentiate for Adolescent Thinking

Low to High

- Is there a boy in kindergarten named Charles? (S)
- *How do you know that Laurie made up Charles? (elaboration, substantiation)
- How would you compare Laurie's behavior at home with Charles's behavior at school? (A)
- Why does Laurie invent Charles? (A)
- *What clues in the story make you think that? (textual support)
- *Is there another reason why Laurie invented Charles? (extension and redirection of A-level question)

High to Low to High

- Do you think Laurie's teacher should have called his parents? (E)
- Do you think Laurie did all the things he described about Charles? (A)
- What are some of the "bad" things Charles did at school? (S)
- How would you compare Laurie's behavior at home and Charles's behavior at school? (A)
- Do you know someone about Laurie's age? (S)
- Would you consider Laurie to have a behavioral problem? (E)

High to Low to High

- Why do you think Laurie had a relapse just before the P.T.A. meeting? (A)
- Was Laurie having trouble adjusting to kindergarten? (S)
- *How do you know? (support)
- Is there a time when he seems to have adjusted? (S)
- *What indicates that to you? (probing, support)
- Why do you think he became the teacher's helper in the third week? (A)
- Why would he have a relapse just before the P.T.A meeting? (return to original A-level question)

High and Extension

- Why do you think Laurie's parents are more interested in Charles's behavior than the behavior of their own son? (A)
- Why don't Laurie's parents guess that Charles doesn't exist? (A)
- How might the story have changed had Laurie's mother gone to the first P.T.A. meeting? (F)
- *Describe your thinking for that response. (probing, metacognition)
- *Is there something else that might have happened? (extension)
- What do you think Laurie's mother says to Laurie when she arrives home? (F)
- Do you think Laurie should be punished? (E)
- *Explain your response. (probing, substantiation)

Source: Adapted from Beamon, G. W. (1997). *Sparking the Thinking of Students, Ages 10–14*. Thousand Oaks, CA: Corwin Press.

The Role of Assessment

Intertwined closely with knowledge acquisition in the intellectual dimension of the learning environment is assessment. Formative and summative assessments are important opportunities for teachers to give adolescents feedback on their thinking and learning (Bransford, Brown, & Cocking, 2000). Informal, or formative, feedback is most valuable when students have the opportunity to use it to revise their tasks. This practice not only increases student learning and transfer but also teaches them to value revision. Effective teachers also help adolescents develop the skills for self-assessment, an important aspect of metacognition.

Tomlinson and Eidson (2003) urge teachers to become "assessment junkies." While teachers are surrounded by assessment options, they frequently view assessment as something to do *after* learning ends. Assessment is rather "as an ongoing process, conducted in flexible but distinct phases" (p. 14). Essential to a differentiated classroom, as discussed earlier in the Evaluation section in Chapter 4, is pre-assessment. A quiz, an exit card, a journal entry, a Quick-Write, or multiple other measures provide teaches with information about adolescents' knowledge, skills, and understanding related to an upcoming lesson or unit. This information serves as a starting point for curriculum design. Assessment is also important throughout the learning experience to gauge students' level of knowledge, skills, and understanding.

When teachers use more than one form of assessment, such as a test or product, they maximize adolescents' opportunities to demonstrate learning and understanding. Tomlinson and McTighe (2006) note that "reliable assessment demands more than one measure" (p. 60). These educators use the metaphor of a photo album of varying assessments, rather than a snapshot, to give a more accurate and revealing picture of student learning in academically diverse classrooms. They contend that "[u]ltimately, the validity and reliability of our judgments about student achievement are enhanced when we ensure the types of assessment we use are effective for particular learners in providing the evidence of their achievement" (pp. 63–64).

Assessment, when used strategically, also helps adolescents develop the cognitive skills for self-directed learning (Beamon, 2001). As noted in the Chapter 4, the most effective learners are metacognitive: they are aware of "how they learn, set personal learning goals, regularly self-assess and adjust their performance, and use productive strategies to assist their learning" (Tomlinson & McTighe, 2006, p. 79). Following a group inquiry, for example, a teacher asks adolescents to think about which strategies or resources were most helpful, what problems arose and how they were handled, how well they worked together, or what factored into group decisions (Crawford, 2007). Students self-evaluate through reflective journals, such as critiquing the procedures of a lab experiment; stop-n-writes, such as pausing to give a personal reaction to a controversial issue in social studies; and learning logs, where they reflect, for example, on daily progress in understanding key concepts in science.

Self-assessment is particularly important in the differentiated classroom where students need to think about personal learning preferences and strengths, weigh task difficulty, and discern useful cognitive strategies. Furthermore, when students understand what they are expected to learn, they are better able to play an active role in setting immediate and long-range learning goals and in assessing their own progress. The result of this cognitive awareness is a shared mindset for personal growth and continual improvement. Metacognition is cultivated when students regularly respond to reflective questions such as:

- What do you understand about _____?
- What questions or uncertainties do you still have about _____?
- What strategy was most effective in _____?
- What strategy was least effective in _____?
- How difficult was _____ for you?
- What would you do differently next time?

- What are your strengths in _____?
- How does your preferred learning style influence _____?
- How does what you've learned connect with other learning?
- How has what you've learned changed your thinking?

Source: Tomlinson, C. A., & McTighe, J. (2006). *Integrating differentiated instruction and understanding by design* (pp. 79–80). Alexandria, VA: Association for Supervision and Curriculum Development.

Additionally, "[a]s adolescents become more adept at self-assessment, they will be better prepared for success in the world beyond the classroom" (Beamon, 2001, p. 79). Assessments that promote adolescent autonomy include digital and product portfolios, student-led conferences, senior exhibitions, performances, fairs, and publications. When outside experts, business leaders, community members, or college professors assist in the evaluation, these culminating assessments gain added authenticity.

Meaningful Assessment and Differentiation

Wiggins (1993) initially uses the term *authentic* to describe alternative assessments in which students demonstrate understanding and learning. Perkins (1991) defines "understanding performances" as the evidence that reveals a learner's insight into knowledge:

> Suppose, for example, that a learner can explain that law of supply and demand in his or her words (not just recite a canned definition), can exemplify its use in fresh contexts, can make analogies to novel situations (let us say to grades in school rather than costs of goods), can generate the law, recognizing other laws or principles with the same form, and so on. We probably would be pretty impressed by such a learner's insight into the law of supply and demand. (p. 76)

Wiggins and McTighe (2005) identify six facets of understanding as indicators of how student understanding is demonstrated. Box 6.3, "When Adolescents Really Understand," summarizes these processes. When adolescents *apply* what they have learned to a new situation, that is, *use* knowledge and skills appropriately in a new context, and are able to explain or justify this application, they most likely understand.

❖ BOX 6.3 When Adolescents Really Understand

They should be able to:

1. **Explain it.** What is the effect of this war on the nation's economy? How would you explain symbolism to a fourth grader?

2. **Interpret it.** How does this style of writing reflect the political climate of the decade? How does this historical event reflect cultural traditions of the country?

3. **Apply it.** How can I apply this mathematical principle in a real-world context?

4. **Take a perspective on it.** What are the two sides of the debate over stem cell research? What are the strengths and weaknesses of these arguments?

5. **Show empathy about it.** How would you feel if you were in this character's shoes? How do more rigid regulations impact the quality of life of immigrants?

6. **Gain self-knowledge through it.** How might I improve my thinking? What prejudices do I recognize in myself?

As discussed in Chapter 1, a good assessment measure is a learning experience in itself (Gardner, 1993). Students bring a set of learned knowledge and skills to the assessment experience, and their involvement in the assessment extends, solidifies, and advances this knowledge. Assessment that is authentic supports a variety of learning preferences and meaningfully extends learning within a real-world context (Crawford, 2007). Adolescents who enact a model United Nations, for example, better understand the concepts of negotiation and interdependence. Those who adopt a local creek; monitor the variables of clarity, temperature, odor, and velocity; and observe the activity of plants and creatures, gain authentic, hands-on knowledge of ecological balance. Those who run a class business or simulate a town meeting to debate an issue learn more deeply about consumer mathematics and civic responsibility.

Adolescents additionally need a good representation, or mental model, of what comprises exemplary performance. When teachers work with students to establish clear guidelines and criteria for evaluation, generally in the form of a rubric, adolescents are better able to gauge personal progress. As Beamon (2001) writes, "A good rubric, collaboratively created based on tangible examples of real work, becomes an important cognitive tool" (p. 79). She offers several tips for rubric design that enhance adolescent cognitive development. These are as follows:

- **Select criteria that are teachable and measurable.** Criteria for a debate, for example, include "presentation of argument," "validity of information sources," "verbal delivery," and "involvement in counter-questioning." Those for a multimedia production include "screen design," "content knowledge," "originality," and "mechanics."
- **Choose descriptors that clearly convey what the criteria levels mean.** Quality words communicate what is exemplary or needs improvement. Descriptors such as "authentic," "detailed," "varied," and "well-documented," for example, denote strong evidence, whereas word such as "superficial" or "undocumented" indicate work that is unacceptable or still "in progress."
- **Limit the number of criteria and the number of levels for each.** Five criteria and four levels are recommended and manageable.
- **Involve students in the rubric design.** Adolescents thus gain cognitive "sense" of the benchmarks along a continuum of personal progress.
- **Don't reinvent the wheel.** Numerous rubric models are available to modify and adapt. Rubistar (http://rubistar.4teachers.org/index.php) and The National Center for Research on Evaluation, Standards, and Student Testing (CRESST), (http://www.cse.ucla.edu/resources/justforteachers_set.htm), for example, have available online rubrics. (p. 79)

In a differentiated classroom, all students have regular opportunities to show their understanding of important content goals. Tomlinson and McTighe

(2006) suggest that teachers design performances or products of understanding according to the *GRASPS* framework, accordingly:

- A real-world *goal*
- A meaningful *role* for the student
- *Authentic* (or simulated) real-world audience
- A contextualized *situation* that involves real-world application
- Student-generated *products* and performances
- Consensus-driven performance *standards* or criteria for judging success. (p. 70)

GRASPS

A differentiation strategy for the design of authentic products or performances. Components are a real-world *goal*; a meaningful student *role*; an *authentic* (or simulated) audience; a contextualized *situation* with real-world application; student-generated *products* or performance; and consensus-driven performance *standards* or evaluation criteria.

While some of the task parameters and the amount of teacher scaffolding may vary for some groups of learners, all students have the opportunity to demonstrate learning through *meaningful assessments* aligned with essential content goals. Keeping these important learning goals in mind, a teacher differentiates, or tiers, the amount of abstraction or complexity. The reader may recall the tiered tasks designed by Mr. Wirt in the Tiananmen Square unit example in Chapter 1. In the following example, a social studies teacher at the middle school level classroom, Ms. Delancy, designs a tiered assessment that follows the GRASPS model and differentiates in level of complexity for student learning readiness.

A Differentiation Application

Ms. Delancy's seventh graders have been studying the Egyptian culture. They have learned about the ancient Egyptian reverence for cultural antiquity and the related religious beliefs and customs. They have also explored the contemporary issues inherent in the excavation and conservation of historical sites, which are frequently in conflict with the country's struggle for economic progress. The unit learning goals are these:

- Students will explore and gain knowledge of ancient Egypt's religious beliefs, values, and customs through readings, research, media, and discussion.
- Students will acquire an understanding of the current and ongoing environmental and economic issues that bring conflict to Egypt's prosperity.

Over the course of three weeks, the adolescents have discussed the sacred and artful practice of mummification and made their own mummy. They have read about the time-consuming construction of pyramids and temples and seen numerous photos of these antiquities. They have viewed video footage of hieroglyphics on the walls of temples, the color amazingly preserved for thousands of years. They were also intrigued by the fact that visitors to unprotected tombs in the Valley of Kings deposit gallons of sweat daily, attributing to the erosion of the paint and plaster. They have debated the pros and cons of allowing Egyptologists to excavate in the Valley of the Kings and were intrigued by the story of Lord

Carnarvon and his death by a mosquito bite. They have also talked about the successful campaign by UNESCO in the 1960s to move the monument Abu Simbel above the waterline of the Nile River for the construction of the new Aswan Dam.

For the culminating assessment, Ms. Delancy designs the tiered challenge in Box 6.4, "Differentiation Through Tiered Assessment." Each assessment meets the criteria of the GRASPS model suggested by Tomlinson and McTighe (2006). In each of the three assessment scenarios, students are asked to apply their knowledge of Egyptian culture and modern-day challenges to a real-world situation. Each of the three tasks is open-ended and allows students to personalize their responses for an identified audience.

Each scenario is an example of meaningful assessment that is differentiated for learner readiness based on Ms. Delancy's knowledge of the students' learning needs. In Tier 1, for early readiness level students, the task is more concrete and requires a more familiar application of knowledge and skills. According to Northey (2005), Tier 1 tasks have the following features: less difficult independent reading, materials based on the average reading level of the students, have a low level of abstraction, require fewer steps to complete, converge on "right answers" to solve problems, require knowledge and comprehension levels of thinking, and include supportive strategies such as graphic organizers or teacher prompts. Ms. Delancy's Tier 1 task fits these criteria. The students are given a definite number of pros and cons to find and a thinking map to organize their work.

Tier 2 tasks generally include grade-level readings, concrete tasks that help adolescents move toward abstract thinking, a mixture of open-ended and "right answer" questions that have more steps, expect students to infer or draw conclusions, and require knowledge, comprehension, and application (Northey, 2005, p. 76). Tier 3 tasks, on the other hand, usually require more complex and lengthy readings, focus on abstract concepts, use open-ended questions exclusively, and challenge students to analyze, infer, synthesize, and evaluate. In the Tier 2 assessment in the example, students are given more detail and structure than the Tier 3 task. They are asked to compose a persuasive speech but do not have to evaluate the knowledge in order to choose a side. The Tier 3 assessment is less defined and requires adolescents to evaluate the pros and cons of the restoration dilemma, to choose a stance, and to organize for a debate. At all levels, students have the opportunity to express their learning through a task that is focused on essential content understanding.

❖ BOX 6.4 Differentiation Through Tiered Assessment

Tier 1: Least Complex

The tomb of a famous pharaoh has been discovered in the Valley of the Kings. Its excavation, restoration, and maintenance would drain the financial resources of Egypt's struggling economy, yet its boost to Egypt's tourism could be significant. Funds are lacking, however, in Egypt's struggling economy, to bring in the technology necessary to preserve yet another antiquity. You have been asked by the local chamber of commerce to give the pros and cons of the restoration project. Use the Pro-Con graphic organizer to record at least three factors that support the restoration and three that do not.

(Continued)

(Continued)

Tier 2: Grade Level

You have been asked to talk to an international committee formed to decide the fate of the newly discovered tomb of a famous pharaoh in the Valley of the Kings. Excavation and restoration would allow the tomb to be opened to the public, a boost to Egypt's important tourist industry. Funds are lacking, however, in Egypt's struggling economy, to bring in the technology necessary to preserve yet another antiquity. Write a persuasive speech that addresses why the restoration would be important historically and economically to the Egyptians, and how international support could help to protect the ancient site from pollution and neglect.

Tier 3: Most Complex

The tomb of a famous pharaoh has been discovered in the Valley of the Kings. Its excavation, restoration, and maintenance would drain the financial resources of Egypt's struggling economy, yet its boost to Egypt's tourism could be significant. You have been summoned, as a native citizen of the country, by the local chamber of commerce for advice. Choose one side and prepare for a debate concerning the fate of this newly found cultural treasure.

Source: Adapted from Beamon, G. W. (1997). *Sparking the thinking of students, ages 10–14: Strategies for teachers*. Thousand Oaks, CA: Corwin Press.

Grading in the Differentiated Classroom

Wormeli (2006), in his book, *Fair Isn't Always Equal: Assessing & Grading in the Differentiated Classroom*, writes that, "A grade represents a clear and accurate indicator of what a student knows and is able to do—-mastery. With grades, we document the progress of students and our teaching, we provide feedback to students and their parents, and we make instructional decisions regarding the students" (p. 103). He contends that any grading practice that hinders a student's development or expression of learning should be questioned.

Teachers in differentiated classrooms continually examine and reexamine what grades mean and how they affect students' lives. They are careful to minimize subjectivity and maximize usefulness of grades by removing nonacademic factors, such as work habits. He proffers that the issue in differentiated classrooms is not about equitably assigning grades across diverse populations but about fairness for each student. "[S]uccessful differentiating teachers focus on criterion-based mastery in relation to essential understandings and their learning objectives" (p. 160).

Wormeli warns that "[s]chools should never be a place where students who learn differently from their classmates—in pace, style, method, or tools—-are made to suffer for that difference" (p. 159). Differentiating teachers create a culture in which grades assess students as feedback to learning. They should report trends, patterns, and mastery of content and not be reflective of student behavior. He recommends several guiding principles for assessment practices for teachers in differentiated classrooms:

- **Do what is fair and developmentally appropriate for students each year**. Instruction is inseparable from assessment, thus grading policies in differentiated classrooms are also responsive to students' learning needs.
- **Do different things for different students.** Equality does not equate to fairness. Teachers scaffold for and support students who need it and increase the level of challenge for others. They design pre-, formative,

and summative assessments that provide feedback, document progress, and inform instructional decisions.

- **Do whatever it takes to maximize student learning.** Teachers recognize that students learn at different paces, in different manners, within different cultures, and with different tools and provide them with the tools to achieve.

- **Allow students more than one chance to master material.** Teachers recognize the developmental nature of adolescent learning and create vivid and compelling expectations for achievement and accountability. They give full credit for the highest level of mastery.

- **Use students' patterns of achievements over time to determine mastery.** Rather than grading daily homework, teachers provide ample feedback. They grade summative demonstrations of proficiency.

- **Separate nonacademic factors.** Teachers do not use distorting factors such as work habits, effort, citizenship, or attendance determine grades. They are cautious with extra credit or bonus points that may substitute or significantly alter grades.

- **Provide ample opportunity for students to assess themselves.** Teachers are clear about the evidence that constitutes content mastery. They realize that some students are working on concept attainment while others require experiences that extend the application of the concept.

- **Use rubrics more than percentage grading.** Teachers tie achievement to specific learning and not the number of correct test items. They record zeros as a sixty or upper F range to prevent the skewing of grade averages.

- **Keep records based on criterion-based assessment.** Teachers do not compare students by grading on a curve or giving many group grades. They find ways other than a report card to convey appropriate student achievement, such as narrative comments, a separate report card or addendum, a conference, or a portfolio analysis.

- **Design test items that are clear enough for intelligent response.** Teachers do not attempt to thwart students with confusing or misleading formats or prompts. They design tests for efficient and useful feedback as progress toward mastery.

- **Collaborate and envision pragmatically.** Teachers are open to observation and advice of colleagues and strive to teach in ways students learn best. They do whatever is realistic and necessary to help students thrive. They teach well. (pp. 195–198)

INTERACTION IN THE DIFFERENTIATED LEARNING ENVIRONMENT

Beamon (1990, 1997) identifies twenty research-based teacher-student interaction practices that support and challenge adolescent thinking and learning. These follow in Box 6.5, "Classroom Climate and Teacher Questioning Strategies," and serve as a conclusion for this section. With their emphasis on equitable response opportunity, cognitive challenge, and cognitive processing, these affective and intellectual practices are appropriate for the differentiated classroom. The model includes the SAFE levels of teacher questioning and guided cognitive processing.

❖ BOX 6.5 Classroom Climate and Teacher Questioning Strategies

Response Opportunity

The teacher:

- offers questions to the class before specific students
- accepts all valid student responses (nonjudgmental)
- gives sustaining feedback when needed
- allows/queries for more than one student's point of view
- elicits students' questions
- permits students to answer each other's questions
- distributes questions equably

Cognitive Level of Questioning

The teacher:

- asks questions that help students set up the knowledge base (remember facts, make connections)
- asks questions that help students analyze new information (interpret, infer, compare, explain)
- asks questions that helps students focus knowledge in a new direction (predict, hypothesize)
- asks questions that help students evaluate new information (judge, appraise, evaluate)

Cognitive Processing

The teacher:

- gives adequate wait time for cognitive level of question
- elicits student thinking appropriate for question
- pauses after student responses (at least three seconds)
- asks student probing questions for more extensive or complex responses
- asks students to explain why or give proof for answers
- asks follow-up questions at same or lower cognitive level
- asks follow-up questions at a higher cognitive level
- asks students how they arrived at an answer or to explain thinking (metacognition)
- elicits higher level questions from students

Source: Beamon, G. W. (1990). *Classroom climate and teacher questioning strategies: Relationship to student cognitive development.* Unpublished doctoral dissertation, University of North Carolina at Greensboro.

THE NEW GEOGRAPHY OF LEARNING

Over the beat of rap music, three of Ms. Hinton's seventh graders talk about a chair leg that bent and spilled a classmate onto the ground (Hayhurst, 2006). Photographs of desks flash by on their iPod presentation, or podcast. The students suggest that some money be set aside from school fundraisers to pay for new classroom furniture. This lively podcast is one of several that students in Ms. Hinton's language arts class have prepared on the topic of school problems. Ms. Hinton admits knowing little about iPods before making the assignment, yet she recognized an opportunity to prepare students for the seventh-grade writing test "without making them groan" (p. A2).

With the assistance of the school's media specialist, the adolescents quickly learned to combine recordings of their written papers with music and images. They enjoyed taking digital photos around the school and adding popular music. For Ms. Hinton, this high-interest instructional strategy was a motivational and effective way to teach writing. "You have to be able to write to do the other parts,"' she offers. '"I think they didn't realize they were doing a writing assignment. It was a lot of fun. After I saw how excited they were about it, I think I will use these more" (p. A2).

Using iPods for podcasts is one of the many ways teachers integrate technology into the adolescent learning environment, and it's a natural fit. Adolescents live in a culture defined by speed, color, sound, and movement (Crawford, 2007). Fast-paced, interactive video games have long challenged adolescents' mental acuity and dexterity, and information comes easily and quickly to their fingertips. With new digital tools such as Weblogs, wikis, Really Simple Syndication (RSS), and podcasting, adolescents construct new Web environments where they interact and construct learning. According to Prensky (2005/2006), digital tools are like extensions of adolescents' brains. Teachers who want relevance in this century engage students in the 21st century way . . . electronically:

> They're already busy adopting new systems for communicating (instant messaging), sharing (blogs), buying and selling (eBay), exchanging (peer-to-peer technology), creating (Flash), meeting (3D worlds), collecting (downloads), coordinating (wikis), evaluating (reputation systems), searching (Google), analyzing (SETI), reporting (camera phones), programming (modding), socializing (chat rooms), and even learning (Web surfing). (p. 10)

Weblogs, or blogs, enable students to create personal or group sites without having to learn hypertext markup language. Wikis are open-content creation tools that anyone can contribute to or edit at any time. Instructional gaming is another technological phenomenon that builds on the intrinsically motivating attraction of recreational video games (Jenkins 2000). Social studies simulations and strategy games, for example, immerse adolescents in authentic social contexts as they explore and think critically about historical issues and current events.

Web-Based Learning Environments

In their book, *Literacy, Technology, and Diversity: Teaching for Success in Changing Times,* Cummins, Brown, and Sayers (2007) emphasize that learning is not "simply a cognitive process that takes place in the heads of individual students; it also involves socialization into particular communities of practice" (p. 44). Through electronic media, this community extends virtually from the classroom to the global community.

Technology-supported instruction brings real-world problems into the classroom for adolescents to investigate in collaboration with experts in the global community (Bransford, Brown, & Cocking 1999, 2000; Donavan & Bransford, 2005). Databases provide real-time, efficient data collection allowing novice investigators access to weather satellites, space probes, and topographical maps (Howard, 2004a). Students sort and retrieve information and compute it into spreadsheets for content interpretation and analysis. Virtual libraries afford ready access to reference materials including magazines, encyclopedias, professional journals, historical and primary documents, and newspapers.

Powerful search engines guide student investigators to sites where they can view authentic documents, photographs, and video clips. Laptops and hand-held computers allow them to use electronic probes and sensors in the field. Visualization tools enable students to construct graphs and representation models, while multimedia tools add audio and video to text. As Howard writes, "The world is literally at their fingertips" (p. 1).

Through teleconferencing and networking, students interact and collaborate with peers and experts, including scientists and engineers, across time and space (Crawford, 2007). In The GLOBE (Global Learning and Observations to Benefit the Environment), for example, an international community of schools forms an electronic network to research large-scale global problems related to earth science. Adolescents research a local problem, share findings with international peers, and interactively identify common environmental phenomena across the world. These students collaborate with real scientists to design experiments, conduct peer reviews, and publish findings.

Simulations permit adolescents to generate information, hypothesize, and test predictions. With geographic information systems (GIS), for example, adolescents determine the vulnerability of a geographic region to natural disaster by identifying constraints and creating an alternative land use option. The free tool, Google Earth, enables them to scan historical photos of a specific city and superimpose the images onto a current satellite view to contrast topography (Burns, 2005, 2006).

Technology and Cognitive Engagement

Instructional technology is also a natural fit with the functioning of the adolescent brain, and when used meaningfully, it can be a tool to develop students' thinking and learning. Jonassen and Carr (2000) coined the term "mindtool" to highlight the power of instructional technology to support knowledge construction and critical thinking. Arguing against the passive use of technology (presentation mode or "cut and paste" exercises) they propose that technologies be used as tools that students learn *with* and not *from.* They write accordingly:

> In this way, learners function as designers, and the computers function as Mindtools for interpreting and organizing their personal knowledge. Mindtools are computer applications that, when used by learners to represent what they know, necessarily engage in critical thinking about the content they are studying. (p. 24)

Jonassen (2000) specifies that mindtools enable students to take control over their own learning as they actively generate knowledge. When technology is used as a tool to cultivate higher-order thinking skills, students and teachers become creators of information and ideas, not simply users of technology (Burns 2005/2006). Used actively and interactively, technology is intellectually challenging tool for shared inquiry, critical thinking, and collaborative problem solving.

Problem-based learning through WebQuests, ThinkQuests, and ClassAct Portals are examples of powerful technology-enhanced approaches that require students to think, collaborate, problem solve, and build new knowledge (Crawford, 2007). Teams of adolescents investigate authentic contemporary problems—such as global warming—create final products in their chosen mode of expression, and reflect upon the experience. Teachers differentiate these inquiry-based strategies with jigsaw or other flexible student groupings, through tiered tasks, and through metacognitive extension.

Tom March (2005/2006), widely associated with WebQuests, incorporates many new technologies, including blogs and wikis, into the highly interactive ClassAct Portal. These sites are built around a topic of high interest that engages students. March cites an example entitled "Child Slave Labor News" (http://ihscslnews.org) created by adolescents in a U.S. History course. This site provides links to organizations that oppose child labor, invites responses, and contains an archive of articles written by the high school students.

March's (2005) site, (http://classactportal.com/), offers suggestions for ClassAct Portals topics and includes user-friendly tutorials for building personal blogs or wikis. He suggests these steps for building ClassAct Portals:

- Locate a site from a free online blog, such as Blogger or WordPress, or set up a personal web space through a web host that provides "cPanel" and "Partastico."
- Create content for the portal by gathering hotlists of links from the Internet and having students critique or annotate these links.
- Build community by having students e-mail appreciation to hosts of the most interesting sites.
- Grow the site by adding wikis or photo galleries.
- Personalize the site with extensions of lesson plans, bulletin boards, student written work, and classroom persona. (p. 18)

Box 6.6, "Web Environment for Adolescent Learning," defines and offers links for several effective instructional tools supported by technology.

❖ BOX 6.6 Web Environment for Adolescent Learning

WebQuest: A web-based scaffolding tool for interactive real-world problem solving that promotes collaborative group work through authentic roles, research skills, and higher-level thinking skills

Selected WebQuests Resources

Tom March's Portal: http://tommarch.com
The central location for all of Tom's "Bright Ideas for Education"

Celebrating the Best iWebQuests: http://bestwebquests.com/
Highly-rated WebQuests and personal feedback from Tom March

Bernie Dodge's Portal: http://webquest.org
Interactive WebQuest community from Bernie Dodge

Filamentality: http://www.kn.pacbell.com/wired/fil/
An online WebQuest maker

Web-and-Flow: http://www.web-and-flow.com/
A comprehensive WebQuest maker

(Continued)

(Continued)

Weblog: Referred to as blogs, this tool enables the creation of personal or group web sites for content sharing and online conversations. Graphic and multimedia can be incorporated (Richardson, 2005, 2006).

Weblog Resources

WordPress: http://wordpress.org/
Blogger: www.blogger.com
Edublogs: www.edublogs.org
Schoolblogs: www.schoolblogs.com
Movable Type: www.sixapart.com/moveabletype

Web Portals: Interactive Internet sites constructed and grown by a group around a common interest or curriculum topic. Content includes pertinent web links to databases, blogs, student communication, and archives of student writing.

Web Portal Resources

ClassAct Portal: http://classactportal.com/
Sample ClassAct Portal: http://ihscslnews.org

Wiki: Hawaiian for "quick," a wiki is a collaborative content creation tool that enables contributors to share and access resources, such as Wikipedia.org, an online encyclopedia of half-a-million entries (Richardson, 2005/2006).

Wiki Resources

Online Research Encyclopedia: www.wikipedia.org
Seed Wiki: www.seedwiki.com
Wiki Software List: http://en.wikipedia.org/wiki/List_of_wiki_software

Podcasting: An audio program broadcast over the Internet that is downloaded to a portable MP3 player (Halderson, 2006). It features class-produced talk shows, audiofiles of books, vocabulary, articles, and poems.

Podcasting Resources

Podcast Directory: www.podcast.net
Sample Podcast: www.netc.org/focus/examples/record.pdp

Resources for Technology-Supported Learning Communities

The GLOBE Program (Global Learning and Observations to Benefit the Environment: http://www.nsf.gov/pubs/2006/nsf06515/nsf06515.htm
Global Schoolhouse Project: http://www.virtualschool.edu/mon/Academia/GlobalSchoolhouseProject.html
Journey North (Annenberg/Center for Public Broadcasting): http://www.learner.org/jnorth/
The Knowledge Integration Environment (KIE): http://www.kie.berkeley.edu/KIE.html
Global SchoolNet: http://www.gsn.org/cu/

Resources for ThinkQuests and Other Inquiry-Based Learning

International Society for Technology in Education: http://www.iste.org/
ThinkQuest Internet Challenge: http://www.thinkquest.org/
Classroom Connect: http://www.classroomconnect.com/
The Exploratorium: Institute for Inquiry: http://www.exploratorium.net/IFI/index.html
Center for Problem-Based Learning: http://www.imsa.edu/team/cpbl/cpbl.htm

Source: Adapted from Crawford, G. B. (2007). *Brain-based teaching with adolescent learning in mind.* Thousand Oaks, CA: Corwin Press.

Technology and Diverse Learners

Cummins, Brown, and Sayers (2007) document case studies where technology-supported practice is highly effective with low-income and linguistically diverse students. They note that when teachers build consistently on the cultural and social capital students bring to the classroom, they "focus their instruction on expanding students' intelligence, imagination, and multilingual talents, using technology as powerful amplifiers" (p. v). Their research also reveals that students of poverty or minority group status are often denied access to "powerful" technology-enhanced learning because teachers assume these populations have limited technology resources at home. While the "digital divide" persists, it has narrowed in recent years. They contend that the disparity between high- and low-income students has been "largely replaced by a pedagogical divide in the way new technologies are used to support instruction and a corresponding cognitive divide in the way students use the new technologies to support different forms of learning" (p. 98).

Cummins, Brown, and Sayers (2007) propose this set of six design principles for technology that support instruction in diverse classrooms. Supportive technology does the following:

- Provides cognitive challenge and opportunities for deep processing of meaning.
- Relates instruction to prior knowledge and experiences derived from students' homes and communities.
- Promotes active and self-regulated collaborative inquiry.
- Promotes extensive engaged reading and writing across the curriculum.
- Helps students develop strategies for effective reading, writing, and learning.
- Promotes affective involvement and identity investment on the part of students. (pp. 109–110)

Technology to Scaffold Adolescent Learning

Differentiated classroom technology's use is twofold: (1) to give students access to powerful learning experiences, as Cummins, Brown, and Sayers (2007) describe in the previous section and (2) to create cognitive access in an equitable manner, as suggested by the principles of Universal Design for Learning (Rose & Meyer, 2002). Unlike a printed book, digital media displays content in many formats, such as text, sound, and still and moving images. The multiple options and versatility in the way information is represented is a necessary step in meeting students' diverse learning needs.

Adolescents who access the same web site, for example, may adjust the appearance of text or images or adjust the sound or use embedded tools, such as speech recognition software, that automatically translates spoken language into text or text-to-speech software that transforms written content into speech. Students with visual impairments enlarge the text for readability; others who have difficulty understanding speech slow the speech down or increase the volume. Hypertext language (HTML) enables teachers to "mark" or "tag" text to alter font, such as the use of italics or under lining to emphasize key content.

> **Content Enhancements**
>
> Differentiation tools that can be digitized to "pop up" through digital overlay to provide built-in options to remind students of a particular strategy or to assist in thinking through a task.

Digital media literally transforms the learning process for students by reducing the barriers inherent in the printed medium (Rose & Meyer, 2002). "Wizards" or "intelligent tutors," for example, are available on most software that make it possible for students to create a graph, design a table, or publish a brochure with little or no experience (Howard, 2004c). As illustrated in the Project T[2] problem-based learning units, *content enhancements* "pop up" through digital overlay to provide built-in options to remind students of a particular strategy or to assist in thinking through a task. By offering multiple levels of tasks, as illustrated in the jigsaw example earlier in Chapter 5, teachers differentiate for complexity or interest. Some students read government documents, for example, while others use software that reads the documents aloud. The Project T[2] units also build in various cognitive software tools that assist adolescents in organizing and representing information, such as Geometer's Sketchpad, Inspiration, and other graphic organizers.

Digital tools allow teachers in differentiated classrooms "to tailor media to the task, to different kinds of learning, and to different kinds of students, reducing the barriers and inefficiencies inherent in one-size-fits-all textbooks" (Rose and Meyer, 2002, p. 67). The use of digital tools transforms the capacity of students to access important knowledge. Putting certain students on equal footing with others thus maximizes their opportunity to learn and gain competence. Box 6.7, "The Digital Tools for Learning," provides a few selected annotated links for sources for digital text and cognitive tools.

❖ BOX 6.7 The Digital Tools for Learning

Sources for Digital Text

Alex: http://www.infomotions.com/alex/
A catalog of electronic texts on the Internet, with roughly 2,000 entries of e-texts, mostly on gopher servers

American Library Association Great Sites: http://www.ala.org/parentspage/greatsites/lit.html (color version)
Comprehensive list of links to literature and language web sites for children

Children's Literature Web Guide (University of Calgary): http://www.acs.ucalgary.ca/~dkbrown/
Internet resources related to books for children and young adults

The Electronic Text Center: http://etext.lib.virginia.edu/english.html
An extensive listing of prose and poetry e-text available for downloading

E-text Archive: http://www.etext.org/
Eclectic subject matter available to download as e-text

Internet Public Library: http://www.ipl.org/
Links to picture books, short stories, poetry, myths, fables, magazines, and information about authors

Literature Online from Chadwyck: http://lion.chadwyck.com/
A fully searchable library of over 250,000 works of English and American literature

On-Line Books Page: http://digital.library.upenn.edu/books/
Directory of sources for over 6000 online books

Project Gutenberg: http://www.gutenberg.net/
Light literature (such as Alice in Wonderland, Peter Pan, or Aesop's Fables), heavy literature (such as Moby Dick or Paradise Lost), and references (such as almanacs, encyclopedias, or dictionaries) in downloadable formats

Weller Media Products: http://dlcwest.com/~wmp/Books.html
Directory of electronic books

Cognitive Tools for Learning

Geometer's Sketchpad: http://www.keypress.com/sketchpad/
Geometry exploration software used to learn about transformations and tessellations.

The Geometer's Sketchpad and Tessellations: http://mathforum.org/sum95/suzanne/tess.gsp.tutorial.html
Interactive software that assists with creation of tessellations, using vectors and parallel lines

Sketchpad Three Labs: http://mathforum.org/sketchpad/Intro/riedy.labs.html
Interactive software that assists with rotation and exploration, creation of cycloids, and the calculation of the areas of parallelograms and rectangles

Geometer's Sketchpad in the Classroom:
http://mathforum.org/dynamic/geometry_turned_on/download/07-gar/
Interactive software that provides hands-on assistance with geometry exploration and calculation

INSPIRATION (7.0) for Concept Mapping and Idea Organization: http://www.Inspiration.com
An interactive tool for concept mapping and idea organizing to use in upper elementary, secondary, and college/university classrooms

Other Sites for Differentiation

LDOnline: http://www.ldonline.org/ld_indepth/general_info/three_steps.html
An article by Margaret King-Sears that details a three-step process for adapting curriculum for special education students and includes helpful resources

Study Spanish: http://www.studyspanish.com/vocab
An interactive site that provides the Spanish word or phrase when English words are entered

SUMMARY AND LOOKING AHEAD

Chapter 6 extends the discussion of the differentiated learning environment that supports the adolescents' affective, cognitive, social, and physical needs. Its focus is on the intellectual dimension. Adolescents thrive in an intellectually charged environment where they are appropriately challenged and intentionally supported. Important in the intellectual dimension is ongoing assessment and differentiated grading that promotes cognitive growth and mastery.

The chapter introduces two key instructional strategies that differentiate for student readiness: sequenced teacher questioning using the SAFE framework and tiered assessment. It proposes research-based affective and cognitive interaction practices that differentiate through equitable response opportunities and cognitive support. Technology is a critical scaffolding and "mindtool" with the potential to give adolescents equitable cognitive access to meaningful learning. With the power to connect with learning communities across the world, technology-enhanced instruction is motivational and developmentally appropriate for adolescent learning.

Table 6.1, "A Developmentally Appropriate Learning Environment," categorizes a sampling of research-based, interrelated practices for structuring and managing a supportive classroom learning environment (Crawford, 2004).

Chapter 7 focuses on differentiation for three clusters of populations that prevalently comprise the diverse heterogeneous classroom: advanced or gifted, English language learners, and students with learning challenges that affect reading comprehension and literacy development. The chapter presents multiple strategies to help these cluster groups succeed academically through cognitive access to meaningful knowledge.

Table 6.1   A Developmentally Appropriate Learning Environment

Physical Dimension	Affective Dimension	Social Dimension	Cognitive Dimension
• Clear directions and time frames • Clear procedures • Available and labeled materials and resources • Space for movement • Clearly communicated transitions • Codes and color • Weekly checklists • Individual work folders • Daily board agenda • Flexible furniture • Technology enhancement	• Journaling • Firm expectations for appropriate behavior • Humor • Fairness and equitable treatment • Acceptance and inclusion • Respect for individual differences • Cultural celebrations • Timely feedback • Supportive classroom climate • Relationship building	• Flexible grouping • Literature circles • Stations • Jigsaw • Numbered heads • Tribes • Reading buddies • Group investigation • Learning clubs • Peer helpers • Clock and compass partners • Process partners • Peer editing partners	• Challenging content • Student-led research and presentations • Reduced or increased complexity • Simulation, debate, role play • Problem/project-based learning • ThinkQuests • WebQuests • Academic service-learning projects • Peer/self-assessment • Enrichment resources

7

Learning Patterns and Profiles

Chapter 6 concluded a discussion of the sixth and last "E" of the adolescent-centered differentiation framework, Environment. The learning environment consists of four interrelated dimensions: affective, social-emotional, physical, and intellectual. Adolescents learn best in a climate of acceptance and support. They are motivated to learn when they are engaged in meaningful instructional experiences that are appropriately challenging and differentiated. They are eager to interact socially and purposefully in structured tasks that invite inquiry and promote personal learning management.

Adolescents also thrive in a physical environment that is visually appealing, flexible, organized, and stimulating. Technology provides a vital and natural extension of adolescents' intellectual and social beings. When used in a relevant context as an opportunity for thinking and collaborative inquiry, technology promotes self-direction and personal learning management. As a flexible and versatile learning medium, technology has the power to transform the differentiated learning environment by giving adolescents cognitive access to meaningful learning.

Chapter 7 focuses on instructional differentiation for three clusters of adolescent populations prevalent in contemporary heterogeneous classrooms. These are gifted or advanced learners, English language learners, and students with learning challenges that affect reading comprehension and literacy development. The chapter presents numerous strategies that build on strengths to enable these cluster groups to succeed academically.

PATTERNS OF RESPONSIVE TEACHING

As discussed in the previous chapters, differentiation requires that teachers be familiar with students' varied learning needs and make modifications in how students access important curriculum content, process new knowledge, and demonstrate understanding (Tomlinson & McTigue, 2006). Differentiation also demands that teachers create a learning environment that maximizes the success of all students. Differentiation, nevertheless, is *not* individualized instruction, which is a common misconception. What differentiation feasibly advocates is that teachers implement *patterns* of instruction and procedures that are, in the spirit of Universal Design for Learning (UDL), likely to benefit students with similar needs. Tomlinson and McTighe (2006) suggest these ten teaching patterns, which summarize the approaches discussed in the previous chapters:

1. **Be intentional about getting to know students.** Stand at the door and address students by name as they enter and exit, use dialogue journals to establish written interchange, and take observation notes as students are working or discussing.

2. **Incorporate small-group teaching regularly.** When students grow accustomed to consistent procedures for small and independent work, the teacher is able to target those who learn in a different way, need assistance with basic skills, or who may need more challenge.

3. **Teach to the high end.** The vast majorities of students benefit from learning tasks that foster complex and creative thinking, support for increased independence, involve self-assessment, and promote metacognitive development. The best differentiation begins with high expectations and continues with the supports for achievement at high levels.

4. **Offer more ways for students to explore and express learning.** Have routine opportunities for students to process ideas (e.g., analytical, creative, practical) and to express learning through varied products and performances that best suit their strengths and interests (e.g., visually, orally, or through acting or writing).

5. **Use informal assessments to monitor students understanding regularly.** Use a nongraded "exit card," for example, for students to respond in writing to one or two questions as the class period ends as a "snapshot" for targeted instructional planning.

6. **Teach in multiple ways.** Use words, images, models, and demonstrations. Use analogies, stories, examples, and illustrations from students' experiences. Multiple representations reach a wider audience who learn in certain ways and reinforce learning for others.

7. **Use basic reading strategies regularly.** Read-alouds, graphic organizers, and double entry comprehension journals help students read with better purpose and comprehension.

8. **Allow students to work independently or collaboratively.** Giving students the choice improves the learning for many with both preferences.

9. **Use rubrics that clearly instruct for quality.** Design rubrics that clearly explain the expectations for quality work and work habits. Include space for students to add personal goals for success or for you to add in a student-specific goal.

10. **Cultivate acceptance for diversity.** Pose questions that invite multiple perspectives, ask students to find multiple approaches to problems or explore multiple possibilities, and consistently use examples and illustrations from varying cultures. (pp. 20–22)

DETERMINING STUDENT VARIANCE

Tomlinson and McTighe (2006) identify four categories that organize the many ways students vary. These are (1) *biology,* which determines gender differences, the unique way individual brains are "wired" for learning, and the range of ability and developmental levels; (2) *degree of privilege,* which is impacted by economic status and associated negatively or positively with race, culture, language, adult support systems, and opportunity; (3) *positioning for learning,* which is constructively linked to motivation, self-concept, trust, temperament, and interpersonal skills; and (4) *preferences,* which influence variations in interests across subjects and topics, variations in the way students receive and demonstrate knowledge, and differences in the way they relate to each other and to teachers. These variations suggest the many reasons adolescents succeed or struggle academically in school. The barriers to learning include low motivation, absenteeism, particular cognitive challenges, learning English as a second language, poverty, stressful family life, cultural capital, and low expectations from adults, to name a few (Scherer, 2006).

Tomlinson and colleagues (2003) observe that "while most, if not all, learners share a common need for higher-level, meaning-focused curriculum and instruction, there will be variance in how students should encounter and interact with the curriculum" (p. 13). As the previous chapters impress, students learn best when instruction is reasonably challenging, personally interesting, and compatible with favored learning preferences. In response to apparent learner variability, teachers make instructional adjustments for students' current readiness level, tap into and/or develop students' interests, and teach with effectual learning strategies. As students become more advanced in their knowledge, understanding, and skills in a content area, "the challenge level of materials and tasks will necessitate escalation" or what Tomlinson and others refer to as "'ascending intellectual demand'" (p. 13). The teacher's role is to support, scaffold, and coach as students complete tasks successfully and become more independent, self-directed learners.

Building on Learning Strengths

Chapter 1 heralds the conversations of differentiation that evolve from a deficit model to the more positive language of inclusion, cognitive access, equity, and opportunity. The research on intelligence in the latter part of the 20th century broadens this construct to include a range of human talents and endeavors (Tomlinson, 2003). As Chapter 1 portends, Gardner (1993) identifies nine ways that individuals may excel. These are logical/mathematical, verbal/linguistic, musical, spatial, bodily-kinesthetic, interpersonal, intrapersonal, naturalistic, and existential. Sternberg (1985) similarly proposes the Triarchic Theory that recognizes the analytical, practical, and creative dimensions of intelligence. In addition, various cultures conceive and express intelligence in different ways. African American students, for example, manifest intelligence through oral language, colorful speech, creative storytelling, or humor (Torrance, 1989). Interpersonal skills such as sensitivity, empathy, and mediation evidence intelligence among Native American students. Furthermore, adolescents as an age group vary developmentally in level of cognitive growth. More traditional, narrow views of intelligence, therefore, limit the capacity for some students to thrive if their learning strengths go untapped or unexpressed.

Historically, curriculum for high-ability learners in gifted education programs is characterized by discovery, critical thinking, manipulation of ideas, thematic integration of subjects, and product-based assessment (Tomlinson et al., 2003). Conversely, general education has been typified by presentation, practice, and replication. Tomlinson and colleagues advocate that high-quality curriculum be available for all learners and that teachers "attend to specific needs of students who exemplify varying degrees of advance potential or performance" (p. 4). While advanced learners need certain accommodations, as this chapter later discusses, all students possess promise as learners, leaders, producers, and contributors to society. Accordingly, these educators advise four important guidelines for curriculum design in the differentiated classroom that reflect a broadened view of intelligence and human potential. These guidelines include:

1. Because intelligence can be affected by environment and opportunity, curriculum for all learners should be rich in opportunity for learners to explore and expand a wide range of intelligences and abilities.

2. Curriculum should be designed in ways that both identify and develop high capacity in the widest feasible range of intelligences.

3. Curriculum should be flexible enough to address both variability in manifestations of high ability and variability in how talent develops over time in a broad range of learners and talent areas.

4. Curriculum should plan for development of intelligences in ways that are valid for an intelligence area and domains in which it is expressed. (p. 3)

Only when a maximum number of students consistently experience the highest quality of curriculum, with the addition of appropriate support, coaching, and mentoring, will these individuals benefit academically.

CLUSTERS OF COMMONALITY

The movement from elementary to middle and high school brings higher expectations for content area reading and vocabulary building. Students face greater demands to read from textbooks, take notes, work independently, and express their understanding through writing (Schumaker & Deschler, 1984). Tomlinson and McTighe (2006) encourage teachers to identify and anticipate common patterns among students' learning strengths and needs and to plan proactively for instructional adjustments. With the goal of maximizing all students' learning capacities and with high demand on instructional time, teachers in differentiated classrooms focus realistically and reasonably on ways that students *cluster* by similar learning propensities and tailor instructional techniques responsively.

Advanced learners for example, comprehend reading materials well beyond grade level, are readily capable of more complexity and depth, and need stimulation at an accelerated pace or they will not achieve to their capabilities. Students at various proficiency levels in learning English face several linguistic, literacy, and cultural challenges. Students with learning challenges need explicit assistance in the attainment of strategies for information acquisition, reading comprehension, memory, and expression or demonstration of understanding. The following sections describe the common learning needs of three clusters prevalent in contemporary mixed-ability classrooms: gifted or advanced learners, English language learners, and students with learning challenges. Notably, there is a large amount of variation within each cluster and there are also similar learning needs across clusters. Each section offers differentiation strategies pertinent to the targeted cluster; however, the strategies, with appropriate support, benefit all learners.

CLUSTER 1: GIFTED OR ADVANCED LEARNERS

The terminology for giftedness varies from state to state, generally depending on beliefs about intelligence and how giftedness is measured (Stephens & Karnes, 2000). Students may be "intellectually" or "academically gifted," with intellectual proclivity or "creatively gifted or talented," with advanced skills in the visual or performing arts (Vaughn, Bos, & Schumm, 2003). Other definitions explain giftedness as the intersection among ability, creativity, and task commitment (Renzulli & Delcourt, 1986). Sternberg and Wagner (1982) view gifted students as effective problem solvers who process information rapidly and insightfully. The earliest definition by the Marland task force (1972) describes giftedness as potential abilities in the areas of general intellectual ability, specific academic aptitude, creative or productive thinking, leadership ability, visual or performing arts, and psychomotor ability. This last indicator, psychomotor ability, was dropped in a 1978 definition. Regardless of terminology, each definition emphasizes that gifted students need differentiated classroom experiences or services to meet their full potential. This definition by Gallagher (as cited in Vaughn, Bos, & Schumm, 2003) illustrates:

> Giftedness refers to cognitive (intellectual) superiority (not necessarily of genius caliber), creativity, and motivation and of sufficient magnitude to set the child apart from the vast majority of age-mates and makes it possible for him or her to contribute something of particular value to society and to be identified for special services. (p. 316)

Winebrenner (2000) writes that gifted students in mixed-ability classrooms learn differently from classroom peers in five important ways. These students (1) learn new material in much less time; (2) remember more readily what they've learned; (3) perceive ideas and concepts at more abstract and complex levels; (4) become more passionately interested in specific topics and have difficulty moving on to other learning tasks; and (5) are able to operate many levels of concentration simultaneously. Other characteristics include large vocabularies, extensive knowledge, and expertise in certain areas; more advanced and effective cognitive processing, including formal operational thought, and metacognitive skills; heightened sensitivity to beauty and the feelings of others; greater flexibility in ideas and approaches to tasks; high motivation to achieve on challenging tasks; high standards regarding performance; positive self-concept related to academic endeavors; above average social and emotional adjustment; and intense curiosity (Ormrod, 2000; Vaughn, Bos, & Schumm, 2003).

Differentiation and Gifted Learners

In its position statement, "Differentiation of Curriculum and Instruction" (1994), the National Association for Gifted Children (NAGC) recommends that differentiation for gifted students include acceleration of instruction, in-depth study, a high degree of complexity, advanced content, and/or variety in content and form. NAGC offers the following description of differentiated instruction for gifted learners:

> Differentiation for gifted students consists of carefully planned, coordinated learning experiences that extend beyond the core curriculum to meet specific learning needs evidenced by the student. It combines the curricular strategies for enrichment and acceleration and provides flexibility and diversity. Appropriate differentiation allows for increasing levels of advanced, abstract, and complex curriculum that are substantive and that respond to the learner's needs. (p. 2)

Educators in gifted education have historically placed strong emphasis on qualitative modifications around the interrelated elements of content, process, product, and learning environment (Gallagher, 1991; Kaplan, 1986; Maker, 1982; Van Tassel-Baska, 1986). A summary of these recommendations follows:

- **Content.** Kaplan (1986) advocates for the development of thematic, integrative, and multidisciplinary units. Gallagher (1985) recommends these content modifications: content *acceleration* by giving more complex matters to students earlier or providing them with special topics to study in greater depth; content *enrichment* by extending the general curriculum; content *sophistication* through more complex concepts or theories; and content *novelty* by involving students in unique studies in which they think in a creative way.

- **Process.** Kaplan (1986) calls for the inclusion of productive thinking and research skills in addition to basic skills. Maker (1982) recommends process modifications defined by higher-level thinking, open-endedness, group interactions, choice, discovery, variety, simulations, and pacing. VanTassel-Baska (1989) voices the need for students to take an active role in planning and carrying out learning experiences, to work independently or in problem-solving groups, and to make connections to the world beyond the school.
- **Product.** Kaplan (1986) contends that units culminate with products that function as a learning tool that communicates student learning through a range of media. Maker (1982) advocates for real-world problems directed toward real audiences and evaluated authentically.
- **Environment.** Maker (1982) proposes that the learning context be student-centered, open, accepting, with complex settings that encourage independent learning and allow high mobility.

Implications for the Mixed-Ability Classroom

These curricular recommendations for gifted learners are familiar elements of effective instructional practice and the components for differentiation proposed in Chapter 1. With the more recent educational movement for inclusion, gifted learners are increasingly clustered in the regular classroom rather than separate resource rooms. Additionally, as this chapter discusses earlier, newer theories of intelligence view giftedness more broadly, and complex instruction, differentiated appropriately for all learners, is more typical of mixed-ability classrooms. As Erb (1992), editor of *The Middle School Journal*, contends, "Higher order thinking skills, collaboration skills, problem-solving skills, and inquiring habits of mind are characteristics necessary for success in the more complex society that our ten-fourteen-year-olds will inhabit in the future" (pp. 20–21). With appropriate degrees of challenge, adjustment, and support, teachers bring rich content and meaningful learning to all students.

An additional reality is that a great deal of variation exists in highly able students. Their abilities may be strong in one area or many, or their learning preferences may be influenced by gender, culture, or development. Their potential develops in differing degrees and on varying timetables, and the level of support needed for academic success varies accordingly. Ormrod (2000) suggests that gifted students in mixed-ability classrooms be viewed as "students with advanced cognitive development on a continuum of abilities" rather than contained within a separate category (p. 207). Similarly, Tomlinson (2001), in a move from formal labeling, uses the term "advanced learners" to distinguish this cluster. As Tomlinson (2003) asserts, "Curriculum designed to be a catalyst for developing advanced capacity in young people must be flexible enough to provide them with appropriate challenge and support at all points in their evolution as learners" (p. 6). As this book proposes, meaningful content, respectful tasks, and authentic products in a flexible and supportive learning environment are important for all learners. Accordingly, NAGC (1996) supports this belief in the uniqueness of all individuals in a democratic society, as indicated by its position statement on differentiation:

> NAGC is fully committed to national goals that advocate both excellence and equity for all students, and we believe that the best way to achieve these goals is through differentiated educational opportunities, resources, and encouragement for all students. (p. 2)

Suggested Differentiation Strategies for Advanced Learners

Several differentiation strategies support gifted learners' unique need for advanced knowledge, complexity, and self-paced learning. These are curriculum compacting, tiered assignments, learning contracts, and learning centers. A brief discussion of these with examples follows.

Curriculum Compacting

Curriculum compacting is a three-stage strategy that helps to maximize learning time by streamlining content that advanced learners may already know (Reis & Renzulli, 1992). In the first stage, the teacher assesses students' prior knowledge about a topic or skill prior to or early in the study. This assessment may be formal, such as a written posttest, or informal, such as observed performance. If a student shows reasonable mastery, for example, 70 to 75 percent or more knowledge of the content, they are "exempted" from whole-class instruction and activities in the particular content area (Tomlinson, 2001). In stage two, the teacher determines any skills or knowledge covered in the learning unit over which the student does not demonstrate mastery and outlines a plan of study that varies when the student joins classmates for instruction, does homework to practice the missing skills, or completes a product that shows understanding.

In the third stage of curriculum compacting, teachers and students collaboratively design an investigation or in-depth study, complete with learning goals, time parameters, procedures, and evaluation criteria, into an area of high interest, such as fantasy or science fiction, or content extension, such as using advanced mathematics software. Tomlinson (2001) recommends that teachers carefully document the compacting in order for parents to understand the reasons for an alternative task and to help students gain awareness of particular learning preferences. In support of curriculum compacting, she cites a common problem for advanced learners in mixed-ability classrooms:

Curriculum Compacting

A three-stage strategy that maximizes learning time by the streamlining of content that advanced learners already know. In the first stage, the teacher assesses knowledge or skill level, in the second, the teacher determines knowledge or skills not already mastered and outlines a plan of study, and the third, teachers and students design an in-depth study.

Advanced learners gain little by continuing to relearn the known, but they gain much from the expectation that they will continually engage in challenging and productive learning in school. Compacting helps eliminate the former and facilitate the latter. (p. 75)

Tiered Assignments

Chapter 1 first introduced the differentiation strategy, *tiered assignments*, in the Tiananmen Square example. Following pre-assessment, teachers assign tasks to small groups of students; the tasks vary in complexity, abstractness, concreteness, number of steps, and/or level of independence (Tomlinson, 2001). Kingore (2006) likens tiered instruction to a stairwell that provides "access within the large building of learning" (p. 2). The stairwell begins with learning tasks for students with fewer skills or less readiness and continues with tiers that are increasingly complex and appropriately challenging for others. He offers these guidelines:

- **Ensure for flexible student groups**. Vary tier groups with each assignment so that all students learn the same essential content in different ways.
- **Plan the number of tier levels most appropriate**. Often tiers are thought of in three levels but different curricular levels, concepts, and skills may warrant fewer or more.
- **Note that complexity is relative**. The complexity of tiered levels is determined by the specific readiness of students and varies in different curricular areas.
- **Encourage high-order thinking in each tier**. All students need the opportunity to analyze, synthesize, and evaluate information.
- **Provide teacher support at each tier**. All students benefit from teacher modeling, feedback, instruction, and guidance. (pp. 2–3)

Tomlinson (2001) additionally advises that teachers use a variety of resource materials at differing levels of complexity and relevant to students' differing learning modes, keep each task focused on the key concepts and essential understandings of the study, and communicate clear standards for quality and success.

Learning Contracts

Learning contracts are negotiated agreements between the teacher and individual student and used for several purposes: to compact for unnecessary skill practice; to allow students to work at a varied pace; to blend skill and content according to student readiness; to allow teachers time to work with small groups or other individuals; to help students learn skills for planning, decision making, and independent learning; to encourage extended study of topics of high interest; and to foster research skills, critical and creative thinking, skill application, and integrated learning (Tomlinson, 2001).

Learning Contracts

Negotiated agreements between teachers and individual students for various purposes, such as for review and practice or extended enrichment. Learning contracts have specified timelines and clear expectations aligned with the curriculum and are generally differentiated by readiness.

Learning contracts foster student choice and align task content and skills to readiness, interests, and learning styles. In designing contracts, Tomlinson suggests that teachers establish clear standards, vary the time period for independent work to match student readiness, and, when possible, focus on concepts, themes, or problems.

Table 7.1, "Individualized Contract for Human Genetics Unit," shows an example of a contract developed by an eighth-grade science teacher for a unit on human genetics.

Table 7.1   Individualized Contract for Human Genetics Unit

These activities are to be completed independently and in class. Do not take the folder home or to your locker. If you are not meeting your due dates, see me, and we can make arrangements for you to complete certain assignments at home.

A participation grade will be given. Everyone will start with a 100. Each time you are asked to get started, get back on task, stop talking, etc., 5 points will be removed from your participation grade.

Each time you finish an assignment, bring it to me to be checked. I will then initial and date your checklist. Be sure to keep up with due dates.

Required?	Due date	Assignment	Teacher initial	Grade
	10–10	Make a double bubble map comparing and contrasting photosynthesis and cellular respiration. Include at least 3 similarities and 3 differences.		
	10–11	Read pages 419–424. Complete workbook pages 189–191. (Don't do questions 12 and 13.)		
	10–12	Draw and label all the phases of mitosis. Explain what happens in each stage.		
	10–12	Read pages 428–431. Complete worksheet 102. (See me for worksheet.)		
	10–12	Make a poster that shows a way to prevent cancer. Use white paper, be neat and colorful. Include an illustration.		
	10–13	Worksheets 104, 105, 40, 41 (See me)		
	10–16	p. 435 1–10 p. 436 11–16, 20, p. 437 1, 3		
	10–16	Read pages 425–426. Draw a picture of DNA. Color cytosine yellow, guanine blue, adenine read, and thymine green.		
	10–17	Test on cell theory, cell organelles, osmosis, diffusion, photosynthesis, cellular respiration, cell cycle and cancer.		

Source: Used With Permission From Melanie Rickard, Turrentine Middle School, Burlington, NC.

Learning Centers

Andrews (2005) describes the successful use of *learning centers* in a seventh-grade mathematics classroom. Over the course of a unit on decimals, she set up two-day centers of skills related to place value; comparing, ordering, and modeling decimals; finding equivalent decimals; rounding, addition, subtraction, and multiplication of decimals; and division of decimals and decimal classification. Each class began with a mini lesson on the particular mathematical skill, followed by students working at centers determined by pre-assessed readiness levels. The "kick-off" day focused on place value, for example. The place value learning centers included a clothesline activity, a "Sam's Sweet Shop" activity, activities from www.funbrain.com and www.aaamath.com, and a research activity to find the weights of five animals.

> **Learning Centers**
>
> Stations aligned with course content that are differentiated by interest, readiness, and learning preferences. At the secondary level, learning centers enable in-depth study of special interest topics.

The centers engaged students in games, hands-on activities, and web-based problem solving as the adolescents applied decimals to baseball, phone bills, and the gravity of metals. Some of the centers required independent work, and others asked for small groups of two or three. The "Ticket Out" for each center was a quick quiz task. Through this set-up, the students made choices based on needs and interests. They were actively involved in monitoring their learning progress, gained confidence, and demonstrated high performance of the culminating unit test.

Colleen Willard-Holt (2003) writes that learning centers, used often at the elementary-school level, are an appropriate differentiation tool for adolescents. U.S. history students can explore in-depth topics related to the Civil War such as leaders, battles, camp life, military technology, civilian life, or the role of women or African Americans based on individual interests, for example. Tomlinson (2001) suggests that teachers develop challenging tasks with clear differentiation criteria for success and allow advanced learners long blocks of time to enable greater depth of study.

CLUSTER 2: ENGLISH LANGUAGE LEARNERS (ELLs)

Hill and Flynn (2006) write that 5.5 percent of the school-aged population in the United States speak a language other than English in the home and speak and write English with difficulty. Approximately 50 percent of these students are Hispanic (Comprehensive School Reform Quality Center, 2005). Middle and high school ELLs face considerable challenges as they work toward English proficiency and strive to meet the academic and social demands of school. As they move along the continuum toward English fluency, many ELLs need to acquire the basic skills of reading comprehension, literacy strategies, and basic writing.

In their book, *Classroom Instruction That Works With English Language Learners,* Hill and Flynn (2006) write of the many learning challenges that ELLs bring for teachers in mixed-ability classrooms:

> No two ELLs have the same amount of grounding in their native language, or are at the same stage of English language acquisition. The

language skills of these students vary, making for even greater complexity. Some students are born in the United States but grow up in non-English-speaking households; others arrive in the classroom having received varying amounts of formal education in their country of birth. Still others may have been in U.S. schools for a number of years, but may still be in the early stages of English language acquisition. (p. 3)

The level of these students' exposure to English, their educational backgrounds, the socioeconomic status of their families, even the number of books in the home, affect ELLs' "readiness to learn—and learn *in*—a new language" (p. 3).

Short and Echevarria (2004/2005) similarly remind us of the many ways ELLs' diverse backgrounds, levels of language proficiency, and education profiles impact their potential for school success:

Some read and write above grade level in their own language; others have limited schooling. Some enter school highly motivated to learn because of family support or an innate drive to succeed; others have had negative experiences that squelched their motivation. Many come from middle-class families with high levels of literacy; others live in poverty without books in their homes. Those whose native language is Latin-based can recognize English words with the same Latin derivatives; those who have different language backgrounds, such as Mandarin or Arabic, lack that advantage. Some students' native language does not even have a written form. (pp. 9–10)

Carrier (2005) asserts that it is also important for teachers to acknowledge that ELLs have two jobs in the classroom: learning a new language and learning new academic content. The time needed to acquire conversational proficiency is one to three years compared to the five- to seven-year span necessary to develop English academic content language.

Stages of Second Language Acquisition

Krashen and Terrell (as cited in Hill & Flynn, 2006) recognize five stages of second language acquisition. In stage one, the *preproduction* phase (zero to six months), students have minimal comprehension and verbalization. They generally nod, draw, and point. In the *early production* stage two (six months to one year), students express language in one- or two-word familiar phrases, uses present-tense verbs, and has limited comprehension. In stage three, the *speech emergence* phase (one to three years), students have relatively good comprehension, produce simple sentences, yet make frequent grammar and pronunciation errors, and often misunderstand jokes. In the fourth intermediate fluency stage (three to five years), students have excellent comprehension and make few grammatical errors, and in the last stage, advanced fluency (five to seven years) students have a near-native level of speech (p. 15).

The implication for teachers comes with the level of instructional expectations (Hill & Flynn, 2006). A student in one of the earlier stages will not be able to respond to "how" and "why" questions, for example. At the higher levels, they are capable of demonstrating both knowledge of language and content. They are capable of higher cognitive thinking such as analysis, synthesis, and evaluation. Knowing the level of language acquisition enables teachers to design instruction within the students' zone of proximal development (Vygotsky, 1978). They are then able to scaffold for success by modeling correct grammar, asking challenging, varied, and tiered questions; offering supplemental visuals, demonstrations, and manipulatives; designing a word/picture wall; or providing direct instruction, as needed.

A Basis for Differentiation for English Language Learners

Ellis (1985, as cited in Vaughn, Bos, & Schumm, 2003) provides a differentiation model for second language acquisition based on five interrelated, research-based factors. These are as follows with sample instructional strategies:

- **Situational**. Students learn second language in multiple environments, formal and informal. They need to learn in a nonthreatening context in which they are willing to take risks and play with words. They also need to perceive that their first language and culture are respected and valued.
- **Linguistic Input**. Reading or listening to a second language is more comprehensible if teachers (1) work new concepts into students' current knowledge base; (2) create a context for learning, for example, when studying marine biology, visit a salt water aquarium, view a video, display photos in the room, conduct experiments to test salinity; (3) encourage students to use their first language to discuss new concepts, vocabulary, or learning; and (4) highlight key words and phrases by repeating them or use simpler sentence construction.
- **Learner Characteristics**. The better developed a student's proficiency and conceptual foundation is in the first language, the more readily the student will learn a second. Characteristics also include age (younger students learn language more readily), aptitude for learning language, self-confidence in language learning, and knowledge of learning strategies.
- **The Learning and Developmental Process**. Students learn basic interpersonal communication skills (BICS) before becoming competent with cognitive academic language proficiency (CALP). Effective teachers work to create context by incorporating both BICS and CALP into all lessons.
- **Secondary Language Output**. Students need opportunities to engage in meaningful oral exchanges in the classroom and community, to receive from listeners, and to learn to self-monitor their oral language. They also need a "silent" or nonverbal period during which they absorb information and language before they are comfortable with written expression. (pp. 283–287)

Curtin (2006) asked a group of middle school English language learners about their preferred learning strategies. Their responses were: (1) personalized classrooms where teachers work in examples from their specific cultures; (2) cooperative groups in which they can get help from peers; (3) varied hands-on activities that differentiate for learning styles and preferences; (4) multiple examples to explain new concepts; (5) a focus on face expression and nonverbal communication while teaching; and (6) a democratic environment characterized by structure, movement, order, humor, and collaboration.

Differentiated "Instruction That Works"

Building on the nine categories of research-based instructional strategies that members of the Mid-Continent Research for Education and Learning (McREL) identify in *Classroom Instruction That Works* (Marzano, Pickering, & Pollock, 2001), Hill and Flynn (2006) build a framework of differentiation strategies to meet the learning needs of ELLs. These are as follows with instructional examples and pages for more extended reading and illustration:

- **Set objectives and provide feedback**. Communicate learning goals clearly and combine language goals with content objectives. Identify key concepts and vocabulary. Keep feedback positive, useful, and comprehensible by restating what the students say using correct pronunciation, grammar, or vocabulary. Involve students in the design of rubrics and help them develop skills for self-evaluation and learning management. (Hill & Flynn, 2006, pp. 22–35)
- **Incorporate nonlinguistic representations**. Use media (films, videotapes, CDs, and audiotapes of books) and realia (real objects such as graphs, photos, maps, charts, and demonstrations). Use graphic organizers for vocabulary terms and phrases, time sequencing, episodes, generalizations, and cause and effect) and symbolic representations (pictures, pictographs, and diagrams). Use three-dimensional models, help students visualize mentally, and build in kinesthetic activities. (Hill & Flynn, 2006, pp. 36–43)
- **Use cues, questions, and advance organizers**. Direct cues and questions to help ELLs make connections with what they already know and want to know by activating prior knowledge. Advance organizers put new information into a visual format.

Hill and Flynn (2006) illustrate this differentiation strategy with an example from a sixth-grade class during a study of arthropods. Before showing a video on arthropods, the teacher provides each student with a graphic advance organizer with the main ideas filled in, thus cueing for the information that students will be viewing. The organizer shows the concept "Phylum Arthropoda" as a center bubble with extending arrows to the three classifications, "Arachnida," "Crustacea," and "Insects." Each of these further extends with examples, such as tick, spider, and scorpion under "Arachnida." The teacher then asks the young adolescents to watch the video and add other important information related to the ideas on the organizer.

Hill and Flynn (2006) emphasize the importance of working with ELLs at their appropriate comprehension level as follows:

> For ELLs at the preproduction level, the teacher attaches pictures to help them learn new vocabulary. At the early production level the students should be able to use the vocabulary with the prompt, "Name a kind of insect." At the speech emergence stage, ELLs should comprehend and be able to explain in short sentences with teacher prompts. At the intermediate and advanced fluency level, the students should be able to add pertinent information about the concepts. (pp. 44–54)

- **Encourage cooperative learning**. Form small cooperative learning groups to benefit ELLs by giving them more opportunities and expectations to speak, to negotiate meaning as they speak, to obtain feedback, and to adjust the level of speech in a context of reduced anxiety. (Hill & Flynn, 2006, pp. 55–61)
- **Summarize and share notes.** Summarize lessons to provide explicit instruction for ELLs to gain Cognitive Academic Language Proficiency (CALP) when they are taught, through teacher modeling, to recognize and understand text patterns and to use a rule-based summarization strategy (e.g., keeping, deleting, and substituting). ELLs benefit initially when they see an example of teacher-prepared notes. Two suggested models that they might learn are the informal outline, with indentations, and the webbing model, with visual representations. (Hill & Flynn, 2006, pp. 62–76)
- **Assign homework and practice**. Adjust homework in response to ELLs' learning needs. Useful strategies are to incorporate concrete, nonlinguistic representations such as photographs, objects, graphic organizers; to provide opportunities for questioning and oral discussion of assignments; to establish clear purpose; and to review continuously. (Hill & Flynn, 2006, pp. 77–86)
- **Reinforce effort and provide recognition**. Through explicit instruction and the opportunity to track personal progress and achievement promote ELLs learning with a connection between effort and achievement. (Hill & Flynn, 2006, pp. 87–100)
- **Identify similarities and difference**. Use familiar contexts, visual representations, and modeling to help ELLs to discern differences and similarities in academic content and become more self-directed learners. (Hill & Flynn, 2006, pp. 101–110)
- **Involve parents and community**. Embrace school-wide initiatives to learn about the native language and cultures to help tap into possible support resource of family and others in the community. (Hill & Flynn, 2006, pp. 111–117)

Additional ideas for teaching adolescents who are English Language Learners can be found at the National Clearinghouse for English Language Acquisition (NCELA), accessed at http://www.ncela.gwu.edu/practice/itc/secondary.html.

A Differentiation Strategy for English Language Learners

One differentiation strategy that works well for ELLs is *reciprocal teaching*, an instructional technique developed by Palincsar and Brown (1984). Reciprocal teaching is a dialogue between teachers and students for the purpose of collaboratively constructing meaning from text. The research of Fashola, Slavin, Calderón, and Durán (1997) found reciprocal teaching to contribute to the reading comprehension of elementary and middle school–aged ELLs. The technique consists of four key reading strategies, each of which is modeled by the teacher most often in the form of "thinkalouds" (Howard, 2004b). These are (1) summarizing the main content, (2) formulating questions, (3) clarifying ambiguities, and (4) predicting what may come next.

> **Reciprocal Teaching**
>
> A differentiation strategy that consists of a dialogue between teachers and students to collaboratively construct meaning from text. Reciprocal teaching consists of these four key reading strategies that are modeled through "think-alouds": summarizing the main content, formulating questions, clarifying ambiguities, and predicting what comes next.

In the initial dialogues, the teacher, as the discussion leader, introduces and sets the purpose of each of the strategies. After students have silently or orally read a selection, the teacher, for example, briefly summarizes the reading and raises discussion questions about the main ideas of the content. Students respond to these questions, add questions of their own, and the teacher again summarizes. The teacher's next step is to help elucidate any confusing points by eliciting clarifying questions that ask students to explain the content by examining context clues to understand unfamiliar terms.

In the fourth stage, the teacher asks for or offers predictions about what will come next in the selection. Students use their prior knowledge of the topic and clues in the reading to base their predictions. Throughout this dialogue, the teacher models how to apply the strategies when reading (Howard, 2004b).

As students become more familiar with the strategy use, they rotate as leaders of the discussion, initially with assistance in the form of feedback and encouragement. As students acquire proficiency in the use of the reciprocal teaching strategies, they assume increasing control over the discussion and the teacher's involvement simultaneously decreases. Reciprocal teaching is an excellent example of the cognitive apprenticeship model (Collins, Brown, and Newman, 1989), as discussed in Chapter 4. The teacher models strategies that represent those used by successful readers as they engage and make meaning of text. The goal of metacognitive coaching is to encourage and enable students, through diminishing scaffolding, to become increasingly self-regulating and self-monitoring learners (Brown, 1980).

CLUSTER 3: STUDENTS WITH LEARNING CHALLENGES

The individual differences among adolescents with learning challenges are many. They may be overwhelmed with the difficulty of a task or bored with its lack of relevance or complexity. A learning challenge may evidence in a student's ability to make meaning of reading content or the skills to attack a math computation. They may not recognize a cognitive strategy that would assist in completing a task or know a strategy that would help with memorization of information. Students may have learning strengths that are not typically tapped or expressed in middle and high school classrooms. Other challenges may be behavioral or emotional, affecting concentration or attention, or physical as related to vision or hearing. Still other social, economic, or personal challenges such as absenteeism, frequent moves, homelessness, recent trauma, poverty, and limited home resources and support systems may affect academic achievement. Furthermore, the expectation for content area literary at the secondary level exposes many learning challenges in the areas of comprehension, fluency, and vocabulary knowledge.

Unflagging Expectations

One temptation in teaching students with learning challenges is to try and remediate rather than enhance their learning strengths. A common misconception is that these students think mainly on a basic, concrete level. Conversely, adolescents with learning challenges do not respond positively to a tedious curriculum of basic skills or drill and practice (Cushman, 2006; Ivey & Fisher, 2006). They want to be a part of a meaningful curriculum that is engaging, cognitively compelling, and relative to what they care about. They may need direct instruction in the use of a learning strategy or need to be given a modified task, but they do not want to feel marginalized by work they perceive as different or less significant in comparison to the work of other students in the classroom.

As this book contends, differentiation is a powerful tool that enables teachers to give the most diverse student a pathway to academic success. It embraces the philosophy that all students can succeed. In differentiated classrooms, teachers do not lose sight of the potential in each student. Rather than labeling students "at risk," "slow," or "struggling," teachers in differentiated classrooms consider these learners to be "at promise" (Tomlinson, 2001). They find something in every student to affirm, design tasks that draw on their strengths, and ensure that they use their strengths as a way of compensating for areas of challenge.

Landsman (2006) similarly writes, "The best teachers . . . believe in the brilliance, creativity, and ability of all their students. There is no condescension or sentimentality in their work with these young people, but there is compassion . . ." (p. 27). She quotes a high school teacher who uses the metaphor of a bridge to describe the instructional expectation for teachers in diverse classrooms. "You would never expect kids to traverse huge gaps of physical space without a bridge. It's the same with learning. You, the teacher, are the bridge to help students get from one level of skill to another" (as cited in Landsman, 2006, p. 27).

Learning Motivation and Personal Efficacy

Tomlinson (2001) asserts that students with learning challenges "are more likely to retain motivation to learn when their days allow them to concentrate on tasks that are relevant and make them feel powerful" (p. 13). These adolescents need to be involved in problem solving, decision making, critical thinking, and investigation—instructional methods that promote higher-order thinking. They also need to engage in authentic learning experiences in which they delve into substantive content, construct meaning, and connect with the world beyond the classroom. Particularly for older adolescents, their learning must be relevant to their future (Vaughn, Bos, & Schumm, 2003). One differentiation strategy is an *apprenticeship* or *mentorship* in which high school students work with area businesses. At the middle school level, an adolescent might work with a resource teacher, media specialist, older student, or community member who guides their growth in a particular area (Tomlinson, 2001). Mentors also function as experts on advanced projects, as in the study group strategy in Chapter 6.

The motivational research emphasizes that students need to be engaged to learn, that they need to be committed to subject matter, to want to learn content, to believe in the personal ability to achieve, and to want to share their understanding (Deci, Vallerand, Pelletier, & Ryan, 1991). Intrinsic motivation is enhanced when students feel they have the self-determination and competence to accomplish a learning goal. When adolescents believe they can succeed on a task, for example, they will persist. Bandura (1986) explains self-efficacy as "people's judgment of their abilities to organize and execute courses of action to attain designated types of performance" (p. 391).

> **Apprenticeship/Mentorship**
>
> Adolescents work one-on-one or in small groups with a resource teacher, media specialist, older student, or community member who mentors their growth in a particular area or on advanced projects

Self-efficacy develops when students recognize that they have accomplished a task they may have believed beyond them (Margolis and McCabe, 2004). Teachers can help adolescents with learning challenges be successful through modeled strategy instruction, support, feedback, and encouragement so that the "seemingly unattainable moves within the learners' reach" (Tomlinson, 2001). Particularly in the area of literacy, genuine engagement is "not the product of strategies alone but a fusion of self-efficacy, interest, and strategic learning" (Ivey & Fisher, 2006).

Critical Literacy

At the secondary level, many students' learning challenges surface in content literacy. Students may have the skills for decoding the words on a page of a science book but lack those to make meaning of the text and read for understanding. The publication *Teaching Literacy in the Turning Points Schools* (Center for Collaborative Education, 2001) defines literacy as broader than reading: "Literacy is a social act. It is a process of thinking, questioning, problem posing, and problem solving" (p. 2). Critical literacy is about "understanding the full context of a text and using that understanding to address important issues" (p. 13). Teaching students to be literate prepares them to be active readers who "take the words on the page and interact with them . . . make assumptions as they collect evidence . . . read with feelings and ideas, with intentionality of their own . . . approach a text with their own wants, tastes, opinions, objectives, and purposes" (p. 13).

Critical literacy in subject areas is necessary because reading is a tool to gather information (Shellard & Protheroe, 2000). Students with learning challenges often lack the background knowledge other students have when they approach a text. They also may not have acquired the metacognitive skills, inherent in many students, to monitor their own thinking. Harvey and Goudvis (2000) in their book, *Strategies That Work: Teaching Comprehension to Enhance Understanding,* note that the goal of comprehension is the construction of meaning. Beyond the literal level, the ability to construct meaning helps students acquire and use information, gain understanding, monitor their understanding, and develop the insight to think more deeply and critically.

Adolescents who are less proficient in comprehension strategies benefit when teachers model explicitly the strategies used by proficient readers. These strategies include the following interrelated skills (Harvey & Goudvis, 2000; Keene & Zimmermann, 1997):

- **Making connections between relevant prior knowledge and the text**. Good readers naturally bring prior knowledge and experience but comprehend better when they think about connections between the text, their lives (text-to-self), other readings (text-to-text), and the larger world (text-to-world).
- **Asking questions throughout the reading process.** Good readers ask questions to clarify understanding, to predict what will come next in the text, and to determine an author's intent.
- **Visualizing.** Good readers create visual and other sensory images or mental pictures based on what they read, which enhances comprehension and understanding.
- **Drawing inferences.** Good readers garner clues from the text and, based on what they know, draw conclusions, form interpretations, make judgments, and speculate about what is to come.
- **Determining the most important ideas and themes.** Good readers are able to discern between less important ideas and key ideas that are essential to the meaning of the text.
- **Synthesizing what they have read**. Good readers develop new insights when they order, recall, retell, and recreate important information that they read.
- **Repairing understanding**. Good readers use a variety of "fix-up" strategies when they are having problems understanding what they are reading. They might stop, reread, read aloud, sound out words, examine the context, or read ahead.

Scaffolding for Success

Researchers recommend several instructional practices that benefit adolescents with learning challenges academically. These strategies help students to activate prior knowledge, build connections, construct meaning, and attain cognitive strategies (Vaughn, Bos, & Schumm, 2003). These are:

- **Pre-learning strategies.** These strategies increase students' motivation by activating background knowledge and stimulating thinking and curiosity. They include advance organizers, which orient students to the task and materials (Lenz, 1983; Lenz, Alley, & Schumaker, 1987);

written and oral purpose statements, which capture concisely and powerfully the reason for the lesson or activity (Blanton, Wood, & Moorman, 1990); semantic maps, which organize related content (Pearson & Johnson, 1978); and concept diagrams, which help students determine definitions, characteristics, examples, and nonexamples of a concept (Bulgren, Schumaker, & Deschler, 1988).

- **Modeling and discussion of strategies.** Teachers make learning visible to students through read-alouds, think-alouds, and instructional conversations (Mariage, 2000; Palinscar, 1986b; Englert, Raphael, & Mariage, 1994).

- **Response options.** Written scaffolding, such as hypothetical letter writing, double-entry journals, quick-writes, KWL charts, timelines, Venn diagrams, bar and line graphs, and sketches, and oral strategies, such as book clubs, pair share, think-pair-share, and strategy study groups, help students organize and make meaning of content (Center for Collaborative Learning, 2002).

- **Memory strategies.** Mnemonic devices or acronyms help students rehearse as they learn, associate and categorize information to make it easier to remember, and visualize information mentally (Swanson, 1993; Swanson & Cooney, 1991; Torgesen & Goldman, 1977).

- **Technology as a learning tool.** Students with learning challenges in reading, writing, and math overcome academic learning challenges through technology-enhanced learning tools (Lewis, 1993; Woodward & Reith, 1997). These include word processors with spell checkers, read-along devices, translations, illustrations, and interactive games for review and practice.

Teachers also maximize the success of adolescents with learning challenges when they present information in multiple ways and allow students to demonstrate understanding through multiple modes (Graham & Harris, 1989; Mather & Roberts, 1995). Teachers who ask themselves questions during the learning process and provide extended time for students to practice—often in small groups—the more complex cognitive strategies (Pressley, Rankin, & Yokoi, 1996; Pressley et al., 2001) help to promote self-monitoring, metacognitive awareness, and the transfer of strategies to other learning situations (Kame'enui & Simmons, 1990; Swanson, Hoskyn, & Lee, 1999).

Gradual Release of Responsibility

The ultimate goal of strategy instruction is for all students to assume responsibility for their own learning. To reach this goal, adolescents need to know both how and when to apply cognitive strategies. As this chapter demonstrates earlier through the reciprocal teaching strategy, the goal of metacognitive coaching is for students to begin to use cognitive strategies "automatically and seamlessly" (Harvey & Goudvis, 2000, p. 12). Pearson and Gallagher (as cited in Harvey & Goodvis, 2001) refer to this process as "the gradual release of responsibility approach" (p. 12). Teachers explain and model the strategy, students practice with teacher feedback and support, students apply the strategy independently with continued teacher and peer feedback, and students apply the effective use of the strategy in another or more difficult context (Fielding & Pearson, 1994). Through this approach, adolescents become more aware of their own strengths and become more reflective, strategic learners.

A Differentiation Example for Students With Learning Challenges

Mr. Armstrong has used the differentiation strategy *I-Search* successfully for many years with a range of adolescent learners. Students select any area of interest, formulate related questions, and conduct concentrated research (Crawford, 2004). High-interest topics range from in-line skating, dolphins, and mental illness to the Delta blues. For a month, the eighth graders literally "live" the inquiry. They trek to the media center to search the Internet, view streaming videos, take notes, and write. From the research data, they generate a formal paper. The project culminates with individual oral presentations.

> **I-Search**
>
> Concentrated research on a topic of high interest. The amount of teacher guidance and scaffolding depends on the readiness level of the adolescent. I-Searches generally end with a student-led presentation for classmates.

Mr. Armstrong's mixed-ability classes do not deter his assignment of this high-level task. He admits that some of the students "need more time, more structure, more help to organize information, and more reminders to focus. Their topics may range from tractors to dysphasia, but the task helps them feel a sense of accomplishment" (p. 43). He jokes that while all of the students are headed for the same place, some may take the interstate. For others, "it's like hiking" (p. 43).

The I-Search as a differentiation strategy encourages students to uncover their own curiosity, to delve deeply into an area of personal interest, to locate and use multiple sources to answer questions, and to write up their findings (Joyce & Tallman, 1997; Macrorie, 1988; Tomlinson, 2001). Through the process, the students become more self-directed and are able to evaluate the rigor of their own work. For Mr. Armstrong, the quality of the I-Search projects is a continual astonishment. One student, for example, wrote a 30-page paper on the evolution of African American music into the blues. He demonstrated this transition by alternating the original spiritual music and the corresponding blues piece line for line. According to Mr. Armstrong, "The project gives students a chance to explore something they are really interested in and to share it with other students in an original and creative way . . . He just has to do is sit back and be amazed" (p. 43).

SUMMARY AND LOOKING AHEAD

Chapter 7 focuses on instructional differentiation for three clusters of adolescent populations that are prevalent in contemporary mixed-ability classrooms: gifted or advanced learners, English language learners, and students with learning challenges that affect reading comprehension and literacy development. The chapter presents numerous differentiation and scaffolding strategies that build on strengths and enable all students to succeed academically.

Changing concepts of intelligence expand the notion of giftedness and recognize multiple learning strengths. Advanced learners need increased sophistication and complexity in tasks and extended time to delve into topics of keen interest. The chapter introduces four differentiation strategies that work well with advanced learners. These include curriculum compacting, tiered assignments, learning contracts, and learning centers.

The awareness of diverse backgrounds, levels of language proficiency, and educational profiles helps teachers design appropriate instruction for students whose first language is not English. These strategies provide multiple and varied sensory strategies to maximize linguistic input, making reading or listening to a second language more comprehensible. Using these strategies, teachers are also aware of the time frame needed for ELLs to acquire proficiency in both basic interpersonal communication skills (BICS) and cognitive academic language proficiency (CALP). Teachers can also provide a learning context that is resourceful and socially interactive and encourage adolescents to practice new, more complex learning in their native languages. A strategy that works well with students who have linguistic challenges is reciprocal teaching.

The chapter's underlying message is that teachers view all adolescents as contributing members in the learning environment. Rather than thinking in terms of labels and students "at-risk," teachers in differentiated classrooms regard students' learning strengths as starting points for instructional design. Teachers who differentiate for adolescents with learning challenges provide cognitive access to meaningful content through direct strategy instruction and the interactive support afforded through digital media. At the secondary level where adolescents are expected to read more complex content, critical literacy is necessary. Many students, however, need explicit instruction in reading comprehension strategies to be able to engage critically with content area text. The chapter describes numerous differentiation strategies that help students to activate prior knowledge, build connections, construct meaning, and attain pertinent cognitive strategies. One differentiation strategy that works well all learners, particularly with challenged learners, is I-Search, in which adolescents conduct in-depth research on topics of high interest.

The chapter also reiterates that the goal of adolescent learning is that they become managers of their own learning. The teacher's role is that of cognitive coach who scaffolds less and less as adolescents progress and assume increasing ownership and control in the learning process. The teacher's role is also to help adolescents not only learn strategies but to know when to use them appropriately. This metacognitive knowledge is critical for adolescents to become more independent learners and thinkers.

The last section, the Epilogue, brings closure to the discussion of adolescent-centered differentiation with a focus on collaboration. Through collaboration, teachers in heterogeneous classrooms encourage high levels of respect and concern among students in high levels that transcend intellectual, cultural, and economic differences. The section showcases a collaboration strategy that works well with all adolescent learners: project-based learning.

Epilogue: A Shared Commitment to Equity

The importance of collaboration in adolescent learning is a theme throughout this book. Adolescents who work cooperatively to solve authentic, complex problems they deem relevant or who participate in meaningful group projects are more engaged and motivated to learn (Beamon, 2001; Crawford, 2007). They have the opportunity to explore, question, interact, think critically, construct meaningful knowledge, and to reflect upon and apply new knowledge. Collaboration as a differentiation strategy in heterogeneous classrooms is critical for another reason: it encourages among students high levels of respect and concern that transcends intellectual, cultural, and economic differences (Boaler, 2006).

Boaler (2006) uses the term "relationship equity" to refer to the positive and respectful intellectual relationships afforded through a commitment to the learning of others, the respect of the ideas and contributions of others, and positive, interpersonal communication with others. Through purposeful collaboration, adolescents learn to listen to the perspectives of others, to assume personal responsibility and leadership, and to persist in challenging learning situations. They also learn to respect their peers regardless of ethnicity, social class, or gender. One powerful collaborative learning strategy is *project-based learning*, which often involves service and contribution to the school or local community. As a differentiation tool, project-based learning is cooperative, interactive, and motivational. Adolescents with varying interests and needs work together toward a common goal, and they demonstrate their understanding of important content in multiple ways. The following section briefly describes project-based learning as an effective instructional tool for mixed-ability secondary classrooms.

PROJECT-BASED LEARNING

With a click of a mouse, technology connects adolescents with the world's best thinkers. Each spring, students in a high school geometry class design a state-of-the-art high school for the year 2050 (Armstrong, 2002; Curtis, 2001). In a period of six weeks, they develop a site model, make simple architectural drawings of floor plans and rooms, project costs, and write a narrative report. A Mountlake Terrace High School math teacher issued the following challenge to her geometry students:

Working as a member of an architectural team in the year 2050, you are competing against five other companies to win the contract to design a state-of-the-art high school on a given site. You must present your proposed design to a panel of professional architects who will be awarding the contract. Your design must meet the learning needs of students in the year 2050, must accommodate 2,000 students, and must make use of the natural benefits of the particular site, while also preserving at least half of the existing wetlands. (p. 1)

The geometry students divide into small teams of two to four, apply mathematical knowledge to build scale models, draft site plans, estimate costs, and prepare written and oral proposals for final presentation to the panel of architects. One team researches solar panels and talks with visiting architects. In their investigation, they consider geodesic domes and environmentally-accommodating designs.

Project-Based Learning

Adolescents conduct research on relevant and authentic topics through Internet research, and expert interviews. The three-phased approach involves classroom discussion of the project's topic, fieldwork to gather information, and presentation to authentic audiences. Many project-based learning experiences involve service.

In project-based learning, students tackle relevant and authentic challenges (Curtis, 2001). They conduct research from the Internet, interview experts, and use whatever discipline is necessary—math, science, history, literature—to complete the study. The three-phased approach involves initial discussion in the classroom of the project's topic; fieldwork to gather information, including sessions with experts; and the presentation of the project to an authentic audience. The results are that students learn the concepts deeply enough to apply them over time. They make connections, learn how to collaborate, and improve social skills and confidence.

A Differentiation Example: The Oral History Project

Cummins, Brown, and Sayers (2007) write that homework "took on new meaning" for students in Mr. Green's seventh grade social studies class in California when they engaged in a project to investigate their own family histories. Mr. Green is known for his ability to engage students in his academically diverse class, many of whom are ELLs or who work below grade level, in active learning experiences. To make the factual history textbook more conceptually compelling, for example, Mr. Green involves students in lively discussions, role-plays, readers' theatre, art projects, and presentations about the political, social, and cultural context of historical events. He relates events in the past to relevant current events, for example, the Crusades to present-day terrorism. He supplements the text for his academically diverse class with videos, resources from the Internet, and books with photographs and drawings. His concern was that few of his students held any aspiration for the future.

The oral history project reflects Mr. Green's effort to design instruction that was "identity affirming" for his impressionable adolescents (Cummins, Brown, & Sayers, 2007). Through the project his students assume the authentic role of historians who interview their families about "past events and ways of life" (p. 150) as they deepen the historical skills for perspective taking and meaning making. They construct historical questions, seek information from primary and secondary sources, document findings, reconcile conflicting accounts, construct explanations, reflect, share findings, use digital technologies, and make decisions as true historiographers. They create family trees using the AppleWorks Draw program, which allows more flexibility and individualization for nontraditional family configuration.

Through the process, Mr. Green's seventh graders begin to understand history and increase communication with family members. On presentation day, they share findings on graphs and flow charts with arrows to show family connections. Mr. Green videotaped the presentations, transferred the digital footage to an iMovie, complete with native-language voice-overs so students' families could understand, which he used for parent open house. Mr. Green's students not only gained the skills for critical inquiry by they also developed an enhanced sense of self and personal pride in individual ethnicity.

Resources for Oral History Projects

Cunmings, Brown, and Sayer (2007) offer several useful sites for oral history collections and Internet resources. These are listed in the Box E1, "Resources for Oral History Projects."

❖ BOX E.1 Resources for Oral History Projects

History Matters: http://historymatters.gmu.edu/mse/oral/
A site for students and teachers to begin work on oral history interviews as historical evidence. Includes a guide to find and use oral history online

Step-by-Step Guide to Oral History: www.dohistory.org/on_you_onw/toolkit/oralHistory.html
A site that provides suggestions and strategies for collecting and preserving oral history. It addresses conceptual and ethical issues related to conducting and using oral history.

Digital Historical Inquiry Project: http://dhip.org
A consortium of schools and colleges interested in promoting historical inquiry in the preparation of pre-service social studies teachers. Showcases current and emerging technologies to support alternate approaches to learning history.

The U.S. Holocaust Memorial Museum: http://www.ushmm.org/research/collections/
One of the largest oral history collections related to the Holocaust in the world. Includes video accounts of people who have experienced or perpetrated Holocaust events.

The Schomburg Center for Research in Black Culture: http://www.nypl.org/research/sc/sc.html
Provides information about people of African descent throughout the world and includes a video, oral history gallery, and other audio and video resources.

Putting the Movement Back into Civil Rights Teaching: http://www.civilrightsteaching.org/links.htm
Provides links to oral histories and other web resources for teaching about the Civil Rights Movement.

Source: Cummings, J., Brown, K., & Sayers, D. (2007). *Literacy, technology, and diversity: Teaching for success in changing times* (pp. 152, 158). Boston: Allyn & Bacon.

Other Examples of Project-Based Learning

Across the country, adolescents in secondary classrooms similar to Mr. Green's are actively involved in projects that involve authentic challenge and community contribution. A few examples follow:

- High school students compete to win a redevelopment contract for a simulated decaying neighborhood.

- Younger adolescents learn about the fundamentals of organic gardening and environmental conservation through a school grounds gardening project.
- High school students collaborate on a computer graphics project and receive feedback from a community project manager.
- High school students participate on a robotics team and learn about applied mathematics, engineering, and collaboration.
- Adolescents become stewards of their state's fragile wetland environment through a service-learning project.
- Adolescents engaged in a project on insects collaborate with university scientists to discuss findings.

To view video clips of these and other examples of successful project-based learning projects, see Edutopia, at www.edutopia.org.

IN CONCLUSION

In his book, *The Abolition of Man: How Education Develops Man's Sense of Morality*, noted theologian C. S. Lewis (1947) wrote that "the task of the modern educator is not to cut down jungles but to irrigate deserts" (p. 24). Over half a century later, his words have implication for teaching in the vastly diverse contemporary secondary classrooms. Differentiation is not a divisive but rather an inclusive approach to curriculum design, instruction, and classroom management that supports adolescents' learning needs and maximizes their learning capacities. Adolescent-centered differentiation anticipates and builds on students' learning strengths by offering varied, multiple, and flexible options to learn, to work together, and to succeed academically. It is an ongoing and active effort to match, monitor, and adjust instruction to adolescents' interests, readiness, and unique learning preferences. It is characterized by activity, purpose, relevance, meaningfulness, and challenge. It is filled with inquiry, questioning, exploration, purposeful interaction, and collaboration as adolescents delve deeply into important content knowledge. Differentiation also provides adolescents with the scaffolding, cognitive tools, and metacognitive strategies that enable them to be able to manage, monitor, and independently direct their own thinking and learning.

This book offers an adolescent-centered differentiation framework that honors adolescents' unique developmental and brain-based learning attributes. The six Es of this framework are Evaluation, in the use of initial, formative, and summative assessment to inform instructional planning and determine student progress; Expectation, in the design of curriculum around relevant themes, essential understandings, key questions, and compelling learning experiences; Exploration, in the promotion of active and socially interactive opportunities for inquiry, investigation, and discovery; Extension, in the provision of strategies for metacognitive development, self-regulation, and transfer; Environment, in the creation and maintenance of a supportive and equitable learning community; and Engagement, in the use of varied, multiple, and motivational instructional strategies for students to learn and demonstrate understanding.

In the words of one adolescent (N. McMahon, personal communication), "education should be more about broadening, than a narrowing." In differentiated classrooms, all adolescents have the opportunity to develop as significant individuals.

Glossary of Adolescent-Centered Differentiation Terminology

Adolescence. The transitional time between late childhood and young adulthood characterized by rapid changes in physical, social, emotional, and intellectual development.

Adolescent-Centered Differentiation. A strategic approach to curriculum design and instruction that builds meaningfully and responsively on adolescents' unique development needs and learning strengths. It incorporates the following six E design principles: *Evaluation, Expectation, Engagement, Exploration, Extension,* and *Environment.*

Adolescent Developmental Learning Needs. The developmental needs for personal connection, appropriate intellectual challenge, emotional engagement, purposeful social interaction, metacognitive development, and supportive learning environment.

Amygdala. The area in the middle brain that is stimulated by emotional arousal and processes incoming information based on emotional relevance. Incoming information subsequently travels to the thalamus, another sensory relay station, and on to the prefrontal cortex where rational responses are made. In stressful situations, emotions dominate the ability for higher-level cognitive processing.

Anchor Activity. A differentiation strategy in which most of the class works independently on an activity such as silent reading, journaling, literature discussion logs preparation, or role task work. Anchor activities enable teachers to observe and monitor the small groups, such as literature circles, that are in session.

Apprenticeship/Mentorship. Adolescents work one-on-one or in small groups with a resource teacher, media specialist, older student, or community member who mentors their growth in a particular area or on advanced projects

Brain-Compatible Instruction. Teaching that is responsive to the way the human brain receives and organizes new information through association with prior knowledge, processes information in long-term memory, and retrieves information previously learned. Conditions conducive for brain-compatible instruction include emotional stimulation and cognitive engagement within a supportive and safe learning environment.

Brain Plasticity. The brain's responsiveness to a challenging learning environment by the development of dendrites and new, increasingly synaptic connectivity, which facilitates more integrated brain functioning.

Cerebellum. The small area located about the brain stem responsible for balance, posture, muscle coordination, physical movement, and coordination of thinking processes. The cerebellum is responsive to conditions in the learning environment.

Cognitive Apprenticeship. The process by which teachers model strategic thinking and guide as students practice and obtain the cognitive strategies for self-directed learning. Also referred to as metacognitive coaching. Teacher assistance gradually decreases and student strategic competence increases.

Cognitive Modeling. A scaffolding tool by which teachers talk aloud about their thinking as they demonstrate the use of a cognitive strategy. They guide and give feedback as students practice and internalize the new strategy.

Content Differentiation. Curriculum sources and materials that are differentiated to challenge students to learn and cognitively organize knowledge in a sophisticated manner. Common differentiation strategies based on *readiness* include materials with varied reading levels and formats of varying complexity, highlighted text and translation, supplemental presentations, visuals, reading partners, concept digests, re-teaching, and varied levels of questioning; on *interest* include interest centers, use of student questions, and examples/illustrations based on students interests and prior knowledge; and on *learning profile* include alternate presentations modes, choice related to intelligence preferences, cultural representation, and extended time.

Content Enhancements. Differentiation tools that can be digitized to "pop up" through digital overlay to provide built-in options to remind students of a particular strategy or to assist in thinking a task.

Content, Process, and Product. Curricular components that are differentiated continuously in response to adolescents' interests, readiness levels, and learning profiles.

Curriculum Compacting. A three-stage strategy that maximizes learning time by the streamlining of content that advanced learners already know. In the first stage, the teacher assesses knowledge or skill level, in the second, the teacher determines knowledge or skills not already mastered and outlines a plan of study, and the third, teachers and students design an in-depth study.

Digital Technology. The host of digital media tools that provide flexible scaffolding for cognitive access to learning. These include digitized books, computer-enhanced features for translation, highlighting, and text manipulation and numerous software resources for screen reading, content organization, and visualization, to name a few.

Elaborate Rehearsal Strategies. Strategies that activate the brain's natural capacity to build long-term memory circuits through repeated association. They motivate through movement, emotional stimulation, multisensory engagement, social interaction, and intellectual challenge.

Enduring Understandings. Powerful curricular goals based on the important concepts, themes, and generalizations of a discipline that engage students and link to their life experiences and interests.

Engagement. The adolescent-centered differentiation principle that uses varied, multiple, and engaging instructional strategies for students to learn and demonstrate understanding.

Environment. The adolescent-centered differentiation principle that creates and maintains a learning environment that is supportive of adolescents' intellectual, social, physical, and emotional development.

Essential Questions. Questions broad enough to be generalized across topics of study within a discipline. They serve as connectors among themes and concepts such as, *How does conflict shape history?*

Evaluation. Process seeking to know students' developmental and individual learning needs, strengths, interests, and preferences through initial, multiple, and ongoing assessments.

Expectation. The adolescent-centered differentiation principle that uses assessment knowledge strategically to design meaningful curriculum and appropriately challenging learning opportunities for a range of learners.

Exploration. The adolescent-centered differentiation principle that organizes flexible opportunities for students to collaborate, explore, and practice under guidance and feedback.

Extension. The adolescent-centered differentiation principle that promotes learning management by making cognitive strategies explicit and structuring time for reflection and metacognitive extension.

Flexible Grouping. Heterogeneous and homogenous student groupings determined flexibly by student readiness, interests, learning styles, and skills level. At times, students select work groups, and at other times, the teacher determines the configuration based on pre-assessment knowledge. Groups may be purposeful or random.

Gender Profile. Differences in the functioning of the male and female brain related to proclivities of verbal/spatial, optical/neural, frontal lobe development, neural rest states, cross talk between hemispheres, and natural aggression.

Graphic Organizers and Thinking Maps. Visualization diagrams, sometimes called "think sheets," that organize thinking or provide a "visible" representation of cognitive strategies to assist in learning.

GRASPS. A differentiation strategy for the design of authentic products or performances. Components are a real-world *goal*; a meaningful student *role*; an *authentic* (or simulated) audience; a contextualized *situation* with real-world application; student-generated *products* or performance; and consensus-driven performance *standards* or evaluation criteria.

Guided Metacognitive Inquiry. The prompting of adolescent metacognitive thinking and inquiry through metacognitive extension questions that guide students to think about their learning as it develops.

I-Search. Concentrated research on a topic of high interest. The amount of teacher guidance and scaffolding depends on the readiness level of the adolescent. I-Searches generally end with a student-led presentation for classmates.

Jigsaw. A cooperative learning structure that groups students for task specialization Jigsaw is a powerful differentiation strategy because it gives all students opportunity to contribute in meaningful ways.

Learning Brain. The multifaceted communication network comprised of the smaller networks—recognition, strategic, and affective—which function distinctively and collectively as adolescents learn.

Learning Centers. Stations aligned with course content that are differentiated by interest, readiness, and learning preferences. At the secondary level, learning centers enable in-depth study of special interest topics.

Learning Contracts. Negotiated agreements between teachers and individual students for various purposes, such as for review and practice or extended enrichment. Learning contracts have specified timelines and clear expectations aligned with the curriculum and are generally differentiated by readiness.

Learning Profile. Students' preferred learning style, intelligence strengths, and gender proclivities.

Learning Style. The sensory modes of audio, visual, tactile, and kinesthetic that affect students' individual learning preferences.

Literature Circles. A differentiation strategy in which small groups of students meet regularly to talk about books or other literary works. Students assume assigned roles and keep response journals. Literature circles are generally followed by an extension project that demonstrates understanding.

Metacognition. The deliberate and conscious control of one's cognitive activity. "cognition about cognition." Adolescents' emerging ability for metacognitive thinking enables them to think strategically about their own thinking as they set goals, plan, problem solve, monitor their learning progress, and subsequently evaluate the effectiveness of their thinking direction.

Metacognitive Coaching. The process by which teachers model strategic thinking and guide as students practice and obtain the cognitive strategies for self-directed learning. Also referred to as cognitive apprenticeship. Teacher assistance gradually *decreases* and student strategic competence *increases.*

Multiple Intelligence Theory. Gardner's (1993, 1999, 2006) theory that intelligence comprises nine areas of learning strengths: verbal-linguistic, logical-mathematical, musical, spatial, bodily-kinesthetic, interpersonal, intrapersonal, naturalistic, and existential.

Neural Exuberance. The overproduction of neurons and synaptic connections in the frontal lobes of the cerebral cortex just prior to the onset of puberty.

Neural Sculpting. The phase of circuit refinement following neural exuberance when neural connections that are used frequently strengthen and those less used are lost. Neural sculpting is susceptible to experiences as the adolescent brain matures.

Personal Learning Profile Assessment. A differentiation self-assessment in which adolescents choose from a list of phrases about how they think they learn best. It renders useful information about students' learning preferences and intelligences.

Podcasting. An audio program broadcast over the Internet that is downloaded to a portable MP3 player. It features class-produced talk shows, audiofiles of books, vocabulary, articles, and poems.

Problem-Based Learning. An effective instructional strategy that invites differentiation and encourages metacognitive development. Adolescents assume the persona of authentic roles and interact in investigation teams differentiated for readiness, interest, or learning preference to solve intriguing, open-ended problems.

Process Differentiation. Providing multiple and varied ways for adolescents to process, internalize, and consolidate new learning. Sample strategies include process partners, interactive response journals, thinking maps or graphic organizers, flexible collaborative learning groups, cooperative controversy, mini-workshops, guided note taking, tiered assignments or parallel tasks, and interactive technology.

Product Differentiation. Assessment options that give adolescents varying opportunities to demonstrate learning in response to readiness, interests, or learning profiles. Products may be traditional, as in a differentiated unit test, or authentic and performance-based.

Project-Based Learning. Adolescents conduct research on relevant and authentic topics through Internet research and expert interviews. The three-phased approach involves classroom discussion of the project's topic, fieldwork to gather information, and presentation to authentic audiences. Many project-based learning experiences involve service and community contribution.

RAFT. A differentiation strategy that varies the complexity level of tasks. RAFT stands for the *role* of the writer; the *audience* that the writer will address, the varying *formats* for writing, and the content *task*.

Reciprocal Teaching. A differentiation strategy that consists of a dialogue between teachers and students to collaboratively construct meaning from text. Reciprocal teaching consists of these four key reading strategies that are modeled through "think-alouds": summarizing the main content; formulating questions; clarifying ambiguities; and predicting what comes next.

Scaffolding. Supports in the learning environment that are human, such as the teacher, peers, or other adults, or symbolic, such as computers, graphing calculators, or graphic organizers.

Sequenced Questioning. The teacher's purposeful sequencing of questioning that varies cognitive levels in order to connect with, build on, and extend adolescents' thinking about important content. Cognitive levels include "Setting the Knowledge Base," "Analyzing the New Knowledge," "Focusing the New Knowledge," and "Evaluating the New Knowledge" (SAFE). Sequenced questioning also integrates follow-up questions, as appropriate.

Shared Cognition. The theory that learning and knowledge construction is supported by meaningful social interaction with resources in the learning environment—human and symbolic.

Thematic Units. Curricular units designed around adolescents' developmental needs, social concerns, and age-relevant themes based on content standards. Sample themes include culture, independence, exploration, conflict, interdependence, power, change, relationship, communication, expression, honor, and justice.

Tiered Assignments. A differentiation strategy in which adolescents work at different levels of difficulty on the same essential learning goals. Tiered assignments may be tasks, such as tiered research, or products. Tiers may be adjusted for complexity.

Transfer. The ability to make learning connections from one context to another. Because learning is so *situated*, or *contextualized*, teachers have to make adolescents explicitly aware of pertinent connections through questioning, coaching, and modeling.

Triarchic Intelligence Theory. Sternberg's (1985) theory that intelligence is the composite of analytical, practical, and creative.

Tribes. Social groupings balanced by such factors as gender, ability, leadership, problem solving, creative or artistic talent, cognitive abilities, backgrounds and languages, and energy levels. Tribes are base groups that help with classroom management and instruction.

Unit Menus. A differentiation strategy in which teachers give adolescents an array of creative choices for final performance-based products to extend learning and prepare for traditional testing.

Universal Design for Learning (UDL). A differentiation approach to curriculum design and instruction that responds to the learning brain. It encompasses flexibility in information representation, strategic learning and demonstration of competence, and emotional engagement.

Weblog: Referred to as blogs, this tool enables the creation of personal or group web sites for content sharing and online conversations. Graphic and multimedia can be incorporated.

WebQuest: A web-based scaffolding tool for interactive real-world problem solving that promotes collaborative group work through authentic roles, research skills, and higher-level thinking skills

Web Portals: Interactive Internet sites constructed and grown by a group around a common interest or curriculum topic. Content includes pertinent web links to databases, blogs, student communication, and archives of student writing.

Wiki: Hawaiian for "quick," a wiki is a collaborative content creation tool that enables contributors to share and access resources, such as http://Wikipedia.org, an online encyclopedia of half-a-million entries.

Zone of Proximal Development. Vygotsky's (1978) concept that students can navigate challenge that is one step above their readiness levels with adequate scaffolding.

References

Andrews, G. (August 2005). One size fits all?: Different, differentiated, and daily. *Middle Ground, 9*(1), 16–18.

Armstrong, S. (February 2002). *Geometry in the real world: Students as architects.* Edutopia. Retrieved on November 17, 2006, from http://www.edutopia.org/php/article.php?id=Art_909&key=037

Aronson, E. (1978). *Cooperative learning.* San Juan Capistrano, CA: Resources for Teachers, Inc.

Bandura, A. (1986). *Social foundations of thought and action: A social cognitive theory.* Upper Saddle River, NJ: Prentice Hall.

Barell, J. (1995). *Teaching for thoughtfulness: Classroom strategies to enhance intellectual development* (2nd ed.). White Plains, NY: Longman.

Barell, J. (2007). *Problem-based learning: An inquiry approach* (2nd ed.). Thousand Oaks, CA: Corwin Press.

Beamon, G. W. (1990). *Classroom climate and teacher questioning strategies: Relationship to student cognitive development.* Unpublished doctoral dissertation, University of North Carolina at Greensboro.

Beamon, G. W. (1992–1993). Making classrooms "safe" for thinking: Influence of classroom climate and teaching questioning strategies on level of student cognitive development. *National Forum of Teacher Education Journal, 2*(1), 4–14.

Beamon, G. W. (1993). Is your classroom "SAFE" for thinking?: Introducing and observation instrument to assess classroom climate and teacher questioning strategies. *Journal of Middle Level Research, 17*(1), 4–14.

Beamon, G. W. (1997). *Sparking the thinking of students, ages 10–14: Strategies for teachers.* Thousand Oaks, CA: Corwin Press.

Beamon, G. W. (2001). *Teaching with adolescent learning in mind.* Thousand Oaks, CA: Corwin Press.

Beane, J. (1992). Turning the floor over: Reflections on a middle school curriculum. *Middle School Journal, 23*(3), 34–40.

Benjamin, A. (2002). *Differentiated instruction: A guide for middle and high school teachers.* Larchmont, NY: Eye on Education.

Benjamin, A. (2005). *Differentiated instruction using technology: A guide for middle and high school teachers.* Larchmont, NY: Eye on Education.

Beyer, B. (1987). *Practical strategies for the teaching of thinking.* Boston: Allyn and Bacon.

Blanton, W. E., Wood, K. D., & Moorman, G. B. (1990). The role of purpose in reading instruction. *The Reading Teacher, 43*(7), 486–493.

Blum, D. (1997). *Sex on the brain: The biological differences between men and women.* New York: Viking.

Boaler, J. (February 2006). Promoting respectful learning. *Educational Leadership, 63*(5), 74–78.

Brandt, R. (1998). *Powerful learning.* Alexandria, VA: Association for Supervision and Curriculum Development.

Bransford, J. D., Brown, A. L., & Cocking, R. R. (1999). *How people learn: Brain, mind, experience, and school.* Washington, DC: National Academy Press.

Bransford, J. D., Brown, A. L., & Cocking, R. R. (2000). *How people learn: Brain, mind, experience, and school: Expanded edition.* Washington, DC: National Academy Press. Retrieved June 29, 2006, from http://www.nap.edu/openbook/0309070368/html/

Brooks, J. G., & Brooks, M. G. (1993). *In search of understanding: The case for constructivist classrooms.* Alexandria, VA: Association for Supervision and Curriculum Development.

Brown, A. L. (1980). Metacognitive development and reading. In R. S. Spiro, B. B. Bruce, & W. L. Brewer (Eds.), *Theoretical issues in reading comprehension.* Hillsdale, NJ: Erlbaum.

Bulgren, J., Schumaker, J. B., & Deshler, D. D. (1988). Effectiveness of a concept teaching routine in enhancing the performance of LD students in secondary-level mainstream classes. *Learning Disabilities Quarterly, 11,* 3–17.

Burns, M. (December 2005–January 2006). Tools for the mind. *Educational Leadership, 63*(4), 48–53.

Caine, R. N., & Caine, G. (1994). *Making connections: Teaching and the human brain* (Rev. ed.). Menlo Park, CA: Addison-Wesley.

Caine, R. N., & Caine, G. (1997). *Understanding the power of perceptual change: The potential of brain-based teaching.* Alexandria, VA: Association for Supervision and Curriculum Development.

Caine, R. N., Caine, G., McClintic, C., & Klimek, K. (2005). *12 brain/mind learning principles in action: The fieldbook for making connections, teaching, and the human brain.* Thousand Oaks, CA: Corwin Press.

Carrier, K. A. (November 2005). Key issues for teaching English language learners in academic classrooms. *Middle School Journal, 37*(2), 4–9.

Center for Collaborative Education. (2002). *A common intent to understand: Boston Pilot School directors talk about diversity.* Summary of findings. Boston, Massachusetts: Author.

Chaucer, G. (1957) The Canterbury tales. In F. N. Robinson (Ed.), *The works of Geoffrey Chaucer* (2nd ed.) (pp. 17–265). Boston: Houghton Mifflin.

Collins, A., Beranek, B. & Newman, S. E. (1991). Cognitive apprenticeship and instructional technology. In B. F. Jones & L. Idol (Eds.), *Educational values and cognitive instruction: Implications for reform.* Hillsdale, NJ: Lawrence Erlbaum.

Collins, A., Brown, J. S., & Newman, S. E. (1989). Cognitive apprenticeship: Teaching the crafts of reading, writing, and mathematics. In L. B. Resnick (Ed.), *Knowing, learning, and instruction: Essays in honor of Robert Glaser* (pp. 453–494). Hillsdale, NJ: Lawrence Erlbaum.

Comprehensive School Reform Quality Center (CSR). (2005, January). *Works in progress: A report on middle and high school improvement programs.* Washington, D.C.: Author.

Crawford, G. B. (2004). *Managing the adolescent classroom: Lessons from outstanding teachers.* Thousand Oaks, CA: Corwin Press.

Crawford, G. B. (2007). *Brain-based teaching with adolescent learning in mind* (2nd ed.). Thousand Oaks, CA: Corwin Press.

Crew, L. (1989). *Children of the river.* New York: Bantam Doubleday Dell Books for Young Readers.

Cummings, J., Brown, K., & Sayers, D. (2007). *Literacy, technology, and diversity: Teaching for success in changing times.* Boston: Allyn & Bacon.

Curry, C. (October, 2003). Universal design: Accessibility for all learners. *Educational Leadership, 61*(2), 55–60.

Curtin, E. M. (January 2006). Lesson on effective teaching from middle school ESL students. *Middle School Journal, 37*(3), 38–45.

Curtis, D. (November 2001). *Start with the pyramid.* Edutopia online. Retrieved November 11, 2006, from www.glef.org

Cushman, K. (February 2006). Help us care enough to learn. *Educational Leadership, 63*(5), 34–37.

Damasio, A. (1994). *Descartes' error: Emotion, reason, and the human brain.* New York: Putman.

Daniels, H. (1994). *Literature circles: Voice and choice in the student-centered classroom.* Portland, ME: Stenhouse Publishers.

Daniels, H., & Bizar, M. (1998). *Methods that matter: Six structures for best practice classrooms.* York, ME: Stenhouse Publishers.

Deci, E. L., Vallerand, R. J., Pelletier, L. G., & Ryan, R. (1991). *Motivation and education: The self-determination perspective.* Hillsdale, NJ: Lawrence Erlbaum.

Deshler, D. D., Ellis, E., & Lenz, B. K. (1996). *Teaching adolescents with learning disabilities.* (2nd ed.), Denver, CO: Love.

Diamond, M. C. (1967). Extensive cortical depth measurements and neuron size increases in the cortex of environmentally enriched rats. *Journal of Comparative Neurology, 131,* 357–364.

Diamond, M., & Hopson, J. (1998). *Magic trees of the mind: How to nurture your child's intelligence, creativity, and healthy emotions from birth through adolescence.* New York: Dutton.

Differentiation of curriculum and instruction. (1994). *National Association for Gifted Children (NAGC) Position Statement.* Retrieved December 27, 2006, from http://www.nagc.org/index.aspx?id=387

Donavan, M. S., & Bransford, J. D. (Eds.) (2005). *How people learn: History, mathematics, and science in the classroom.* Washington, DC: National Research Council.

Ellis, E. (2004). *Makes sense strategies—the works.* Retrieved October 22, 2006, from www.GraphicOrganizers.com

Englert, C. S., Raphael, R. E., & Mariage, T. W. (1994). Developing a school-based discourse for literacy: A principled search for understanding. *Learning Disabilities Quarterly, 17,* 2–32.

Erb, T. O. (1992). Encouraging gifted performance in middle schools. *Midpoints, 3*(1), 1–24.

Erikson, E. H. (1968). *Identity, youth, and crisis.* New York: Norton.

Fashola, O. S., Slavin, R. E., Calderón, M., & Durán, R. (1997). *Effective programs for Lationo students in elementary and middle schools.* Paper prepared for the Hispanic Dropout Project, Office of Educational Research and Improvement, U.S. Department of Education, Washington, DC.

Feinstein, S. (2004). *Secrets of the teenage brain: Research-based strategies for reading and teaching today's adolescents.* Thousand Oaks, CA: Corwin Press.

Fielding, L., & Pearson, P. D. (1994). Reading comprehension: What works? *Educational Leadership, 51*(5), 62–67.

Flavell, J. H. (1985). *Cognitive development* (2nd ed.). Upper Saddle River, NJ: Prentice Hall.

Franklin, J. (June 2005). *Mental mileage: Education update.* Alexandria, VA: Association for Supervision and Curriculum Development.

Gallagher, J. J. (1991). Editorial: The gifted: A name with surplus meaning. *Journal for the Education of the Gifted, 14,* 353–365.

Gallagher, J. J. (1997). Preparing the gifted students as independent learners. In J. Leroux (Ed.), *Connecting with the gifted community.* Selected proceedings from the 12th World Conference of the World Council for Gifted and Talented Children, Inc.

Gardner, H. (1993). *Multiple intelligences: The theory in practice.* New York: Basic Books.

Gardner, H. (1999). *The disciplined mind: What all students should understand.* New York: Basic Books.

Gardner, H. (2006). *Multiple intelligences: New horizons.* New York: Basic Books.

Giedd, J. N., Gogtay, N., Lusk, L., Hayashi, K. M., Greenstein, D., Vaituzis, A. C., et al. (2004). *Dynamic mapping of human cortical development during childhood through early adulthood.* Proceedings of the National Academy of Sciences. *627,* 231–247.

Graham, S., & Harris, K. R. (1989). Cognitive training: Implications for written language. In J. Hughes & R. Hall (Eds.), *Cognitive behavioral psychology in the schools: A comprehensive handbook* (pp. 247–279). New York: Guilford.

Greenfield, S. (1995). *Journey to the center of the mind.* New York: W. H. Freeman Company.

Gurian. M. (1996). *The wonder of boys.* New York: Tarcher/Putnam.

Gurian, M., & Stevens, K. (2005). *The minds of boys: Saving our sons from falling behind in school and life.* San Francisco: Jossey-Bass.

Halderson, J. (August 2006). Podcasting: Connecting with a new generation. *Middle Ground, 10*(1), pp. 18–21.

Harvey, S., & Goudvis, A. (2000). *Strategies that work: Teaching comprehension to enhance understanding.* Portland, ME: Stenhouse Publishers.

Havers, F. (March 1995). Rhyming tasks male and female brains differently. *The Yale Herald.*

Hayhurst, B. (December 18, 2006). Teachers use technology to connect with students. *Burlington, NC Times-News*, pp. A1–A2.

Heacox, D. (2002). *Differentiating instruction in the regular classroom: How to reach and teach all learners, Grades 3–12*. Minneapolis, MN: Free Spirit.

Hill, J. D., & Flynn, K. M. (2006). *Classroom instruction that works with English language learners*. Alexandria, VA: Association for Supervision and Curriculum Development.

Houston, J., & Houston, J. (1973). *Farewell to Manzanar*. New York: Random House.

Howard, J. B. (Summer 2003). Universal design for learning: An essential concept for teacher education. *Journal of Computing in Teacher Education, 19*(4), 112–117.

Howard, J. B. (2004a). *The Alhambra restoration*. Elon University, NC: Project T2. Retrieved November 20, 2006, from http://org.elon.edu/t2project/article0001index.htm

Howard, J. B. (2004b). *The malaria mission*. Elon University, NC: Project T2. Retrieved November 20, 2006, from http://org.elon.edu/t2project/article0003/index.htm

Howard, J. B. (2004c). *Metacognitive inquiry*. Elon University, NC Project T2. Retrieved November 20, 2006, from http://org.elon.edu/t2project/index.htm

Howard, J. B. (2004d). *Problem-based learning*. Elon University, NC: Project T2 Retrieved November 20, 2006, from http://org.elon.edu/t2project/index.htm

Howard, J. B. (2004e). *Reciprocal teaching*. Elon University, NC: Project T2. Retrieved November 20, 2006, from http://elon.edu/t2project/index.htm

Howard, J. B. (2004f). *Technology enhancements*. Elon University, NC: Project T2. Retrieved November 20, 2006, from http://org.elon.edu/t2project/index.htm

Howard, J. B. (2004g). *Universal design for learning*. Elon University, NC: Project T2. Retrieved November 20, 2006, from http://org.elon.edu/t2project/index.htm

Ivey, G., & Fisher, D. (October 2006). When thinking skills trump reading skills. *Educational Leadership, 64*(2), 16–21.

Jackson, A. W., & Davis, G. A. (2000). *Turning points 2000: Educating adolescents in the 21st century*. New York: Teachers College Press.

Jackson, S. C. (1951). Charles. In R. M. Stauffer, W. H. Cunningham, & C. Sullivan (Eds.), *Adventures in modern literature*. New York: Harcourt, Brace, & World.

Jenkins, H. (April 2000). Getting into the game. *Educational Leadership, 62*(7), 48–51.

Jensen, E. (1998). *Teaching with the brain in mind*. Alexandria, VA: Association for Supervision and Curriculum Development.

Jensen, E. (2000). *Different brain, different learners*. Thousand Oaks, CA: Corwin Press.

Jensen, E., & Dabney, N. (2003). *Environments for learning*. Thousand Oaks, CA: Corwin Press.

Johassen, D. H., & Carr, C. S., (2000). Mindtools: Affording multiple knowledge representations for learning. In S. Lajoie (ed.), *Computers as cognitive tools* (pp. 165–196). Mahwah, NJ: Lawrence Erlbaum.

Johassen, D. H. (2000). *Computers as mindtools for schools: Engaging critical thinking*. (2nd ed.). Upper Saddle River, NJ: Prentice Hall.

Johnson, D. W. (1976). *Jack and the beanstalk*. Boston: Little, Brown.

Johnson, D. W. (1979). *Educational psychology*. Englewood Cliffs, NJ: Prentice Hall.

Johnson, D. W., & Johnson, R. (1988). Critical thinking through structured controversy. *Educational Leadership, 45*(8), 58–64.

Johnson, D. W., Maruyama, G., Johnson, R., Nelson, D., & Skön, L. (1981). Effects of cooperative, competitive, and individualistic goal structures on achievement: A meta-analysis. *Psychological Bulletin, 89*, 47–62.

Jordan, P. (1971), *Black coach*. New York: Dodd, Mead & Co.

Joyce, M., & Tallman, J. (1997). *Making the writing and research connection with the I-Search process*. New York: Neal-Schuman Publishers.

Kagan, S. (1990). *Cooperative learning resources for teachers*. San Juan Capistrano, CA: Resources for Teachers.

Kagan, S. (1994). *Cooperative learning*. San Juan Capistrano, CA: Resources for Teachers.

Kame'enui, E. J., & Simmons, D. C. (1990). Translating culture: From ethnographic information to educational program. *Anthropology and Education Quarterly, 16*, 105–123.

Kame'enui, E. J., & Simmons, D. C. (1999). *Toward successful inclusion of students with disabilities: The architecture of instruction*. Reston, VA: The Council for Exceptional Children.

Kaplan, S. N. (1986). The grid: A model to construct differentiated curriculum for the gifted. In J. S. Renzulli (Ed.), *Systems and models for developing programs for the gifted and talented* (pp. 180–193). Mansfield, CT: Creative Learning Press.

Kaufeldt, M. (2005). *Teachers, change your bait!: Brain-based differentiated instruction.* Norwalk, CT: Crown House Publishing Company.

Keene, E. O., & Zimmermann, S. (1997). *Mosaic of thought: Teaching comprehension in a reader's workshop.* Portsmouth, NH: Heinemann.

King, K., & Gurian, M. (September 2006). Teaching to the minds of boys. *Educational Leadership, 64*(1), 56–61.

Kingore, B. (2006). *Tiered instruction: Beginning the process.* Retrieved December 27, 2006, from http://www.nagc.org/index.aspx?id=1488.

LaDoux, J. (1996). *The emotional brain.* New York: Simon & Schuster.

Lambros, A. (2004). *Problem-based learning in middle and high school classrooms: A teacher's guide to implementation.* Thousand Oaks, CA: Corwin Press.

Landsman, J. (February 2006). Bearers of hope. *Educational Leadership, 63*(5), 26–33.

Lent, R. (September 2006a). In the company of critical thinkers: Study groups investigating real-world issues energize high school minds. *Educational Leadership, 64*(2), 68–72.

Lent, R. (2006b). *Engaging adolescent learners: A guide for content area teachers.* Portsmouth, NH: Heinemann.

Lenz, B. K. (1983). Promoting active learning through effective instruction: Using advance organizers. *Pointer, 27*(2), 11–13.

Lenz, B. K., Alley, G. R., & Schumaker, J. B. (1987). Activating the inactive learner: Advance organizers in the secondary classroom. *Learning Disabilities Quarterly, 10*, 53–67.

Lewis, C. S. (1947). *The abolition of man: How education develops man's sense of morality.* New York: Macmillan.

Lewis, R. B., (1993). *Special education technology: Classroom applications.* Pacific Grove, CA: Brooks Cole.

Lowry, L. (1989). *Number the stars.* Boston: Houghton Mifflin Company.

Macrorie, K. (1988). *The I-Search paper.* Portsmouth, NH: Boynton/Cook Publishers.

Maker, C. J. (1982). *Curriculum development for the gifted.* Rockville, MD: Aspen.

Mandated educational opportunities for gifted and talented students. (1994). National Association for Gifted Children (NAGC) Position Statement. Retrieved December 27, 2006, from http://www.nagc.org/index.aspx?id=387

March, T. (December 2005–January 2006). The new WWW: Whatever, whenever, wherever. *Educational Leadership, 63*(4), 14–19.

Mariage, T. V. (2000). Constructing educational possibilities: A sociolinguistic examination of meaning-making in "sharing chair." *Learning Disability Quarterly, 23*, 79–103.

Marland, S. (1972). *Education of the gifted and talented.* Report to the Congress of the United States by the U.S. Commissioner of Education. Washington, DC: U.S. Government Printing Office.

Martin, S. J., & Morris, R. G. M. (2002). New life in an old idea: The synaptic plasticity and memory hypothesis revisited. *Hippocampus, 12*, 609–636.

Marzano, R. J., Pickering, D. J., & Pollock, J. E. (2001). Classroom instruction that works. Alexandria, VA: Association for Supervision and Curriculum Development.

Mather, N., & Roberts, R. (1995). *Informal assessment and instruction in written language.* Brandon, VT: Clinical Psychology Publishing Company.

McCarthy. B. (1981, 1982). *The 4Mat system: Teaching to learning styles with right/left mode techniques.* Wauconda: IL: About Learning.

Meichenbaum, D. (1977). *Cognitive behavior modification: An integrated approach.* New York: Plenum.

Morgolis, H., & McCabe, P. P. (2004). Self-efficacy: A key to improving the motivation of struggling learners. *The Clearing House, 77*, 241.

National Association for Gifted Children (NACG). (1994, June). *Mandated educational opportunities for gifted and talented students.* Position statement. Retrieved December 27, 2006, from http://www.nagc.org/index.aspx?id=401.

National Clearinghouse for English Language Acquisition (NCELA). (2006). *In the classroom: A toolkit for effective instruction of English Learners.* Retrieved December 27, 2006, from http://www.ncela.gwu.edu/practice/itc/secondary.html

Nelson, K. (2001). *Teaching in the cyberage: Linking the Internet and brain theory.* Thousand Oaks, CA: Corwin Press.

Northey, S. S. (2005). *Handbook on differentiated instruction for middle and high schools.* Larchmont, NY: Eye on Education.

Ormod, J. E. (2000). *Educational psychology: Developing learners.* (3rd ed.). Upper Saddle River, NJ: Merrill.

Palinscar, A. S. (1986a). Metacognitive strategy instruction. *Exceptional Children, 53,* 118–124.

Palinscar, A. S. (1986b). The role of dialogue in providing scaffolding instruction. *Educational Psychologist, 21*(1/2), 73–98.

Palinscar, A. S., & Brown, A. L. (Spring 1984). Reciprocal teaching of comprehension-fostering and comprehension-monitoring activities. *Cognitive Instruction, 2,* 167–175.

Park, L. S. (2002). *A single shard.* Boston: Clarion Books.

Paulsen, G. (1993). *Nightjohn.* New York: Bantam Doubleday Dell Publishing Group.

Pea, R. D. (1993). Practices of distributed intelligence and designs in education. In G. Saloman (Ed.), *Distributed cognitions: Psychological and educational considerations* (pp. 47–87). Cambridge, England: Cambridge University Press.

Pearson, P. D., & Johnson, D. D. (1978). *Teaching reading comprehension.* New York: Holt, Rineholt, & Winston.

Perkins, R. (1992). *Smart minds: From training memories to educating minds.* New York: The Free Press.

Perkins, R. (1991). Educating for insight. *Educational Leadership, 29*(2), 4–8.

Perkins, R. (1999). The many faces of constructivism. *Educational Leadership, 57*(3), 6–11.

Piaget, J. (1928). *Judgment and reasoning in the child.* (M. Warden, Trans.) New York: Norton.

Polya, G. (1945). *How to solve it.* Princeton, NJ: Princeton University Press (Reprinted 1957, Doubleday, Garden City, NY).

Prensky, M. (December 2005-January 2006). Listen to the natives. *Educational Leadership, 63*(4), 9–13.

Pressley, M. J., Rankin, J., & Yokoi, L. (1996). A survey of instructional practices of outstanding primary-level literacy teachers. *Elementary School Journal, 96,* 363–384.

Pressley, M. J., Wharton-McDonald, R.,Allington, R. Block, C. C., Morrow, L., Tracey, D., Baker, K., Brooks, G., Cronin, J., Nelson, E., & Woo, D. (2001). A study of effective first-grade literacy instruction. *Scientific Studies of Reading, 5,* 35–58.

Price, L. F. (April 2005). The biology of risk taking. *Educational Leadership, 62*(7), 22–26.

Reis, S., & Renzulli, J. (1992). Using curriculum compacting to challenge the above average. *Educational Leadership, 50*(2), 51–57.

Renzulli, J. S., & Delcourt, M. A. B. (1986). The legacy and logic of research on the identification of gifted persons. *Gifted Child Quarterly, 30*(1), 20–23.

Resnick, L. B. (1987). *Education and learning to think.* Washington, DC: National Academy Press.

Rich, B. (2000). *The Dana brain daybook.* New York: The Charles A. Dana Foundation.

Richardson, W. (December 2005-January 2006). The educator's guide to the read/write web. Educational *Leadership, 63*(4), 24–27.

Rose, D. H., & Meyer, A. (2002). *Teaching every student in the digital age: Universal design for learning.* Alexandria, VA: Association for Supervision and Curriculum Development.

Ryan, P. M. (2000). *Esperanza rising.* New York: Scholastic Books.

Santa, C. M. (1988). *Content reading, including study systems: Reading, writing and studying across the curriculum.* Dubuque, IA: Kendall/Hunt Pub. Co.

Sax, L. (2005). *Why gender matters.* New York: Doubleday.

Scherer, M. (September 2006). Discovering strengths. *Educational Leadership, 64*(1), 7.

Schlick Noe, K. L., & Johnson, N. J. (1999). *Getting started with literature circles.* Norwood, MA: Christopher-Gordon Publishers.

Schumaker, J. B., & Deshler, D. D. (1984). Setting demand variables: A major factor in program planning for LD adolescents. *Topics in Language Disorders, 4,* 22–44.

Sharan, S, &, Sharon, Y. (1976). *Small-group teaching.* Englewood Cliffs, NJ: Educational Technology Publications.

Shellard, E., & Protheroe, N. (2000). *The informed educator: Effective teaching: How do we know it when we see it?* Arlington, VA: Educational Research Services.

Short, D., & Echevarria, J. (December 2004-January 2005). Teacher skills to support English language learners. *Educational Leadership, 62*(4), 8–13.

Siegal, D. J. (1999). *The developing mind: Toward a neurobiology of interpersonal experience.* New York: Guilford.

Silver, H. F., Strong, R. W., & Perini, M. J. (2000). *So each may learn: Integrating learning styles and multiple intelligences.* Alexandria, VA: Association for Supervision and Curriculum Development.

Silverman, S. (1993). Student characteristics, practice, and achievement in physical education. *Journal of Educational Research, 87,* 1.

Simmons, S. (December 1995). Drawing as thinking. *Think Magazine,* 23–29.

Sousa, D. A. (2001). *How the brain learns: A classroom teacher's guide.* Thousand Oaks, CA: Corwin Press.

Sousa, D. A. (2003). *How the gifted brain learns.* Thousand Oaks, CA: Corwin Press.

Spinks, S. (2002). *Adolescent brains are works in progress: Here's why.* Retrieved June 25, 2006, from http://www.pbs.org/wgbh/pages/frontline/shows/teenbrain/work/adolescent.html

Sprenger, M. (1999). *Learning and memory: The brain in action.* Alexandria, VA: Association for Supervision and Curriculum Development.

Sprenger, M. (2003). *Differentiation through learning styles and memory.* Thousand Oaks, CA: Corwin Press.

Stephens, K. R., & Karnes, F. A. (Winter 2000). State definitions for the gifted and talented revisited. *Exceptional Children, 66*(2), 219–238.

Stepien, W., & Gallagher, S. (1997). *Problem-based learning across the curriculum: An ASCD professional kit.* Alexandria, VA: Association for Supervision and Curriculum Development.

Sternberg R., (1985). *Beyond IQ: A triarchic theory of human intelligence.* Cambridge, MA: Cambridge University Press.

Sternberg, R., & Wagner, (1982). *Giftedness and the gifted: What's it's all about?* (ERIC EC Digest #E476, 1990). Retrieved January 11, 2007, from http://www.kidsource.com/kidsource/content/giftedness_and_gifted.html

Stevenson, C. (2002). *Teaching ten to fourteen year olds.* (3rd ed.). Boston: Allyn and Bacon.

Strauss, B. (2003). *The primal teen: What the new discoveries about the teenage brain tell us about our kids.* New York: Anchor Books.

Swanson, H. L. (1993). Working memory in learning disability subgroups. *Journal of Experimental Child Psychology, 56,* 87–114.

Swanson, H. L., & Cooney, J. B. (1991). Learning disabilities and memory. In B. Y. L. Wong (Ed.), *Learning about learning disabilities* (pp.103–127). Orlando, FL: Academic Press.

Swanson, H. L., with Hoskyn, M., & Lee, C. (1999). *Interventions for students with learning disabilities: A meta-analysis of treatment outcomes.* New York: Guilford.

Sylwester, R. (1999). *A celebration of neurons: An educator's guide to the human brain.* Alexandria, VA: Association for Supervision and Curriculum Development.

Sylwester, R. (2003). *A biological brain in a cultural classroom: Enhancing cognitive and social development through collaborative classroom management.* (2nd ed.). Thousand Oaks, CA: Corwin Press.

Sylwester, R. (2004). *How to explain a brain: An educator's handbook of brain terms and cognitive processes.* Thousand Oaks, CA: Corwin Press.

Sylwester, R. (2006). Connecting brain processes to school policies and practices. Retrieved June 28, 2006, from http://www.brainconnection.com/library/?main=talkhome/columnists

Taylor, S. (2002). *The tending instinct.* New York: Times Books.

Teaching literacy in the Turning Points schools. (2001). Center for Collaborative Education.

Thompson, P. M., Giedd, J. N., Woods, R. P. et al. (2000). Growth patterns in the developing brain detected by using continuum mechanical tensor maps. *Nature, 404*(6774), 190–193.

Tomlinson, C. A. (2001). *How to differentiate instruction in mixed-ability classrooms.* (2nd ed.). Alexandria, VA: Association for Supervision and Curriculum Development.

Tomlinson, C. A. (2002). Invitations to learn. *Educational Leadership, 60*(1), 6–10.

Tomlinson, C. A. (2003). Deciding to teach them all. *Educational Leadership, 61*(2), 6–11.

Tomlinson, C. A. (August 2005). Differentiating instruction: Why bother. *Middle Ground, 9*(1), 12–15.

Tomlinson, C. A., & Eidson, C. C. (2003). *Differentiation in practice: A resource guide for differentiating the curriculum.* Alexandria, VA: Association for Supervision and Curriculum Development.

Tomlinson, C. A., & Jarvis, J. (September 2006). Teaching beyond the book. *Educational Leadership, 64*(1), 16–21.

Tomlinson, C. A., Kaplan, S. N., Renzulli, J. S., Purcell, J., Leppien, J., & Burns, D. (2003). *The parallel curriculum: A design to develop high potential and challenge high-ability learners.* Thousand Oaks, CA: Corwin Press.

Tomlinson, C. A., & McTighe, J. (2006). *Integrating differentiated instruction + understanding by design.* Alexandria, VA: Association for Supervision and Curriculum Development.

Torgesen, J. K., & Goldman, T. (1977). Rehearsal and short-term memory in second grade reading disabled children. *Child Development, 48,* 56–61.

Torrance, E. P. (1989). A reaction to "Gifted black students: Curriculum and teaching strategies." In C. J. Maker & S. W. Schiever (Eds.), *Critical issues in gifted education: Vol. 2. Defensible programs for cultural and ethnic minorities.* Austin, TX: ProEd.

Torp, L., & Sage, S. (2002). *Problems as possibilities: Problem-based learning for K–16 education.* (2nd ed.). Alexandria, VA: Association for Supervision and Curriculum Development.

VanTassel-Baska, J. (1992). Educational decision making on acceleration and grouping. *Gifted Child Quarterly, 36*(2), 68–72.

Vaughn, S., Bos, C. S., & Schumm, J. S. (2003). *Teaching exceptional, diverse, and at-risk students in the general education classroom.* (3rd ed.) Boston: Allyn & Bacon.

Vygotsky, L. S. (1962). *Thought and language.* Cambridge, MA: MIT Press.

Vygotsky, L. S. (1978). *Mind in society: The development of higher psychological processes.* Cambridge, MA: Harvard University Press.

Weiner, L. (September 2006). Challenging deficit thinking. *Educational Leadership, 64*(1), 42–45.

Wiggins, G. P. (1993). Assessment: Authenticity, context, and validity. *Phi Delta Kappan, 75*(3), 200–214.

Wiggins, G. P., & McTighe, J. (1998). *Understanding by design.* Alexandria, VA: Association for Supervision and Curriculum Development.

Wiggins, C. P., & McTighe, J. (2005). *Understanding by design* (Expanded 2nd ed.). Alexandria, VA: Association for Supervision and Curriculum Development.

Willard-Holt, C. (2003). Raising expectations for the gifted. *Educational Leadership, 61*(2), 72–75.

Willis, J. (2006). *Research-based strategies to ignite student learning: Insights from a neurologist and classroom teacher.* Alexandria, VA: Association for Supervision and Curriculum Development.

Wilson, L. M., & Horch, H. D. (September 2002). Implications of brain research for teaching young adolescents. *Middle School Journal, 34*(1), 57–61.

Winebrenner, S. (September 2000). Gifted students need an education, too. *Educational Leadership, 58*(1), 52–56.

Wolfe, P. (2001). *Brain matters: Translating research into classroom practice.* Alexandria, VA: Association for Supervision and Curriculum Development.

Woodward, J., & Reith, H. (1997). A historical review of technology research in special education. *Review of Educational Research, 67*(4), 503–536.

Wormeli, R. (2006). *Fair isn't always equal: Assessing & grading in the differentiated classroom.* Portland, ME: Stenhouse Publishers & Westerville, Ohio: National Middle School Association.

Index

CORWIN PRESS